TYRANNY OF PARTITION

TYRANNY OF PARTITION

Hindus in Bangladesh and Muslims in India

Kathinka Sinha-Kerkhoff
Asian Development Research Institute

GYAN PUBLISHING HOUSE
New Delhi–110002

Tyranny of Partition: Hindus in Bangladesh and Muslims in India

Rs. 540

ISBN : 81-212-0890-4

Published in 2006 in India by
Gyan Publishing House,
5, Ansari Road, Daryaganj,
New Delhi-110002
E-mail : gyanbook@vsnl.com

Laser Type setting by: Tact Computer Graphics, Delhi
Printed at: Salasar Imaging System, Delhi

Contents

Acknowledgements

This book is the final outcome of research for the most part carried out between September 2000 and September 2003. During these three years, communal relations in both India as well as in Bangladesh did deteriorate drastically. All could, unfortunately, witness this, even if not involved in research on the relation between 'Hindus' and 'Muslims'. Observing the way in which academicians in both nation-states as well as beyond analysed the predicament of the Muslim minority in India as well as the plight of Hindus in Bangladesh, I became even more convinced than at the time of writing my research proposal for a SEPHIS scholarship, of the use of 'memories of partition' to not only 'revise, complete, or even altogether transform' partition historiography, but also to show that and how the past is connected to the present and vice versa. What was lacking in most approaches to contemporary communal relations, and the disturbances thereof, I felt, was a historical approach to the issue. I am extremely happy that the several persons who assisted me during the course of my research changed their attitudes towards the topic as well as main methodology of research. They initially had questioned the necessity of historical research during times when their own futures as Muslims in Jharkhand or as Hindus in Bangladesh were at stake and their current positions in the nation-state endangered. Nevertheless, during the work in progress, they started not only sharing my interest in the narratives of other members of the communities they identified with, but also got interested in listening to the narratives of 'others' who resided in and beyond their own nation-state. Concerning ourselves less with the veracity of the 'memories' of our informants than with the richness and diversity they provided, we all became convinced that these narratives should become part of 'official' historiography in both Bangladesh and India. In this way, we hope, awareness might arise in both nation-states, which can reverse the present trend of the deteriorating conditions to which so-called religious minorities in both countries are subjected. I therefore first of all like to thank Dipankar Mukherjee, Noor Alam, Md. Masoom Reza, Arun Pandit, Md. Tanweer Ahmad, Chandan Roy, Alok Deo Singh, "Rahul" and Atiqur Rahman who though at times concerned about their own safety nevertheless helped me understanding and appreciating the written as well as oral narratives exposed in the present book. I, of course, thank all those whose narrations you find exposed below and all others who provided me with their stories during interview sessions we had with them but which I did not include in this book for various reasons.

I further like to thank a few extremely fine research scholars and professors, activists, friends and family members who have helped me, knowingly and unknowingly, in formulating my arguments: Syed Rafiqul Alam Rumi, Md. Mahbubar Rahman, Imtiaz Ahmed, Abhijit Dasgupta, Mushirul Hasan, Asghar Ali Engineer, Tanvir Mokammel, S.S. Halder, Salam Azad, Haque and Alka Nizamie, Thomas P. Fenton, Sultana F. Nahar, Khushi Kabir, Aroma Dutta, Abul Barkat, Meghna Guhathakurta, Ahmad Sajjad, Abdul Qayum Abdali, Abuzar Usmani, Md. Khurshid Perwez, Syed Shahabuddin, Samrul Haque, Md. Ejaj Anwar, Imtiaz Ali, Javed Akhtar, Priti Kumar Mitra, Neem Chandra Bhowmik, Joke Schrijvers, Peter Gray, Kendrick Oliver, Rajni Palriwala, Jos Mooij, Victor van Bijlert, Bhaswati Bhattacharya, Willem Van Schendel, Gyanendra Pandey, Md. Sajjad, Alpa Shah,

Eyal Ben-Ari, Burkhard Schnepel, Smita Jassal, Alok Bhalla, Ellen Bal, Vinod and Trishla Sinha and Ranabir Samaddar. Some of them I never met or spoke to while others are, also thanks to the internet, part of my daily world, yet they all in their own way helped me to finish this book.

I am also grateful to the help provided by the staff of several institutions, journals and libraries in Bangladesh as well as India. My special thanks to the Library and the Institute of Bangladesh Studies of the Rajshahi University, the Bangladesh National Archives and Library, the University of Dhaka, the Bangladesh Asiatic Society, the Khuda Bakhsh Oriental Public Library and the Patna State Archives in Patna, the National Archives and Library and the West Bengal State Archives in Kolkata, the Nehru Memorial Museum and Library (Teen Murti House) in New Delhi, the Library of the Tribal Research Institute in Ranchi, the Urdu Public Library in Ranchi, the Milli Gazette and Muslim India in New Delhi, the Bangladesh Hindu Buddha Christian Oikya Parishad and the Ain o Salish Kendro (ASK) in Dhaka, the Institute of Objective Studies (IOS), New Delhi, Combat and the Centre for Study of Society and Secularism (CSSS) in Mumbai, Critical Asian Studies (CAS), the South Asian Refugee Watch (SARWATCH), the Indo-Dutch Programme for Alternatives in Development (IDPAD) , the Indian Council for Social Science Research (ICSSR) and the Indian Council for Historical Research (ICHR) in New Delhi, the Centre for Studies in Social Sciences (CSSS) in Kolkata and Heritage in Rajshahi. I also specially like to thank my own institution, the Asian Development Research Institute (ADRI) in Ranchi and Patna. Without the financial support of SEPHIS, neither would the research have been carried out nor would it have resulted in a book. Ulbe Bosma and Ingrid Goedhart of SEPHIS get my special recognition.

Glossary

Adivasis	First inhabitants, sons of the soil. In Jharkhand this term is preferred above 'tribal communities'.
Ajlaf	Descendants of low-caste Hindu converts to Islam.
Ansaris	See: Julahas.
Aqliat suba	Minority province.
Arzal	Low-class Muslim.
Ashraf	Term (as opposed to ajlaf, the 'low-born') to describe those Muslims descended from immigrants in India; the Syeds (descendants of the Prophet) and Shaikhs (descendants of his Companions).
Bahris	Outsiders
Bangabandhu	Lit. Friend of Bengal often used for Sheikh Mujibur Rahman of Bangladesh.
Bazaar	Market place.
Bhadralok	Literate, 'proper', 'civilized' or 'genteel, people used for the upper classes/castes among Bengali Hindus.
Bindhi	Vermillion power placed as a dot on the forehead of Hindu women. Now often replaced by small round (red) stickers.
Biradari	Brotherhood, sub-caste among Muslims.
Bunkar	Weaver.
Burqa	Veil observed by Muslim women.
Dalits	Lower classes/castes.
Diku	Outsiders, foreigner, exploiter.
Eid	Also spelled: Id. Muslim festival at the end of the month of fasting; Id-al Fidr as opposed to Id-al Zuha or Bakr Id, 'the feast of scrifice'.

Goondas	Criminals.
Haat	Local (vegetable) market.
Havildars	Assistant sub-inspectors of police.
Izzat	Honour.
Jagir	Landed property.
Jihadis	Also spelled Jehadis. Those Muslims who undertake a religious war against the unbelievers.
Jizya	The poll-tax levied in dar-al-Islam (the abode of Islam).
Julahas	A Muslim caste of ajlaf status associated with weaving.
Kafir	A non-Muslim; one who practices kufr, infidelity.
Katha	Measurement term of land.
Kolha-Jolha Bhai-Bhai	Phrase emphasising Adivasi-Muslim brotherhood.
Kuffar	Plural of kafir, non-believers.
Lakh	Hundred thousand.
Madrasa	Islamic school.
Malguzar	Tributary.
Malauns	Derogatory term for Hindus in Bangladesh.
Marwaris	Business community originally from Rajasthan.
Moharram	First month of the Muslim lunar calendar, the month in which Hussain was assassinated.
Momins	See: Julahas.
Moolvasis	Local dwellers. Sons of the soil.
Muhajir	Refugees (singular: muhajirin). Those Muslims who migrated from India to Pakistan and Bangladesh.
Mohalla	Quarter of a city or neighbourhood.
Namasoodras	Also spelled: Namasudras. Lower castes among Bengali Hindus. Also called: Chandals (untouchables, low born).
Namaz	The prescribed prayer in Islam.
Paila Baisakh	The Bengali New Year.
Pandal	Covered stage with a statue of a Hindu god or goddess within.

Prasad	Offer (often food offered) to a Hindu deity.
Purdah	Muslim women who are required by religion or custom to be secluded from the male adults.
Qabaristan	Muslim graveyard.
Qaid-e-Azam	Great leader, title attached to M.A. Jinnah, known as the founder of Pakistan.
Puja	Hindu religious worship.
Raj	Ruler.
Ram Lila	Dramatic pageant of the Hindu God Ram, one of the avatars of Vishnu celebrated as a human king in the Sanskrit Ramayana.
Ramzan	Fast from dawn to sunset during the ninth month of the Islamic calendar.
Rathyatra	Hindu religious journey.
Razil	Labourers; lower classes among Muslims.
Sadans	Long-settled and mainly agricultural communities in Jharkhand (India).
Sarna	A semi-Animist faith.
Shakas	White and red glass bangles that married Bengali Hindu women often wear.
Shariat	The Islamic law, including both the teaching
(Sharia)	of the Quran and of the traditional saying of Prophet Mohammad.
Sharif	Lit. 'respectable'; also used for the upper castes among Muslims.
Sindoor	Vermillion powder that married Hindu women apply to the parting of their hair. Signifies a married woman.
Sunnis	Those who follow the 'trodden path'; applied to the largest 'sect' in South Asian Islam.
Ulema	Plural of alim, lit. 'man of knowledge'. Scholars in Islamic jurisprudence.
Vaishnavitess	Followers of Lord Vishnu (Krishna).
Zamindars	Landholders.

List of Map and Photographs

Map. Location of Bihar and Jharkhand in India and Loction of Bangladesh.

Source. Amit Prakash
Jharkhand, Politics of Development and Identity.
(Hyderabad: Orient Longman Limited, 2001): XVI.

1

The Creation of New Nation-States in Partition

Introduction

When the soil, on which people live, suddenly belongs to other rulers, people who stay put might perceive the change as providing increased personal safety or they might feel less secure; they might suffer losses and gain. The new geographical borders often present themselves as walls of stones or barbed wire and do protect some and incarcerate others. There are of course the 'borderlanders' who continue living on both sides of the border (Van Schendel 2005). Besides, on one side of the border, people in the heartland (the heartlanders) are possibly deprived of rivers, roads, fertile lands, (religious) monuments or space yet they might still live with relatives and friends, have jobs and be healthy. The other side of the border will contain a similar mix of a satisfied and disgruntled population. Whatever side, most continue living with the new borders only until their sufferings extend their perceived gains. They will then start to doubt or cross-borders. In this book, I focus on this lot of 'deprived recipients' who live near or farther away from the border of 4,300 kilometres[1] (*Indian Express*, 14 January 2003)[2] and who, or their ancestors, stayed put after the 1947 partition of British India either in the territory that was renamed the Republic of India or in what now is called the People's Republic of Bangladesh. This book is primarily about their 'losses' but also about 'gains'.[3] We are thus concerned with the aftermath of partition and I look into particular processes initiated after the event of partition accomplished by the creation of new geographical boundaries demarcating first two and later three new nation-states and which affect some people's lives in India and Bangladesh till date.[4]

"We live in partitioned times", Ranabir Samaddar (2003: 21) eloquently argued and according to him this "Partition is 'contained' within all dimensions of national politics in territory, citizenship, bureaucracy, group identity, law, literature, language, and now in history". Partition, Samaddar (2003: 22) states: [...] is within our post-colonial being, in our agony, pessimism, and strivings. One can of course write, when writing of Partition, of its prelude, or of the imperial process of divide and quit, or its residue, or the trauma, the violence, the human sufferings, and the catharsis. But this history is lost in quagmire of the present that does not allow Partition to become a thing of the historical past. Partition's history is thus an incomplete one. At once an event of the past and a sign of the present time, Partition lives on in post-colonial times to such extent that we should truly prefer the phrase 'partitioned times' to the more common 'post-colonial times'.

Samaddar (2003: 22) also adds that, "The extent to which the states formed in all these areas [Germany, Korea, Vietnam, Ireland, India, Yemen, Palestine and Cyprus] in the post-war period have been influenced by that mode of origin have yet to be historically measured and appreciated". I have made an effort to carry out such a measurement for India and Bangladesh and the present book is the result.

The establishment of new nation-states (where the state tries to define the 'nation') not only requires new geographical boundaries but also new constitutions, new legislature, written laws. These laws formally define who (legitimately) are included in and who are excluded from the nation, who are citizens and who are not. Yet, as Bhargava (2000: 193-190) shows the making of the nation, "the cultural community and the relation between the two" is not only shaped by laws and constitutions designed through the "political imagination" of nation-builders but also by "emotions" that influence these laws and constitutions and political imagination. Bhargava therefore tried to show how, before partition, "emotions entered the very conception [among historical actors at the time] of community and nationhood":

> The specific nature of estrangement between Hindus and Muslims cannot be understood without a proper grasp of the sentimental component of the Indian conception of community. I do not wish to over-emphasise this point but it is wise not to ignore durable sentiments or deny them some explanatory power. It is surely not my intention to give emotions primacy over other explanatory variables. I want to claim that estrangement and its converse are primarily affective notions and an attempt to reduce them to something else serves no cognitive purpose.

Following Bhargava, in this book I look at how such 'emotions' entered the political imagination of historical political actors such as Muhammad Ali Jinnah for Pakistan, Jawaharlal Nehru for India and Sheikh Mujibur Rahman for Bangladesh and fundamentally influenced their 'cognitive maps' with the result that they could not imagine their nation-states in any other way than 'partitioned'. In other words, besides, laws and constitutions, such nation-builders also need and use rhetoric, mostly unwritten that not only explains the nation but also its relations with other nations and its internal political, socio-cultural, religious and economic organization.[5] In day-to-day life, politicians and more ordinary 'guardians of the nation-state' thus need rhetoric, i.e. narratives of the nation that not only explain the birth of the nation but also legitimise it. They use these narratives (including 'histories') as 'strategies of remembrance and forgetting' to decide who 'belong' and who do not. This partition rhetoric has thus potential to severely impact the lives of some people. This book illustrates that, narratives of the 1947 partition as advanced by various (self-appointed) nation-builders form such rhetoric, which is the baseline understanding of nationhood of countries like India and Bangladesh and a window into identity politics. It is argued that strategies of remembrance and forgetting sanction certain narratives of partition whereas others are silenced and forgotten. The ones 'remembered' are found in day-to-day speech and they, as shown in this book, though not sanctioned by all citizens, have nevertheless become common sense knowledge among citizens in the country. In material form, they are transmitted through school textbooks and partition fiction, academic work on partition, newspapers columns and reproduced by other media, politicians and common citizens. Importantly, severe controversies are generated if there is transgression of these strategies of remembrance and forgetting, i.e. if things are 'remembered' that should be forgotten or 'forgotten' that should be remembered. This could be witnessed in India during the summer of 2005.

During his weeklong visit to India's neighbouring country Pakistan L.K. Advani's comments on M.A. Jinnah (commonly viewed in Pakistan and India alike as the founder of the 'Muslim nation' Pakistan), did ensue such controversies in India. Clearly, this president of the rightist nationalist Bharatiya Janata Party (BJP) had crossed the borders by reminding people of 'other truths', which lay in the field of 'forgotten narratives'. He thus created "mass hysteria in the national press" (Datta 2005: 3000), by labelling Jinnah as "a secularist" (Datta 2005: 3000).[6] His party-fellow and former Prime Minister A.B. Vajpayee later on also joined in by adding that though "Jinnah was later responsible for the country's partition" [...] "Pakistan's founder Mohammed Ali Jinnah was a secular person". In the presence of the chief of the Hindu fundamentalist organisation the Rashtriya Svayamsevak Sangh (RSS) K.S. Sudarshan, Vajpayee even quoted from a book written by another transgressor of the borders and RSS ideologue and entitled "The Tragic Story of Partition", 'proving' that Jinnah himself was not religious (*Hindustan Times*, August 22, 2005). These alternative versions of history narrated by such politicians and (ex) leaders of nation-states of course first of all prove how narratives of partition are used to suit one's own perceived political interests. Yet, and more important for this book, seeing the 'mass-hysteria' that follows such pronouncements, this also shows how clear the borders are between what should be remembered and what should be forgotten and how dear these borders are to many citizens in the country.

In the views of the BJP/RSS leaders, Jinnah remained 'a villain', a person "responsible for the Muslim League, the country's partition and religious fanaticism" (Datta 2005: 3000) yet Advanis' statements seemed unacceptable to his own party members as well as to the opposition. Thus far known for his support of BJP's 'Hindutva nationalism'[7] against 'secular nationalism' supported by some opposition parties such as the Congress, Advani thus challenged the "narratives of nationalism" upheld by both his own party as well as the ruling political parties in the country.[8] His 'historical revisionism' clearly went against the narratives designed and upheld by ruling parties as well as those in the opposition. Communist Party (CPIM) leader and former Chief Minister of West Bengal Jyoti Basu felt for instance that, "Advani is distorting history by branding Pakistan founder...as secular. The country was divided on the basis of a demand of the Muslim League" (*The Asian Age*, June 8, 2005). Basu also recounted Jinnah's role in instigating the terrible riots in Calcutta in August 1946 and blamed the butchery of thousands on his

Muslim League's direct action (*The Milli Gazette*, 16-31 July 2005: 14).

This book studies the character of these kind of narratives that form the baseline of nation-states and their 'organising principles' and which include some people and exclude others and make some people gain and other loose after new geographical boundaries have been enacted.[9] These narratives "have permeated people's cultural and political consciousness at the expense of tolerance, dignity and equality in everyday lives" (Datta 2005: 3001) of citizens of India and Bangladesh alike. I show the workings of what I define as 'narratives of partition' (its tyranny), which function as non-physical 'borders', i.e. 'mental borders' that like geographical borders divide and unite people, tell them who they are and inform them if and where they belong.

I argue that nation-states hemmed in geographical borders depend on these partition narratives that like written laws divide the nations' citizens in majorities and minorities and the latter in 'good minorities' and 'bad minorities' who are informally excluded from the nation. Moreover, these narratives have potential to be translated in written laws and subsequently able to formally exclude so-called bad minorities from the nation. Thus as Samaddar (2003: 30) argued: "Just as borders are the product of Partition, the mental borders conjured up by the geopolitical imagination of the nation-in-the-making gave birth to partition as well". This book studies how this mechanism of narratives, these 'narrative regimes' (Cf. Radstone and Hodgkin 2003) function by affecting these ('good' and 'bad') minorities. In other words, this book describes how through these partition narratives, these mental borders, some people gain and others loose by the creation of new geographical borders, how minorities benefit and suffer; how these narratives teach them about 'their' past; how they should behave as 'a good minority' in present and how these threaten them with expulsion in future, if they behave as 'a bad minority'. Lastly and importantly, this book also narrates the stories formulated by such 'minorities' themselves who often reported increased senses of insecurity after the enactment of these mental borders that divide them as a 'minority' from the 'majority'.

Locating the Study in Partition Historiography

Other scholars of various disciplines and adopting divergent approaches have thoroughly examined the processes that led to the break-up of British India as well as the aftermath of this partition.[10] Historians, for instance, have looked at it as an event as well as process,[11] and scrutinized the role of key actors and institutions. They undertook this work in the context of developments within the discipline such as the inclusion of people's partition memories (including also analyses of 'silences' and 'forgetting'). They also included the (strategies of) remembrance of people in other regions than divided Bengal and Punjab[12] and their work (therefore) reflected a shift in history from 'above' to 'below' and from 'his' stories to 'her' stories and memories. These scholars thus recognised that the partition of 1947 was, "not just a story of causes, but an experience captured in the multiplicity of voices and visions" (Datta 2005: 3001). Indeed, memories of the 1947 partition have recently constituted a pervasive presence in discourses of historians and memory scholars in other disciplines. Through the excavation of partition memories of different nature these scholars hope to revise, complete or even altogether transform (1947) partition historiography. The aim of this book is similar in that it is concerned with 'strategies of remembrances' and is an analysis of 'silences and forgetting', yet its approach and methodology is somewhat different. I do not aim at refuting these voices and visions or the scholarly approaches to them but elaborate on them, categorize them and aim at expanding these narratives as well as the theoretical notions derived from them.[13]

So far, scholars have treated this 1947 break-up of British-India, its consequences for those who stayed put as well as those who migrated including memories of the event, as 'the Partition', i.e. as a unique event and process. I do not deny that in some ways the 1947 partition of British-India does signify uniqueness and can be spelled with a capital P as I have done myself in previous work on the partition of the Indian subcontinent. Having carried out fieldwork in both Bangladesh as well as in the Indian states of Bihar and Jharkhand, I realised however that not only had this 1947 partition of British-India, different meanings for various people, its importance in their lives also varied spatially and in temporal sense. The partition of 1947 was, clearly and shown in this book, not 'the Partition' for all. In Bangladesh, for instance, the Partition signified the division of Pakistan and the birth of Bangladesh and in our Indian case study the Partition denoted the division of Bihar and the birth of Jharkhand. Spelling the partition of British India in 1947 with a capital P would therefore emphasize the 'tyranny' of this partition, which I want to avoid for reasons that become clear by the end of this book.

I believe moreover, that this emphasis on its unique character should not stop scholars from recognizing similarities between the British Indian case and processes in other divided lands (including cities).[14] I therefore felt that in this account on the meaning of partition in the lives of people who stayed put after 1947, I should use the small 'p' to highlight and analyse processes that I assume always take place after divisions of inhabited territory, albeit in various forms and with different consequences. Though I have not embarked on such an endeavour in this book, I hope my approach to partition will stimulate other scholars to try whether this model is useful for analyses of people who stayed back/put after other partitions such as those of Palestine, China, Korea, Ireland, Czechoslovakia, Yugoslavia, Cyprus and Germany.

Like other studies on the aftermath of the event of the 1947 partition of British-India, my study too started as an effort to collect more 'partition memories' of different kind of communities in alternative regions. Though India as well as Bangladesh faced huge migrations flows of so-called religious minorities that travelled to and from the two countries and which continue, there never was an exchange of population on religious lines. The percentage of Muslims in India is presently about 12 per cent[15] and that of Hindus in Bangladesh about 11 per cent.[16] In other words, though in India after 1947, the percentage of Muslims had dropped and similarly in Bangladesh the percentage of Hindus many have stayed put/back and are living as a 'minority' among a 'Muslim majority' in Bangladesh and a 'Hindu majority' in India. After having carried out research among 'displaced people' in Bihar who had migrated from areas of Bangladesh (Sinha-Kerkhoff 2000) and with these percentages and ideas about 'minorities and majorities' in mind, I embarked on a new research project.

Between September 2000 and September 2003, I was involved in a three years (part-time) research project called "Partition Memories, Identities and Those Who Stayed: A Comparison of Muslims in India and Hindus in Bangladesh". The South-South Exchange Programme for Research on the History of Development (SEPHIS) sponsored the research during which I had in-depth discussions with 113 Muslims in Jharkhand and 95 Hindus in Bangladesh. Besides, in Jharkhand,[17] during 2003-2003, I also carried out two large surveys in Ranchi, its capital, among another 200 Muslims and organised a workshop on Muslims in Jharkhand after 9/11 (*The Milli Gazette*, 16-30 November 2002). I interviewed (Sunni) Muslims of various categories residing in different blocks and districts of the relatively new state of Jharkhand. Of the in-depth-interviews, a little less than half (50) of the narratives used to compose this book, identified themselves as male *ansaris*. Other informants identified with other 'caste-like' (*biradari*) categories that claim backward class status for themselves and 25 said they belonged to the 'Muslim upper classes/castes'. Yet, 15 of the latter were nevertheless and relatively poor. The total number of women we interviewed in Jharkhand was 15 only.

Though I had carried out fieldwork in Bangladesh before, for the purpose of this research, I visited Bangladesh[18] trice and interviewed Hindus living in the rural and urban districts of Sylhet, Dhaka, Bagerhat, Pirojpur, Khustia and Rajshahi. Among those interviewed, 72 identified as scheduled castes and the total number of women we interviewed in Bangladesh was 32. Apart from these interviews, for the purpose of this book I also incorporated some of the interviews I had carried out during earlier fieldwork in Bihar/ Jharkhand and Bangladesh that were related to a different project supported by the Indo-Dutch Programme on Alternatives and Development (IDPAD) (Ahmed; Dasgupta and Sinha-Kerkhoff 2004 and Sinha-Kerkhoff 2004c).[19]

Formal interviews with a list of (qualitative) questions were accompanied by informal talks about different matters and lasted somewhere in between two and five hours. A few informants were interviewed more than once and some became permanent friends with whom I still interact.[20] In September 2000 I thus set out to collect 'partition narratives' of Hindus in Bangladesh and Muslims in Jharkhand who, or their ancestors, had stayed put after the soil on which they lived became differently ruled and changed names. The bulk of migrants from East Pakistan in India, I had concluded from my previous work on partition, had initially been upper castes. Similarly, the majority of Muslim migrants who left Bihar for Pakistan were ashraf. Therefore, I deduced the majority of those who stayed put in Bangladesh must have been lower-caste Hindus and most of those who stayed put in Jharkhand were likely to be ajlaf. I thus set out to talk with these 'lower-class' groups in Bangladesh and Jharkhand and to listen to their 'memories of the Partition'. These partition memories of lower-caste Hindus and Muslims who did not leave their homes after 1947 would, I presumed, complement and enrich the growing literature on 'Partition'.

Yet, though these interviews, along with other primary and secondary sources, form the basis of the arguments in this book, they did so in a very different way than hypothesized. Actually, most of the informants did not (directly) talk about the 1947 partition. In fact, we[21] encountered, disinterest, irritation, sadness and even anger when we asked people to recount their memories of 'The Partition'.[22] Many also asked us to explain about which partition we wanted to talk as in India they were unsure whether we meant the partition of Bihar in 2000 and the subsequent establishment of Jharkhand and in Bangladesh they often thought we meant the partition of Pakistan and the creation of Bangladesh in 1971. When we made it clear that we wanted to know what they remembered of 1947 or how they viewed the partition of British India and the establishment of two new nations, India and Pakistan, many answered they were not able or did not want to talk about that. Instead, they said I should ask about their present-day problems in India and Bangladesh, which, they believed, were many. For them the 1947 partition of British India was an event of the past that did not concern them. I found out however rather than an event, partition is a process that continues to influence the lives of my informants in both Bangladesh and India in similar fashion. One of the most frequently mentioned complaints communicated to us was the feeling of insecurity these informants went through, sometimes all the time a bit but more frequently suddenly very much. These informants almost all felt that they had not been and were still not treated 'at par' with 'other' citizens and they provided us with examples when and where and on which occasions they felt such discrimination, unequal treatment and subsequent feelings of dejection often along with insecurity. It was only after listening and analysis of these stories, which were in fact not 'partition narratives' but rather 'narratives of independence', and at the end of the research period in 2003 that I understood the great significance of these narratives for the meaning of the 1947 partition in the lives of my informants; an event that did not however frequently and explicitly occur in the narratives I had collected.

Geographical and Mental Borders

Common to all 'partitions' is the redrafting of geographical borders. As a result, people who shared territorial space are redistributed over two or more and often renamed places. At times, total population exchanges take place after such partitions, yet after most partitions most people just remain where they were before. Significantly, so-called border studies have traditionally paid attention to flows and attempted flows. Such studies tell us a lot about mobility and even about curtailed mobility yet overlook the fact that newly created borders also allow people to remain where they are. Besides, for those who stay back they provide 'security' to some yet form a 'threat' to others. These borders thus divide people in the newly created territory between those who stay put (i.e. those who want to remain where they are) and those who stay behind (i.e. those who want to leave but cannot) (Sinha-Kerkhoff 2003). The former category looks upon the new borders as 'lines of security' and the latter considers them as 'precincts'.[23] These physical borders that map the new nations are more or less permanent. Yet, though designed to provide 'security' to people living on one side of the border, or to contain them, as well as to prevent international 'illegal' trespassing, for many people who reside in the borderland, these boundaries are unclear or do not exist. Some try, and at times successfully, to ignore them.[24]

In this book however, I present the life-worlds of so-called legal citizens (i.e. those citizens whose position is not formally contested) who opt to stay put in the country of their birth, remain and make a living there. It was through the narratives of the people I interviewed that the idea of this book took shape. During the three-year long research carried out with support of SEPHIS, I realised the continuously enactment[25] of certain and state-sponsored partition narratives, the 'partition rhetoric', in the day-to-day lives of our informants as well as during so-called communal riots. Elsewhere, I have described this as an enactment of 'Partition memory', which occurred only after the actual division of British India in 1947 and changed the event of partition in a process that continues even at present. In this book I elaborate more on this kind of 'enactment of Partition memory' and present an ethnographic account of Muslims we interviewed in Jharkhand and Hindus in Bangladesh. The narratives presented in this book show that during the aftermath of partitions, other than geographical borders are at play that are even more difficult to ignore than the physical ones. Actually, the narratives presented in this book are the result of processes of negotiation with and contestation of state-supported partition rhetoric enacted in the lives of the people I interviewed (and I myself enacted this rhetoric by inviting my informants to talk about the 1947 partition). These collected narratives show that this enactment of partition rhetoric created new and symbolic boundaries, so-called mental borders as my informants seemed to have reacted to and contested other 'partition narratives' with which 'boundaries' they did not identify.

Partition, in fact, caused a permanent division of these two nations into 'majorities' and 'minorities' based on religious differences (Cf. Samaddar 2003: 22). Thus as Bharucha (2003: 4241) wrote, "even though the political geographies of India and Pakistan were ruptured and sealed, the cultural geography of the subcontinent remained wayward and alive". After partition, mental borders created order in 'wayward societies' and in India in the way described by Bharucha (2003: 4240):

> Some communities were more 'foreign' than others: while the Buddhists, Jains, and Sikhs could claim India as the *janmabhumi* (land of birth) of their religious identities and traditions, this was not true for the Christians, Parsis, and Jews, who have a distinct ancestry, culture, and tradition outside of India. Yet, these communities could be more tolerated than their Muslim counterparts because they had, in their own ways, accepted India as their country or contributed to its development, unlike Muslims, whose loyalties allegedly lay elsewhere in Arabia, Persia, Turkey, and most ignominiously, Pakistan. The very proximity to, if not equation of Muslims with Hindus, before their conversion, contributed to their image as 'traitors'.

In Pakistan and Bangladesh it was non-Muslims, in particular Hindus, who were construed as 'second class citizens' by such mental borders and as Meghna Guhathakurta (2002: 72) argued:

> Hindus not only formed the majority of this group [of second class citizens in East Pakistan] but also became politically more vulnerable since India, the Hindu dominated nation was considered the natural enemy of Pakistan. The status of Hindus in Pakistan therefore became marginalized. They became hostages to the politics of the dominant society and state.

Motivated by 'border scholars' but influenced by empirical findings, I therefore propose an approach to borders that while acknowledging the analytical importance and relevance of border theory, I nonetheless strongly support a better balance between historical empiricism and the more symbolic appropriations of borders. I thus underscore "the importance of pursuing empirically informed research how social, political, and economic relations are produced at and in the context of specific borders" (Cunningham and Heyman 2004: 291). This book concentrates on these 'mental borders' and argues that they are in fact part of a particular kind of historiography that changes 'tales of independence' into tales partition that do not decolonize the land and its people but rather recolonize some of the people living in the land (Cf. Samaddar 2003: 23). I argue that this historiography constitutes a rhetoric that forms the baseline understanding of nationhood by so-called guardians of the state and which is internalized by many but to which the Muslims and Hindus we interviewed do not always or fully ascribed. To the contrary, they felt, this is part of 'other people's history' that burdened them.[26] I describe that in fact these partition narratives constitute 'mental borders' for those we interviewed that not only sanction the geographical borders but also guide their functioning and separate them mentally from the 'majority' as 'religious minorities' (the 'other') and therefore repeatedly 'reopens' the partition question (Cf. Samaddar 2003: 22).

Narrative Regimes: Partition, Nation-States and Narratives of Independence

In some respects, the differences that existed between the Hindus we interviewed in certain regions of Bangladesh on the one hand and the Muslims we interviewed in Jharkhand on the other were many and make a comparative effort on the basis of similarity unlikely. Firstly, the by us interviewed Hindus are part of a religious community of which the absolute number is not only much less than the number of their counterparts in India, but which is also rapidly declining in numbers. In contrast, the population of Muslims in India remains stable. Secondly, whereas the Hindus we interviewed in Bangladesh mostly possessed some relatives or friends who resided in India, the opposite was not true. Almost none of the Muslims we interviewed in Jharkhand had any relatives or friends in Bangladesh or for that matter in Pakistan. Lastly, scholarly work on the 'sufferings' of Hindus in Bangladesh is relatively extensive. In fact, almost all literature on Hindus in Bangladesh is concerned with their 'sufferings'. The contrary is true in the case of Muslims in Jharkhand or rather there are, apart from my own writings (Sinha-Kerkhoff 2004d), no studies that explicitly focuses on Muslims in the so-called Chhota Nagpur area of Southern Bihar that in 2000 was separated and became the state known as Jharkhand. Whereas there is a considerable literature on 'the sufferings of Indian Muslims after the partition of 1947', Muslims in Jharkhand are only moderately discussed in literature on Muslims in Bihar (Cf. Ghosh 1997 and 1998; Sajjad 2002). This literature moreover does not concern the position, or 'sufferings', of Muslims that stayed put in Bihar after 1947 or for that matter Muslims in the newly created state of Jharkhand. Besides, one can also wonder at the seemingly 'strange', or even reject as invalid, comparison between members of a nation-state and members of a state within a nation-state.

Narratives of our informants indicate however, as illustrated in this book, that resemblances between the two groups were greater than the differences. Apart from the fact that the Hindus we interviewed in Bangladesh and the Muslims in India are both labelled as religious minorities in their respective countries of residence, these informants resembled each other in other respects too.

Firstly, they inhabited nations where the meaning of 'secularism' has been the subject of long-lasting controversies.[27] Secondly, they all were people, who or whose ancestors had been left behind or stayed put after the partition of 1947 and who (still) reside in the country of their birth. Thirdly, they almost all belonged to the lower echelons of the class or caste hierarchies of their respective religious communities.

Lastly, and importantly, they all narrated 'partition stories' that greatly differed from the 'veracities' that were embedded in what for them constituted 'Partition History' and which they perceived as a burden in their lives and about which they were unwilling to talk. In fact, these 'lower-caste' Hindus interviewed in Bangladesh and Muslims in Jharkhand, in reply to questions of 'partition' all told us tales of independence and tales of being partitioned, followed by narratives with alternative borders. In this way these narratives are compared with each other.

In this book, I show how our informants perceive this 'Partition History' as mental borders where geographical borders have assumed symbolical meaning informing these people who they are and where they belong. Besides, these mental borders enact behaviour rules expelling those who do not conform as those who do not belong. Our informants could not identify with such narratives of the 1947 partition, as found, for instance, in curricula, partition fiction, reports and statements of various kinds, published by various media and (re) presented in and by several public institutions as well as during private meetings. They also felt extremely offended and humiliated during so-called communal riots when they were confronted with parts of such narratives in the shape of pamphlets, newspaper reports and slogans shouted in public by common people, police officials and formulated in public speeches by political leaders. Actually, they perceived these narratives as 'alien' and not part of their own life-worlds and not part of the own history. Instead, they contested this partition rhetoric as "they have against them so much which is set up to silence them" (Foucault 1981: 8). They told us about their pasts in their own voices formulating their own narratives with alternative borders that placed them, at times, along with the so-called 'majorities' against other 'others'.

There therefore exist many narratives of independence this book shows. Whereas nation-states are based on narratives that foreground 'partition' either because this signified the dawn of independence in the case of Bangladesh or the 'price of independence' in the case of India, in this book I show that there are other tales of independence to be told. Yet, as is also illustrated, not all these narratives do have an equal status. Our informants felt that their narratives, their histories and memories of 1947, were at odds with those they disliked and even perceived as threatening and which consequently made them feel insecure. Besides, they saw their voices ignored, surpassed and even quietened. In their view, there was a hierarchy of narratives in society,[28] a 'narrative regime' (Cf. Radstone and Hodgkin 2003) through which certain partition narratives (part of state-sponsored 'history') got preference over others and which silenced their voices. It is this common burden that constitutes the sufferings of both Hindus we interviewed in Bangladesh and interviewed Muslims in Jharkhand.

In this book, I show that both in India as well as in Bangladesh, there indeed exist state-supported partition historiography, which presents histories of minorities (i.e., Hindus in Bangladesh and Muslims in Jharkhand) that are at odds with the regional versions of 'the partition stories' we collected. These regional and personal histories also present different identities and ideas of rooting than those found in what we here define as state-supported partition rhetoric (including historiography). These state-supported partition narratives form 'mental borders' that separate 'the majority' from the 'minority' and inform the latter about who they were "and" are. They also subscribe to a set of behaviour rules for present and future.

Although multiple divisions characterized the population of British India in 1947, 'Hindus of Pakistan' and 'Muslims of India' were, in 1947 separated through geographical borders accompanied by written laws and regulations as embodied in the new constitutions of these two nation-states. The Governments in these two newly created nation-states offered their citizens labels as religious minorities with which many among them have hence identified. The constitutions in both Pakistan and India included their own 'minorities' in their concepts of the nation and accordingly they now belong to these nation-states, as citizens with, officially, equal rights and duties. Actually, after 1947 both new nations had envisioned secular states with clear provisions for the so-called religious minorities, i.e. Hindus in Pakistan and Muslims in India (Cf. Sheth and Muhajan 1999). Besides, the so-called Nehru-Liaquat Ali agreement (also known as the Delhi Pact) officially provided Hindu and Muslim minorities with machinery that could put forward their complaints and seek redress during the early 1950s (Cf. Banerjee 1999).

To guide the process of nation building, these nation-states have not only constitutions and written laws however. They also have narratives, grand-narratives, rhetoric, that tell who is included in and who excluded from the nation. These state-supported "national histories" thus, "create their own heroes and villains and survive on the spectre of the fear of the 'Other'" (Datta 2005: 3002). The state-supported partition narratives exposed in this book, and here defined as 'mental borders', were exposed by our informants during our oral history project, yet are also reflected in collected primary and secondary sources on the 1947 partition as well as encountered in so-called minority reports and reports on communal riots. What these narratives have in common is that they partition the land and people that reside in it into religious 'minorities' and 'majorities' and 'colonize' the former by linking them to 'partition'. They thus create and sustain 'partitioned nation-states and societies'. Many scholarly and semi-scholarly treatises on post-partition 'Muslims in India' and Hindus in Bangladesh do the same and describe the suffering of the minorities caused by partition.

Internet sides are in particular favourite media to fan 'evidence' concerning these suffering minorities. In an article on "atrocities" against Hindus in Bangladesh Rahul Gupta on the web[29] and himself a Hindu, defines this as "ethnic cleansing" due to a "Bangladesh über Alles syndrome" where the "Desher Bhabmurti" is more important than "a few thousand 'Malaun's lives'":

Hindus are subjected to the same types of atrocities after 1971 as they were during 1947-1971. There is an all-pervasive feeling of insecurity. As far as Hindus are concerned, nothing is safe-fishes in the ponds, paddy in the fields or valuables at home. Hindu women can be harassed or subjected to threats of kidnapping, to be followed by actual kidnapping, if the potential victims do not leave Bangladesh for India. It is nearly impossible for Hindus to sell anything at a fair price-cattle, paddy or land. They are forced to sell their lands at incredibly low prices. Even the plea for a fair price can provoke threats of murder or kidnapping. Moreover, even the price that is fixed at an unwarrantedly low level is not fully paid. False cases are started against Hindus. Police torture follows. Neither the Police apparatus nor the village community has any interest in coming to the rescue of beleaguered Hindus. There is, consequently, no option before Hindus except, leaving Bangladesh for India.

Similarly, Muslims who stayed put in India have become the 'victims' after 1947 according to many. Safeed Suhrawardy in an article on "Muslims after independence" (*Milli Gazette*, 16-30 June 2003) writes for instance:

Misinformation about Muslims was there during the British period also. However, that became an organized campaign of vilification after freedom. They were initially blamed for partition of the country. Suspicious about their patriotism and loyalty to the country continue with revisions, additions and subtractions. Now the common theme of anti-Muslim tirade is their 'alleged' links with ISI of Pakistan. Their religious institutions are being targeted for training and supporting terrorism.

Likewise, Rafiq Zakaria, a Muslim scholar, in his book entitled 'The Price of Partitions' laments the sufferings of 'Muslims' ever after partition. In his book "The Break-up of India, India Muslims: Where have they gone wrong?" he wrote bitterly advising Indian Muslims to chart a new path:

Indian Muslims must open their eyes to the ground reality that an increasing number of Hindus have begun to hate them...Indian Muslims must now see the light of the day and move in a different direction.

In "Muslim Indians— Yesterday, Today and Tomorrow" Zakaria describes the pre-1947 "paradise" in which the Muslims of the sub-continent lived and which is destroyed by the partition that was "the greatest tragedy that befell the Muslims" as now Muslims who stayed put in India, "In every field, sphere and sector, whether political, educational, social or economic, they have been reduced to be 'hewers of wood and drawers of water'" (*The Milli Gazette*, 16-30 June 2003: 12-13). Ironically, such writers though they are right about the sufferings of Hindus in Bangladesh and Muslims in India, reproduce the same 'two-nation theory' they themselves denounce as their entire perception is based on "we-they" syndrome and the resulting dichotomy between the 'minority' and the majority', the 'Hindus' and the Muslims'.

In this book we are also concerned with the sufferings (their 'losses') of the by us interviewed Hindus in Bangladesh and Muslims in Jharkhand but argue that their sufferings are based on this "substitution of the logic of majority for that of plurality" (Samaddar 2003: 25) through the enactment of the partition rhetoric which is often but certainly not always as the above examples illustrate, done consciously and with the malicious intent to let Muslims in India and Hindus in Bangladesh pay 'the price of partition'.

Our informants indicated that many people around them seem to listen to and even create and reproduce these narratives that endorse other 'truths' than those that are embedded in the respective legal systems of both countries. Our informants perceived these 'truths' as 'mental borders', which, they felt, separate them from the 'majority', discriminate them and cause insecurity among them as citizens. These borders make the reproducers the 'heroes' and them the 'Other' or even worse: 'villains'. Whereas the legislature in both nation-states is designed to protect the interests of these 'others', the so-called 'minorities', these 'unwritten laws' embodied in these partition narratives, often jeopardize these safeguards of citizens rights. Embodied in state-supported partition narratives and similar to 'prejudice' causing 'discrimination', these mental borders on people's minds, are difficult to expose as, precisely, they are mostly though not totally, 'unwritten'. They are erected or at least protected by those who identify as the 'claimants, makers and managers of states' who are often, though not necessarily so, part of the 'majority' as well.

Besides, geographical borders of the nation-states do not confine the workings of these mental borders. Many, who often identify as part of a religious majority in their own country, do perceive the religious minority of the neighbouring state as being their 'own', as belonging to 'us', and include them in their concept of the nation-state. In other words, these majorities advance a particular version of partition history that includes Muslims of India as 'we' in Bangladesh and Hindus in Bangladesh as 'we' in India. What is more, the rhetoric in both countries connects Muslims in India with Muslims 'there' (i.e. in Bangladesh/Pakistan) and Hindus in Bangladesh are amalgamated with Hindus in India. The by the 'religious majority' supported mental borders of partition furthermore separate Muslims from Hindus in India and Hindus from Muslims in Bangladesh. In fact, as shown in this book, the concern of the two nations over their 'own' minorities is influenced and often overshadowed by this much bigger concern over 'each other's minorities', which often creates tussles between the two nations. Along the long road of nation building, and through use of partition narratives, both countries thus claim the minorities of the other state in their concepts of 'we' and offer them refugee (Cf. Mishra and Majumdar 2003 and Roy 2001) whereas others, through the same narratives, are expelled as 'infiltrators' (Ramachandran 1999: 235-255).

Examples are numerous and last till date.[30] One such example of 'claiming the other's minority' is provided by R.M. Pal who wrote that, the West Bengal Government must remember that it is the *bhadralok* Hindus in Bengal like Jyoti Basu who wanted Bengal to be partitioned; after partition in 1947 they all migrated to West Bengal (leaving the poor and the working-class plebeian behind) and began to enjoy the fruits and benefits of partition— they became the rulers of West Bengal. The poor Hindus, Buddhists and Christians who stayed back in East Pakistan did not want Bengal to be partitioned'. Pal therefore felt that, 'The *bhadralok* Hindus in West Bengal have the moral duty and responsibility to come to the rescue of the poor from Bangladesh' (*Main Stream*, January 26, 2002: 17-18). These efforts are often done with the good intensions of providing minorities with a sense of security, but as will be shown in this book, such enactment of partition narratives to safeguard the interest of the other country's minorities, which are included as 'we' in these narratives, are not always welcomed by these "poor and plebeian Hindus" who were "left behind by the *bhadralok*". In particular not if these *bhadralok* in India claim "their fellow Hindus" in Bangladesh. This, it is shown, can trigger off repressive measures from the side of the Bangladesh Government who might castigate those Hindus in Bangladesh through their own mental borders. In their rhetoric they exclude those Hindus who do accept such 'help from India', separate them from the majority Muslims and depict them as 'traitors to the nation'. The other way round also happens, i.e. the effect of 'help' extended by Muslims in Bangladesh/Pakistan to their 'fellow Muslims in India'. This might trigger off the fear of the Indian Government over its 'internal security' and sometimes leads to arrests of Muslims in India depicted as 'infiltrators', 'spies' or 'terrorists' working against the 'interests of the nation-state'.

After the event of partition in 1947, these 'mental borders' that guide such 'inclusions and 'exclusions' by nation-states became more explicit and somewhat more 'formalized' through their inclusion in textbooks (Cf. Kumar 2001 and Rosser 2004), government and media reports and history books.[31] Yet, these 'mental borders' did not come about as sudden as the geographical borders in 1947 and in fact, have a long history of slow growth. Rather, the geographical partition seemed to have been the logical outcome of this increased workings of mental borders, which were already embedded in two centuries of divide and rule politics of the colonial state and worked during five decades of communal mobilization, needed to bring two new nations called India and Pakistan into being. In 1947, Sir Cyril Radcliffe, an English barrister who had never even visited South Asia before, drew lines on his map of what had till then been known as British India (Chatterji 1999: 185-242). As a result, some areas dominated by Muslims and others by non-Muslims, as determined by statistical census data, separated, and became part of different nation-states. In this way, Bengal was physically partitioned and the eastern part that what dominated by Muslims became part of the new nation Pakistan whereas the western part of Bengal where Hindus constituted the majority became part of the new nation India. Yet before this partition, religion had already become a primary criterion for the categorization not only of time but also of society (Gottschalk 2000: 27) and had separated 'Muslims' from 'Hindus'. The barrister's borderlines looked therefore to be a logical element in Britain's long reign over the Indian subcontinent. A reign guided by these mental borders on the minds of the British rulers and which created a binary opposition between Muslims and Hindus now perpetuated by the process of partition.

From the first census of the whole of British India taken in 1871, it becomes clear that society was divided mainly on basis of caste and religion (Van Bijlert 2002: 38-39). Though previously, neither the Muslim nor the Hindu community seem to have constituted homogeneous communities,[32] the census process itself presented Hindus and Muslims as fixed categories. Accordingly, Muslims were imagined to constitute one homogeneous group and Hindus were imagined as another group. This process also divided history into Hindu and Muslim periods and led to a bifurcation of space according to this religious divide. Later, when Ramsay MacDonald gave his famous award known as the Communal Award on August 16, 1932 representational politics were introduced (Mahajan 1970: 29-30). Consequently, population size became most important and religion became the basis on which the majority Hindus of British started campaigning against the minority Muslims. In short, by that time imagined communities had become somewhat real communities (Kaviraj 1992). Mental borders that divided Hindus and Muslims were somewhat accepted by some, though certainly not by all.[33]

During the 1930s, when the struggle for independence from British rule was in full flung, serious differences developed within and between some members of Hindu and Muslim communities, with some in each group arguing that Hindus and Muslims could never live peacefully together in one nation, according to any power-sharing formula. Syed Sifarish Husain Rizvi (1998: 170) narrated that, 'When Lord Wavell left India, the country was a boat whose sails had blown off; anchor lifted and was drifting towards a wreck. The Congress was busy with her strategy; the League was skeptical whether the British would divide India'. With the failure of a last-ditch attempt to build a political alliance between the Indian National Congress Party and the Muslim League in 1947, Muhammad Ali Jinnah, president of the Muslim League as well as Jawaharlal Nehru of the Congress Party, concluded that they had no other choice than to accept a partition of British India and support the establishment of two independent nations (Hasan 2002: 10 and Cf. Jalal 1985).

In other words some, in particular so-called leaders of the country, allowed borders of the mind to affect geographical borders. The spatial division of British India in 1947 according to religious labelling by the colonial rulers, though there was not necessarily an identification with this label among the masses of people, corresponded with the borders drawn by Barrister Radcliffe and became known as 'the Partition' among many. This "Partition", Radhika Desai (2002: 3459), added, created "Hindu and Muslim majority states, each with an official version of history". Pakistan was thus created for the Muslims with two wings, one in the East called East Bengal or Muslim Bengal and later on known as East Pakistan (Samad 1995: 126-167) the other wing became known as West Pakistan (Ibid: 118). The Hindus kept their 'Hindustan' (India or *Bharat*), situated between these two wings (Pandey 2001: 21).

Thosugh 1947 initiated new processes of nation building, 'triumph shook therefore hands with trauma'

(Cf. Bagchi and Dasgupta 2003). Though there were gains for some, there were losses for many others and 'the freedom attained had its price' in both countries (Cf. Khan quoted in Noorani 2003: 3). The violence that constituted and constitutes partition (Cf. Pandey 2001) was therefore the result of these mental borders, which also caused and in the case of Bangladesh causes migration of Muslims from India to East and West Pakistan and Hindus towards India[34] as well as 'ghettoization' of Muslims in India. These mental borders that existed before 1947 and which British rulers had used to separate 'Muslims' from 'Hindus', did not change. In fact, embodied in the partition narratives, the new rulers in both nation-states used them to initiate new processes of nation building. These narratives still do their work in dividing Muslims from Hindus in both countries and make the 'event of partition' a 'process of partition' that continues till date.

Though in present-day India and Bangladesh some legalisation recognises differences, laws are, still, designed to make the 'national' minorities in both countries more secure as citizens. Yet, religious minorities, as evidenced in this book feel in practice and with the rise of so-called religious fundamentalism in both nation-states increasingly so, insecure; at times all the time a bit and sometimes suddenly very much. The present book that explains the 'tyrannical' workings of narrative regimes in East Pakistan, Bangladesh and India shows how and why. I illustrate that partition narratives as supported by these nation-states encompass three types of mental borders enacted in both countries:

1. A border that separates the religious communities in 'minorities' and 'majorities'.

2. A border that separates these 'minorities' as 'non-indigenous' ('outsiders') from the 'indigenous' ('insiders').

3. A border that links these 'minorities' through transnational migration to the other nation and

threatens to make them or in fact makes them 'foreigners' ('non-citizens').

Sometimes, 'claimants, makers and managers of states' stop at the enactment of only the first border but they also perform 'full enactment'. Mostly this is an 'informal practice' yet I also show that the assiduous enactment of these mental borders by professed nation-state supporters, also influences written laws and are formalized in textbooks, reports and other documents. At times therefore, and because of this enactment of an 'unwritten law', even the legitimate rights of these minorities in India and Bangladesh as citizens are under threat.

On the one hand, therefore, there are the laws that define the legal status of minorities and the geographical boundaries, which include these minorities in the nation. On the other hand there are the narratives (mostly unwritten) that are incorporated in 'partition rhetoric' as subscribed to by managers of states and which borders do symbolically exclude these minorities from the nation and even threaten to do so legally. There is thus a contradiction between the two, which makes it possible, that, though laws guarantee equality, the population within the nation is divided by the workings of this narrative regime. Religious minorities in both countries, who are legal citizens according to the map, are thus separated, as 'outsiders', from the 'insiders'. The 'invisible' but very real and effective (mental) borders might even have potential to expel these 'outsiders' from the nation, literally or symbolically. These mental borders certainly constitute burdens for these minorities therefore.

Narratives of Rooting and Organization of the Book

Both India and Bangladesh, in principle and as observed in their democratic constitutions, treat their citizens at par. What now constitutes Bangladesh however was part of Pakistan. In Chapter 2 of this book, I show that the genesis of Bangladesh carved out of Pakistan with the geographical borders that demarcated East Pakistan becoming new international borders, was caused by the workings of mental borders at play in Pakistan after 1947. In that chapter I show that these mental borders as embodied in partition narratives and propagated by the new Pakistani leaders, did not only divide Hindus from Muslims but also East Pakistanis from West Pakistanis. Though outnumbering West-Pakistanis, these East Pakistanis felt treated, as illustrated, as 'minorities' and felt discriminated and dejected as citizens in their own country. Consequently, they started arguing against these mental borders and finally claimed and fought for new international geographical borders.

In chapter 3, I illustrate that when Bangladesh was established in 1971, it seemed that nation building could go on without mental borders that separated Hindus from Muslims since the 1947 partition. Yet, as shown in that chapter for Bangladesh and for India in Chapters 5 and 6, these mental borders rather than vanishing were strengthened and more formalized and eventually, even embedded in some written laws and regulations supported by the two nation-states.

In Chapters 6 and 7, we look into the lives of ordinary people who stayed put after the soil on which they lived suddenly belonged to different rulers. Scholars wrote about these masses of people who were "directly or peripherally affected following the sudden changes in the political map of India" that, "some were passive but interested observers. Some represented the elites", but most were, argues Mushirul Hasan (quoted in Chakrabarty 2003: 76), "ordinary folks whose fortunes and destinies were changed without taking into account their feelings and interests". In this chapter we listen to these 'untold stories of partition' (Ahmed, Dasgupta and Sinha-Kerkhoff 2004: 245-279) of Muslims who as Bharucha (2003: 4240) argues form "a blanket, undifferentiated" category in India, "who increasingly after independence, have had to prove their patriotic credentials before they can be regarded as 'Indian', and not open or closed Pakistanis". In Chapter 4, we do the same for Hindus in Bangladesh and look how these people, who spoke in "different voices", expressed "varying concern" and chose "separate and distinct points of identification" (Chakrabarty 2003: 76). As with Pandey (2002: 1032) we feel that, '[it] may indeed be the case that the "small voice" [...], of human variety and human dignity, is in greater danger than ever before [...]'. Subsequently, Pandey therefore rightly asks: 'Will these leave no room for anything other than desperate and symbolic statements of an undying and unchanging religious affiliation as identity?' In Chapters 4 and 7, I show that our informants did have other (national) selves than such based on an "unchanging religious affiliation" which were based on ethnicity, region, class and even gender and which created bonds in their minds with 'other locals'.

As mentioned before, our informants in India as well as those in Bangladesh were initially indifferent to, troubled by, or even hostile towards the topic of research. They wondered about the use of such a study, doubted our intensions or were even angered over the fact that we, like others before us, wanted them to "relive their pain, trauma, anger" (Alam and Sharma 1998: 98). They sometimes ignored my request therefore or replied with anger and agony as will be illustrated in Chapters 4 (for Bangladesh) and 7 (for India). Subsequently, the understanding of these sufferings became the main aim of my research. I wanted to know what caused this agony. This is explained in this book and in the conclusion (Chapter 8) some suggestions are given that might release some of this 'pain, anger and trauma'. Yet, more than others, including myself, it was our informants who provided the answer to the attenuation of their sufferings. In Chapter 4 (for Bangladesh) and Chapter 7 (for India) 'counter narratives' of our informants are presented that fundamentally question the 'truths' of the mental borders and their dividing workings. These narratives also evidence the 'tyranny' of the partition rhetoric in their lives. Instead, our informants came up with narratives (of independence) embodying new or alternative mental borders that:

1. United them, as 'minorities', with the majorities' against 'non-citizens'.
2. Separated them from others identifying as 'minorities'.
3. Rooted them firmly as 'insiders'/'locals' and separated them from 'outsiders'.

In other words, these narratives are all designed by alternative cognitive maps that legitimate their existence as citizens in the country/state in which they live and to veto their rhetorical or literal expulsion from the country/state. One can look upon these narratives as 'other nationalisms' (Datta 2005: 3000), as an alternative rhetoric with different mental borders that do not only unite these 'minorities' with the 'majorities' but also include them in these nation-states. They are thus part of the 'narrative regimes' but occupy a different position in the hierarchical ordering of such partition narratives in the two nation-states. This also explains the anger and agony among our informants, as they feel 'burdened' by these 'other people's narratives', which clearly, as experienced in day-to-day lives all the time a bit and during so-called communal riots suddenly very much, do not pay much heed to their (counter) narratives. In case they do, 'state guardians' try to silence them as they are seen as a threat to the mental borders they upheld and even, at times, to the geographical borders that they sustain.

References

1. These are thus strictly speaking both 'borderlanders' as well as 'heartlanders'. This study does not concern however those who come across international geographical borders in their day-to-day lives. The experiences of these 'borderlanders' form the subject of so-called borderland studies of which Van Schendel (2005) provides an admirable example.
2. This Indo-Bangladesh border is porous and consists of land as well as maritime borders. Besides, there is also a stretch of land that is yet to be demarcated. This causes problems between India and Bangladesh and is also the reason for controversy on the actual size of the borders, which some feel is, for instance, 4096 km long (Gupta and Chanda 2001). There are also border disputes between the two nation-states over the so-called enclaves. See for this, for instance, Alok Kumar Gupta and Saswati Chanda (2001), India and Bangladesh: Enclaves Dispute, on: http//www.ipcs.org/issues/articles/493-ban-alok.html and also Van Schendel (2002: 115-147).
3. Related to this see also Sinha-Kerkhoff (2004a); Sinha-Kerkhoff (2004b) and Chakravarty (2005) who evaluate the 'losses and gains' that partition engenders among those who stayed put and those who migrated. The 'gains' were in terms of increased class and/or gender awareness among lower classes, castes, or (widowed) women who experienced partition. This awareness did even engender movements that empowered these groups marginalized even before partition.
4. This book is thus not directly concerned with transnational migration flows but instead concentrates on the effect of partition on those who stayed put after the event. See Pandey (1997) for a similar focus.
5. I here draw on an analysis made by Bruner (2002).
6. See, for instance, *Hindustan Times* (Ranchi edition): June 2, 2005; June 3, 2005; June 6, 2005; June 20, 2005; June 22, 2005; June 25, 2005; July 6, 2005 and July 26, 2005. See also Muralidharan (2005); the editorial "Advani's 'saffron

secularism', in: Communalism Combat 2005, year 11, no. 108, June: 5 and Ram Puniyani 2005, "Partition culprit: to each one's own", in: *The Milli Gazette*, 131, vol. 6, no. 13, 1-15 July.

7. See for a good discussion of this kind of 'Hindu nationalism' the omnibus edited by Zavos, Jaffrelot and Hansen (2004).

8. See Datta (2005) for an excellent analysis of this controversy from the historian's point of view on which I also draw.

9. It should be remembered that partition brought apart from 'losses' also 'gains' for more powerful groups both among those who were relocated as well as among those who had stayed put. In this respect see also Rahman and Van Schendel (2004: 207-244).

10. The list of books on partition is long and does not allow full enumeration. I have, for instance, gone through the following that are mostly concerned with the so-called aftermath of partition: Niaz Zaman, A Divided Legacy: The Partition in Selected Novels of India, Pakistan, and Bangladesh (New Delhi: Manohar, 2000); Ravikant and Tarun K. Saint (eds.), Translating Partition (New Delhi: Katha, 2001); Ritu Menon (ed.), "The Partition of the Indian Sub-Continent", Interventions (Special Issue), vol. 1, no. 2 (1999): 157-235; Urvashi Butalia, The Other Side of Silence: Voices from the Partition of India (New Delhi: Penguin Viking, 1998); Muhammad Umar Memon, An Epic Unwritten: The Penguin Book of Partition Stories (New Delhi: Penguin India, 1988); Bimal Prasad, Pathway to India's Partition. The Foundations of Muslim Nationalism (Volume I); A Nation Within a Nation (Volume II) (Delhi: Manohar Books, 1999/2000); Mushirul Hasan (ed.), India's Partition. Processes, Strategy and Mobilization (New Delhi: Oxford University Press, 1993); Sukrita Paul Kumar and Muhammad Ali Siddiqui (eds.), Mapping Memories: Urdu stories from India and Pakistan (New Delhi: Katha, 1998); Tai Yong Tan and Gyanesh Kudaisiya (eds.), The Aftermath of Partition in South Asia (London/New York: Routledge, 2000); Ahmad Salim (ed.), Lahore 1947 (Delhi: Swankit India Research Press, 2001); Sucheta Mahajan, Independence and Partition:

The Erosion of Colonial Power in India (New Delhi: Sage Publications, 2000); Khadija Mastur (Translated from Urdu by Neelam Hussain), Inner Courtyard (Lahore: Simorgh, 2000); Alok Bhalla, "Memory, History and Fictional Representations of the Partition", Economic and Political Weekly, vol. xxxiv, no. 44 (30 October to 5 November 1999): 3119-3128; Mushirul Hasan, Adjustment and Accommodation: Indian Muslims after Partition. Occasional papers on history and society, 2nd series, no. 31 (New Delhi: Nehru Memorial Museum and Library, 1990); Gyanendra Pandey, Memory, History and the Question of Violence: Reflections on the Reconstruction of Partition (Calcutta: Centre for Studies in Social Sciences, 1999). David Gilmartin, "Partition, Pakistan, and South Asian History: In Search of a Narrative", The Journal of Asian Studies, 57, no. 4 (November 1998): 1068-1095; Rajeev Bhargava, "History, Nation and Community. Reflections on Nationalist Historiography of India and Pakistan", *Economic and Political Weekly*, vol. xxxv, no. 4 (22-28 January 2000): 193-2000; C. Emdad Haque, "The Dilemma of 'Nationhood' and Religion: A Survey and Critique of Studies on Population Displacement Resulting from the Partition of the Indian Subcontinent", *Journal of Refugee Studies*, vol. 8, no. 2 (1995): 185-209 and Ayesha Jalal, "Secularists, Subalterns and Stigma of 'Communalism': Partition Historiography Revised", in Modern Asian Studies, vol. 30, no. 3 (1996): 681-689 and Jasodhara Bagchi and Subhoranjan Dasgupta (eds.), The Trauma and the Triumph. Gender and Partition in Eastern India (Kolkata: Stree, 2003); Ritu Menon and Kamla Bhasin, Borders and Boundaries: Women in India's Partition (Delhi: Kali for Women, 1998); Suvir Kaul (ed.), The Partitions of Memory: The Afterlife of Partition (Delhi: Permanent Black, 2001); Ranabir Samaddar (ed.), Reflections on Partition in the East (Calcutta: Calcutta Research Group/Vikas, 1997); Amrik Singh (ed.), The Partition in Retrospect (New Delhi: Anamika/ Publishers/National Institute of Panjab Studies, 2000); Mushirul Hasan, Inventing Boundaries. Gender, Politics and the Partition (New Delhi: Oxford University Press, 2000); Imtiaz Ahmed (ed.) Memories of Genocidal Partition: The Haunting Tales of Victims, Witnesses and Perpetrators (Colombo: Fellowship in South

Asian Alternatives/Regional Centre for Strategic Studies, 2002); Ritu Menon (ed.) No Woman's Land. Women from Pakistan, India and Bangladesh write on the Partition of India (New Delhi: Women Unlimited and Associate of Kali for Women, 2004); Verma, Meenakshie, Aftermath. An Oral History of Violence (New Delhi: Penguin, 2004) and Bhalla, Alok and Vishwamitter Adil (translators), A Chronicle of the Peacocks. Stories of Partition, Exile and Lost Memories by Intizar Husain (New Delhi: Oxford University Press, 2004). Most of these studies concentrate on those who had 'moved' rather than on those 'who stayed put/behind'. Significantly, most scholars focus on partition's aftermath in India rather than in Bangladesh (or Pakistan) and comparative studies are extremely rare if not altogether absent. Note: the titles of those books fully enumerated here and elsewhere in notes and which are not referred to later on in the main texts have not been included in the bibliography at the end of this book.

11. Most of the recently published studies have described partition as a process rather than an event. See, for instance Ghosh (1998: 33-62). I go along with Samaddar's (2003: 23) interpretation of partition who stated that, "Thus, what we have to deal with is not a historical event subject to death, but a signed event, an event signed into the present, therefore an event not yet over –not yet even an event". See also my conclusions in chapter 8 where I argue that unless we make partition an event, embodied sufferings of so-called religious minorities in India and Bangladesh will continue. This will require complete different cognitive maps on the minds of nation-builders that do imagine 'departitioned' instead of 'partitioned states'.

12. Most scholars describe the lives, experiences and memories of people who resided in the Punjab. Related to this see, Ayesha Jalal, "Nation, Reason and Religion: Punjab's Role in the Partition of India", *Economic and Political Weekly*, vol. xxxiii, no. 32 (8 August 1998): 2183-2190. Yet, now scholarly work is also available that focus, 'on the human dimension of the second partition of Bengal (1947) with a clear emphasis on the gender perspective' to fill the 'serious gap'. See, for example, Jasodhara Bagchi and Subhoranjan Dasgupta (eds.) "Porous

Borders, Divided Selves", in Seminar (Special Issue), 510 (February 2002): 12-93 and also: Dipesh Chakrabarty, "Remembered Villages. Representation of Hindu-Bengali Memories in the Aftermath of the Partition", in Economic and Political Weekly (10 August 1996): 2140-2151.

13. Mushirul Hasan (1998: 2667) remains my great source of inspiration. He once wrote though in somewhat different context that, "if the 'histories of partition are to be rewritten, there are several reasons why we must judiciously draw upon the intellectual resources made available to us by such creative writers. They expose the inadequacy of numerous narratives on independence and partition, compel us to explore fresh themes and adopt new approaches that have eluded the grasp of social scientists, and provide a foundation for developing an alternative discourse to the current expositions of a general theory on inter-community relations".

14. Yet, so far, not many attempts have been made to compare the Indian case with other divided countries. Some recent, notable and outstanding exceptions are however: Deschaumes and Ivekoviæ (2003) and Greenberg (2004). For an effort in that comparative direction see also: 'Borders of the Mind: Changing Geographical Borders and their Mental Impact on People in India and Bangladesh after the Partition of 1947', a paper prepared by Sinha-Kerkhoff and Ellen Bal and presented during an international conference on "Memory and the Partition Motif in Contemporary Conflicts (Germany, India, Israel)", Institute of Social Anthropology, Martin–Luther-University, Halle-Wittenberg, Germany: 14-17 July 2005. To be revised and included in an edited volume published by Sage and edited by Eyal Ben-Ari, Smita Jassal and Burkhard Schnepel.

15. See, for instance: www. censusindia.net/religion.html (last downloaded on 19/8/2005). Indian census figures of 2004 inspired 'hysteria' among many and remain the source of controversies. See, for instance: Economic and Political Weekly, vol. xxxix, no. 39 (September 25-October 1) 2004: 4292-4304.

16. See, for instance: www.bmm.org/BMM/WhereWeServe/Asia (18/8/2005).

17. Jharkhand covers an area of 74677 square kilometers that is divided in 18 (plus 4) districts with a total population of about 22 million (see, for instance: www.Jharkhandyellowpages.net/statistics.php?file=population.html (last downloaded on 19/8/2005).

18. Bangladesh covers an area of 143,998 square kilometers that is divided in 64 districts with a total population of 138.44 million (see, for instance: en.wikipedia.org/wiki/Bangladesh (last downloaded on 19/8/2005).

19. In terms of numbers, this study does not represent therefore the 'majority' views and experiences of so-called religious minorities in the two countries, and certainly not that of females among them, yet I feel that it provides us with alternative narratives and the main argument remains applicable and can be used for more and other examples of 'alternative narratives' such as, for instance, narrated by Bal (2004) and Mehdi (2003).

20. Yet, I confess that in terms of numbers and as I continue living in Ranchi (Jharkhand), there is a certain bias in this study in favor of Muslims in Jharkhand with whom I interact on a more frequent basis than Hindus in Bangladesh who I have 'only' encountered in less numerous and 'formal' field work visits.

21. I conducted the interviews along with several research assistants mentioned and accredited in the acknowledgements.

22. Of relevance here is the remark by Gyanendra Pandey (2001: 13-14) that, "In spite of occasional objections, however, historians belonging to both India and Pakistan continue to write of the Partition of India, or of British India, in 1947. Indeed, the proper noun, 'Partition', has passed untranslated into several South Asian languages (including languages spoken in Pakistan and Bangladesh) as the name of a significant break that occurred in or about 1947".

23. See Cunningham and Heyman (2004: 289-302) for such an approach to the outcome of geographical borders in terms of the "mobilities" as well as "enclosures" they engender.

24. We here refer to the fact that many borders, including the Indo-Bangladesh border here discussed, are quite porous and trespassing finds place on daily basis. In an Amnesty International Report of 2003, it is also described how these physical borders are used by 'security forces' on both sides of the border to "push-in" and "push out" those groups of people whose nationality is disputed, quoted in: Muslim India Journal of Research, Documentation and Reference, 241-247, vol. 21, nos. 1-7, January-July 2003: 369.

25. By enactment I mean the conscious as well as unconscious endorsement of the 'truths' embedded in the narratives that are included in state-sponsored partition narratives ('partition rhetoric') as well as the acting upon these so-called truths, here defined as 'mental borders'.

26. This refers to the title of an unpublished report prepared for SEPHIS in 2003: 'The Burden of Other People's History: The Enactment of Partition Memory and Narratives of Religious Minorities in Jharkhand, India and in Bangladesh'.

27. In the case of India see for instance, Shefali Jha, "Secularism in the Constituent Assembly Debates, 1946-1950", *Economic and Political Weekly*, Vol. xxxvii, no. 30 (27 July to 2 August 2002): 3175-3180; Neera Chandhoke, Beyond Secularism: The Rights of Religious Minorities (New Delhi: Oxford University Press, 1999); Rajeev Bhargava (ed.), Secularism and Its Critics (New Delhi: Oxford University Press, 1998); Jacob De Roover, "The Vacuity of Secularism: On the Indian Debate and Its Western Origins", *Economic and Political Weekly*, Vol. xxxvii, no. 39 (28 September to 4 October 2002): 4047-4053 and its rejoinder by Kushal Deb, "Vacuous Critics of Indian Secularism", *Economic and Political Weekly*, Vol. xxxvii, no. 43 (26 October to 1 November 2002): 4466-4467. In the case of Bangladesh see for instance, Amena Mohsin "Democracy and the Marginalisation of Minorities", in B.K. Jahangir (ed.) *The Journal of Social Studies*, no. 78 (Dhaka: Center for Social Studies, October 1997); Barun De and Ranabir Samaddar (ed.) State, Development and Political Culture: Bangladesh and India (New Delhi: Har Anand Publications Pvt. Ltd, 1997);

Rafiuddin Ahmed (ed.), Religion, Nationalism and Politics in Bangladesh (New Delhi: South Asian Publishers, 1990); Sheikh Hafizur Rahman Karzon, "Secularism and Bangladesh Constitution, in Bangladesh Political Science Review, Vol. 1, no. 1 (June 2001), 105-132 and Joseph T. O' Connell, "The Bengali Muslims and the State: Secularism or Humanity for Bangladesh?", in Rafiuddin Ahmed (ed.), Understanding the Bengal Muslims. Interpretative Essays (New Delhi: Oxford University Press, 2001): 179-209.

28. We here are thus concerned with 'political societies' as they exist in India and Bangladesh and which work outside the framework of legality and constitutional norms, and its representatives are citizens only in a nominal sense. These are different from 'civil society', which Partha Chatterjee defined as "the domain of citizenship and civic and social organizations based on contractual agreements, mutual understanding, and consent", quoted in Bharucha (2003: 4250n28).

29. This article triggered off a huge debate on the web regarding the issue with people arguing that the violence directed against and oppression of 'Hindus' in Bangladesh' should be called 'ethnic cleansing' and others who denied such violence or did define and analyze it otherwise. See, for instance: www.mukto-mona.com/human rights/index.html

30. Just to get the 'smack' of this process see, for instance, historic example provided by the *Pakistan Observer*, which during a period of extreme communal violence in Bangladesh reported that, 'the Hindus are safe and secure in East Pakistan' (*Pakistan Observer*, 3 February 1964) but at the same instance it also reported 'mounting tension' among Muslims in India and reported that these Muslims were being threatened to 'quit the area' (*Pakistan Observer*, 20 March 1964). Besides, it also reported a message sent by the All Pakistan Press (APP) that 'Pakistan has protested to India for tempting Pakistani minorities to migrate from their homes in East Pakistan and cross into India with a view to unsettling the minorities in Pakistan and bringing a bad name to Pakistan' (*Pakistan Observer*, 5 March 1964). Identical examples can be given

for India where newspapers during the same time reported that in India, where communal riots had also broken out, the Muslim minority had nothing to fear but that India was worried about the lives of Hindus in East-Pakistan. See for instance, *Ananda Bazar Patrika*, 29 March 1964, which reported that peace had been restored in Jamshedpur a steel city in Jharkhand and that the minority was taken care of. *The Ananda BazarPatrika* of 30 March 1964 reported however that at the same time in East Pakistan Hindu girls had been sold to Arabs.

31. Ranabir Samaddar (2003: 25 and 35-36) shows that partition created "majoritarian states" that may be referred to as "ethnocracies" in which ethnic and religious conflicts only increased. Samaddar therefore regrets that, "Even perceptive observers miss the role of 1947 in the development of Indian geopolitical thinking–an event that marked the shift of the nation from marking out a cultural region/area to a geopolitical area as its 'natural habitat".

32. Bidyut Chrakrabarty (2003: 109) quoted Mushirul Hasan who once argued that it had now been a well-established fact that there had never been, 'despite the rhetoric of theologians and publicists', 'a single, inalienable Muslim identity'. He added that 'identities are inclusive and often rooted in local cultures, languages, oral traditions, influenced by complex historical processes'. On religious fusion and social bondings between and among Muslims and Hindus in South Asia see also for instance: Ahmad and Reifeld (2004).

33. Scholars have shown that in pre-independent as well as post-independent India there were and are cordial relations among many 'Hindus' and 'Muslims' and that "Even in localities where people clearly identified themselves as either Hindu or Muslim, there are numerous examples of saints and places that attracted both Hindus and Muslims", or of "Hindu patronage of Muslim institutions and vice versa [...] and of participation in religious rituals of the other community". Besides, there often was no "clear-cut division between Hindus and Muslims" and that "As late as towards the end of the nineteenth century, a number

of communities were as influenced by Islamic beliefs as by Hindu practices" (Frøystad 2005: 160-161).

34. Statistics provided by both nation-states are not very reliable as generally, both countries wanted to show that the in-flow of 'refugees' to their country was much more than the out flow. This downplaying of the numbers of people crossing the international borders could be political expedient in certain instances yet not in other cases and in the latter instance numbers were accordingly inflated. Generally, reports from West Bengal mentioned that 'huge flows' of Hindu refugees had arrived from East Bengal (see, for instance, West Bengal Papers, B Proceedings, Public Relations. vol. 2, first half of September 1951). Reports from East Bengal, which now belonged to Pakistan, mentioned that the flow of Hindus out of the country was much less than those of Muslim refugees from in particular the north eastern areas of India to East Bengal (see, for instance, East Bengal Papers, B Proceedings, Public Relations, vol. 2, part I, first half of July 1951). Reasons for high enumeration of in-coming refugees were for instance the claim both governments could lay on territory that had been awarded to the neighboring country in order to 'rehabilitate' these 'newcomers'. In short, one can argue that the workings of 'mental borders' also influenced statistics and it is difficult therefore to give any exact enumeration of people who crossed the borders or even of those who died on their way or before they even could start off. In this connection see also Pandey's excellent exposition on the impact of rumor on statistics concerning these 'Partition victims'. Pandey (1991: 91) concluded that, "The accounts live on in this form, rooted as they are in deeply held suspicions and beliefs, which are of course further reinforced by such 'remoured histories', 'truths' produced by prejudice that further accentuate prejudice".

2

The Working of Mental Borders in Pakistan

The Idea of Pakistan

Pakistan was a novel experiment in the history of nation building. With its two wings separated by 15,000 kilometres of foreign territory (India), it was obvious that its first Governor-General the Quad-i-Azam Mohammad Ali Jinnah would have a tremendous task to forge a nation. During the almost twenty-five years that the nation existed in this peculiar geographical disposition, guardians of the nation-state took to task to make Pakistan an "independent, democratic, sovereign Islamic state, which its founding fathers had envisaged" (Datta 2004: 4329). Yet, though Jinnah had spoken of equal rights for all citizens of Pakistan thus signalling a democratic state[1] he or Pakistan's first Prime Minister Liaquat Ali Khan were not able to make much headway with the formation of a Constituent Assembly. It was only after the death of Jinnah in September 1948 that decisions were taken and in March 1949, an Objectives Resolution was passed by the Constituent Assembly. It was declared that sovereignty belonged to Allah, but the same was to be exercised in Pakistan by its people according to the dictates of the Koran and Sunnah. Pakistan was to be a federation and the principles of democracy, freedom, equality, tolerance and social justice as enunciated by Islam were to be fully observed. In the Pakistan constitution of 1956 the rights and legitimate interests of the minorities were to be protected and they were free to profess and practise their religion and develop their culture. The state guardians guaranteed that all the citizens of Pakistan would get equal fundamental rights (Mahajan 1970: 282-285). Yet, this constitution did not bring the desired 'unity', 'welfare' and 'happiness' among all 'people of the country'. Another constitution therefore replaced it in 1962, which declared Pakistan a Republic and the fundamental human rights of citizens preserved if they were "consistent with the security of the state, public interest and requirements of morality" (Ibid: 292). Yet, in Pakistan the democratic process did not develop and "her growth as a sovereign, democratic republic was stunted and mutilated due to long military rule clamped on Pakistan" (Datta 2004: 4333).

What is more, all through its more than two-decade history, there remained a contradiction between these laws and constitutions that should have guaranteed equality among those who were included in the nation-state and the "the 'idea' of Pakistan" (Datta 2004: 4332). Clearly, there were other borders at work than the geographical that circumscribed Pakistan and that should have 'united' and 'protected' people living inside them against the 'outsiders', the 'others' (i.e. Indians). This 'internal bordering' by enacting borders here defined as mental borders, or borders of the mind, caused in fact a "symbolisation and (discursive) institutionalisation of differences" (Houtum and Naerssen 2001: 125). As explained below, the mental borders included in the grand-narrative of the nation, though translated in laws that professed inclusion, actually alienated a majority of the population from the nation-state. This disgruntled lot not only challenged these mental borders by which they found themselves excluded from the nation and which simultaneously provided the raison d'être of Pakistan but also started a campaign to transform the geographical boundaries that circumscribed the nation-state.

When on 14 August 1947 Pakistan emerged, there was sadness as well as happiness. Many were killed just before, during and after partition. Observing the tremendous losses of lives, property and 'honour', partition narratives embodied these traumatic experiences. Jinnah, for instance, deplored "the human madness that had overwhelmed people and brought misery to many homes" (Noorani 2003: 55). Judged from reports and fiction written by Pakistani Muslims at the time, though they now had become a 'majority' in their own nation-state, many remembered partition as a catastrophic event (Anisuzzaman 1999: 23-42). Pakistan had emerged through the separation of the Muslim-majority North Western and North Eastern zones from the rest of British India and their amalgamation into a single state. Altogether, Pakistan received 23 per cent of the territory and 19 per cent of the population of British India. West Pakistan had a population of 33.70 million and East Pakistan 42 million (Ahmed 1996: 169). Many Pakistani Muslims perceived that the 'deal' had not been fair however and there was anger as many felt the Radcliffe Awards had been the unjust and illegal result of a conspiracy hatched between Lord Mountbatten and Nehru. This sadness and anger did not vanish. It remains responsible for traumas and border tussles between India and Pakistan.

Yet, though attained at a price, which people on both sides of the borders still are paying, in Pakistan the leaders of the newly established nation-state were jubilant over the newly received freedom. For them the year 1947 signalled the end of British colonialism and Hindu domination and the beginning of new processes of nation building during which partition became looked upon as a necessary evil while the new borders would provide many Muslims with security, mental as well as physical. These new geographical boundaries would thus provide the majority of Pakistanis with (inner) space to develop identities and constitute groups that would empower them.

The demand for Pakistan thus was, as Tanveer Fazal concluded, "raised on behalf of the [British] Indian Muslims in their entirety. Yet, in retrospect, the creation of Pakistan foreclosed any neat equation between the demand and the reality" (Fazal 2004: 278). For one, well after 1947, millions of Hindus still lived in Pakistan and the 1951 census recorded their numbers at as high as around 14 per cent, with the largest chunk residing in East Pakistan (Gankovsky and Polanskaya 1964: 97). The new guardians of the nation-state would have a tremendous task to unite whole of the population under the nomenclature 'Pakistanis'. This was, however, the task the self-appointed 'jubilant' leaders of Pakistan had set themselves. On 11 August 1947 Jinnah delivered his famous and often quoted address to the Pakistan Constituent assembly in Karachi, in which he had said:

> You may belong to any religion or caste or creed – that has nothing to do with business of the state – we are starting with the fundamental principle that we are all citizens of one state. I think we should keep that in front of us as our idea and you will find that in course of time, Hindus will cease to be Hindus, and Muslims will cease to be Muslims, not in religious sense because that is the personal faith of each individual but in the political sense, a citizen of the state (quoted in Datta 2004: 4332).

Jinnah envisaged a welfare state in Pakistan by incorporating in the constitution the principles of a free representative government, constitutional liberalism, strong rule of law and equitable social justice and he regarded Islamic values and liberal ideals as the "guiding principles of the Pakistan state" (Datta 2004: 4332). The new leaders thus presented Pakistan as "the embodiment of the unity of the Muslim nation" (Nauriya 1999: 98). What is more, what was clear to these state guardians after the "euphoria" of Independence was over, that national identity and nation building had to be formulated through a framework, 'a mental map', that distinguished itself from India (Cf. Ahmed 2002: 20). While this framework's mental border, 'of course', excluded non-Muslims, it would unite all Muslims in Pakistan who were supposed to maintain distinctiveness from "secular India" (Cf. Ahmed 2002: 21). In this way, a grand-narrative of the nation, the 'idea of Pakistan, was framed which separated Pakistan from 'Hindu India' while it would unite all Muslims in Pakistan. This grand-narrative of the nation was embodied in educational, religious and other associated institutions of civil society in Pakistan and was reproduced in speeches, textbooks, historical projects and transmitted by other media in other to mould "cognitive structures" (Fazal 2004: 281) of all Pakistani citizens.

In order, to properly dissipate these mental borders as embodied in this idea of Pakistan, Pakistani leadership needed "the invention of a distinct historical past" that could justify Pakistan's separate existence as a Muslim nation and in contrast to India (Cf. Ahmed 2002: 21). Therefore, the new leadership propagated new narratives of the nations reproduced by state-owned educational institutions and other media. A Radio Pakistan broadcast, for instance, declared that:

The foundations of Pakistan were laid with the arrival of the first Muslim in subcontinent. Pakistan has at its back the historical heritage of a thousand years. The strength of Pakistan lies in the political, cultural and religious supremacy of the Muslims [...] The people of Pakistan are firm in their belief in Islamic principles (quoted in Fazal 2004: 281).

Apart from geographical borders and written laws that contained Muslims in Pakistan in one nation-state, Pakistan thus also reproduced the rhetoric of partition in order to contain its Muslim population within its geographical borders as well as to attract certain wealthy and well-known Muslim (leaders) of neighbouring India. Immediately after the Dominion of Pakistan came into existence on 14 August 1947 the new nation-state was in great need of a means to forge unity among its citizens in both wings (Cf. Choudhury 1997: 1-39). The formulation of a common constitution alone proved not sufficient however and a rhetoric was needed that could not only legitimate the establishment of a separate nation truncated from British India, but also its somewhat odd shape. Partition narratives with their mental borders constituted such rhetoric in post-independent Pakistan that was used by guardians of the nation-state to establish a collective 'memory-community'. The early leaders in Karachi realized the difficulty as President Ayub Khan admitted:

> [Pakistani nationalism was] based more on an idea than any territorial definition. Till then ideologically we were Muslims, territorially we happened to be Indians and parochially we were a conglomeration of at least eleven smaller provincial loyalties. But then Pakistan emerged as a reality, (we) were faced with the task of transforming all out traditional territorial and political loyalties into one great loyalty for the new state of Pakistan (quoted in Fazal 2004: 278).

Yet, apart from other internal as well as external problems that threatened the nation-state, it proved in particular difficult to keep the two wings of Pakistan together as East Pakistan resented the domination of West Pakistan. After protest from Dhaka, the new constitution provided however for the establishment of the seat of the National Assembly at Dhaka and the Headquarters of the Government of Pakistan at Islamabad in West Pakistan. Both Urdu and Bengali became the national languages of Pakistan in order to give satisfaction to the people of East Pakistan. Similarly, after Dhaka severely criticized Karachi's efforts at power domination, East and West Pakistan became equally represented in the National Assembly. Yet, in spite of all this, opposition persisted among the majority in East Pakistan and leaders among them formed the Pakistan Democratic Movement in 1967 that demanded more regional autonomy. Opposition in East Pakistan increased however and finally cumulated in a movement for total liberation from West Pakistan, which East Pakistanis achieved in 1971 with the establishment of the new nation of Bangladesh. The mental borders that had been created by the guardians of the Pakistani nation-state and had guided and sustained the geographical borders that circumscribed Pakistan between 1947 and 1971, had thus proved unable to separate 'Hindu and Muslim Bengalis' in East Pakistan and include the latter in the independent Muslim state. In other words, the project of "homogenization" (Fazal 2004: 276) as envisioned by Jinnah and other guardians of the nation-state clearly failed. After 1947, Jinnah and others supported 'centralised consociational accommodation' (Cf. Adeney 2002: 8-33) but already in 1941 Jinnah had clearly foreseen that it would be difficult to contain non-Muslims in the imagined Muslim-state after partition as he had the said inter alia:

> It is obvious that if the Hindu minorities in Pakistan wish to emigrate and go to their homelands of Hindustan they will be at liberty to do so and vice versa those Muslims who wish to emigrate from Hindustan can do so and go to Pakistan and sooner or later exchange of population will have to take place and the Constituent Assemblies of Pakistan and Hindustan can take the matter and subsequently the respective governments in Pakistan and Hindustan can effectively carry out the exchange of population wherever it may be necessary and feasible (Sheth and Mahajan 1999: 91) [emphasis added in original quotation].

Yet, what was not 'logic' was, the new leaders in Karachi thought that the Bengali Muslims who formed a majority in Pakistan did want a third nation and separate state for themselves. As Hamza Alavi (1973: 166) described:

In Pakistan the ruling, predominantly Punjabi, bureaucratic-military oligarchy has taken over and put to its own particular use the slogans of Muslim nationalism, the slogans of the movement on whose strength Pakistan was brought into being. It extols the virtues of "Islamic solidarity" and denounces linguistic or regional opposition movements as divisive provincialism. In this way, since the creation of Pakistan, the nature and political role of Muslim nationalism and the significance of its slogans have altered. Muslim nationalism in [British] India propagated the cause of the underprivileged Muslim educated middle classes in India, who were numerically small and educationally less advanced than those of the Hindus. The creation of Pakistan, the separate homeland of the Muslims, was the fulfillment of that cause. Therefore, after the state of Pakistan had been created, the raison d'être of that movement ceased to exit. At that point the Muslim League, the principal organ of the movement, disintegrated. The surviving faction, which appropriated the mantle of the Muslims League, then began to propagate its ideology on behalf of the privileged groups, especially the Punjabi oligarchs, in opposition to regional challenges. The ideology of Islamic unity was now employed to deny the validity of the claims and demands of the less privileged groups— the Bengalis, Sindhis, Pathans, and Baluchis-for recognition of their distinct identity and needs.

Thus, the new state of Pakistan was not simply based on Islam, or the ideal of "Muslim unity", but, "more precisely, on a particular interpretation of Islam that stressed the importance of modern education leading to an individual *Bildung* into modern citizens and the ability of independent reasoning concerning religious matters (*ijtehad*)". Yet, in this nationalist ideology, "particular practices were rejected as being traditional, backward, syncretic, a remainder of Hindu or colonial influence, and therefore un- or not quite-Islamic" (Verkaaik 2001: 350). In other words, the 'military-bureaucratic oligarchy' in Karachi had propagated mental borders that were expected to have had separated these Bengali Muslims East Pakistan from 'Hindus' and unite them with the other Pakistani Muslims in one nation-state. Yet, in practice these mental borders were embodied in narratives of the nation that alienated these East Pakistanis as they only referred to a history version and interests of the ruling Urdu-speaking, Muslims called *Muhajir* who had migrated and the Punjabi-Pukhtun military-bureaucratic oligarchy (Cf. Ahmed 1996: 174) with rooting in West Pakistan. The history and ideology as formulated by Bengalis was not included in these narratives of the Pakistani nation-state, these East Pakistanis felt and they therefore started contesting the mental borders included in these narratives.

The Exclusion of East Pakistanis from the Nation and the State

In the 'grand narrative of Pakistan' that had the 'Two-Nation Theory' as its organizing principle as argued above, Bengali Muslims were prompted to behave as 'Muslims', and Muslims only, who constituted a separate nation and stood in binary opposition to 'Hindu India'. Besides, these narratives did either not include the views of those who valued differently or these were reprimanded. To use Fazal's (2004: 276) apt description:

> In their effort to create an appropriate phantasmagoria, the cultural moorings of the 'nation' came to be defined in terms of the symbols and ethos of the dominant group, this led to the 'ethnification' of the weak and the marginal national and ethnic groups.

Clearly, the traditions and history of Bengal were not embodied in the narratives of the Pakistani nation-state and mental borders on the minds of its rulers divided the nation in East and West Pakistanis. In fact, these borders made East Pakistanis 'minorities' and as a result made them feel "colonized" in their own country (Cf. Fazal 2004: 283).[2]

The 'official nationalism' as propagated by the guardians of the nation-state and transmitted through speeches, textbooks and other media, attempted "to fix and objectify an essentialized sense of 'Muslim identity'", which in essence was the Punjabi identity that "fused into the identity of Pakistan" (Fazal 2004: 280). Besides, "while essentializing Islam as the sole determinant of Muslim predilections", simultaneously "a monolingual Islam" was propagated and reified and "Scriptural [i.e. in Urdu] Islam was idealized at the cost of other social practices" (Fazal 2004: 281). Clearly, such a 'one-tunnel view' of national identity (Cf. Bagchi quoted in Datta 2004: 4333) excluded other conceptions of Islam and practices of Muslims such as those followed by Muslims in Bengal. These narratives clearly excluded them from the (Muslim) state and even somewhat relegated them to (Hindu) India. The contempt for the Bengali form of Islam is clear when President Md. Ayub Khan observed that,

> East Bengalis, who constitute the bulk of the population, probably belong to the very original Indian races...they have been and still are under considerable Hindu cultural and linguistic influence. As such, they have all the inhibitions of downtrodden races.

While the *Muhajir* filled the bureaucracy along with Punjabis, "the Punjabi domination in the military, a colonial legacy, remained unperturbed" (Fazal 2004: 280). Besides, these two groups were also at the top of the machinery that spread the state-approved narratives of the nation. The mental borders incorporated in the narratives of the nation and reproduced through various media therefore also separated the non-Bengali Urdu-speaking *ashraf* from the vernacular (Bengali speaking) *ajlaf*, urban as well as rural in East Pakistan. In their efforts to order the society, Pakistani leaders in Karachi, tried to include the 'other' in their concept of the nation but only if these 'others' would accept their 'idea of Pakistan', fundamentally based on the partition ideology where partition "appears as the final act, perhaps undesirable but unavoidable, perhaps bloody but necessary to avert more bloodshed, perhaps an unhappy separation but a separation to prevent genocide" and this "irreversibility of partition" overwhelmed "the nation, its leaders and public". Samaddar (2003: 31) continued:

> In this situation, the public mind becomes an ethnic mind, for the nationalist public discovers itself in the comic form of identity, which can only assume an ethnic form. To the extent that democracy becomes a victim of the nationalist strategy to use Partition to achieve statehood, ethnicity wins out. Partition inverts the relationship between nationalism and ethnicity on the one hand and democracy on the other. It is the irreversibility of the act that makes this inversion possible.

What is more, during these two decades of Pakistan's existence, as civil authority was continuously broken, these Pakistani leaders had ample space for 'compulsive reference' (Cf. Ahmed 1996: 171) to their idea of the nation-state and thus a free flow of the mental borders embodied in it. Though the laws in Pakistan supported 'inclusion' or ('voluntary') "assimilation of some" (Cf. Van Houtum and Naerssen 2002: 126), the East Pakistani Muslims were thus effectively excluded by these mostly 'invisible borders'. It is difficult to 'prove' the existence of such a 'symbolization of differences' (Cf. Van Houtum and Naerssen 2002: 125) unless these differences are somehow registered at the time. Apart from institutionalization in laws and constitutions, mental borders can also be detected through examination of different media. One can get a 'taste' of such borders through the analysis of, for instance, Pakistani textbooks that were prescribed in educational institutions during the fifties and sixties in East Pakistan.

These textbooks were certainly without 'B' (Cf. Rosser 2004: 15). Modern history focused more on the Western wing and central India and East Bengal was "tacked on to the two-nation theory" (Rosser 2004: 15).

Other narratives were forgotten or forbidden, silenced. Indeed, the narratives gave some credit to the eastern wing of helping the creation of the nation and it was recognized that "the Muslim League was founded in Dhaka" (Rosser 2004: 15). Yet, the main concern in the narratives incorporated in these textbooks was "to foster a Pakistani-Islamic identity defined negatively, as a contrast to India" (Ahmed 2002: 21). Only some parts of Bengali history was included in the textbooks and only a few Bengalis 'remembered' while others conveniently 'forgotten' or their deeds denounced as being 'India-centric' or being against the interests of the Pakistani-nation state. The fact, for instance, that Hussein Shaheed Suhrawardy, chief minister of United Bengal, had also, i.e., along with Fazlul Huq, attended the All India Muslim League Conference in Lahore was completely omitted in these textbooks. During this meeting in 1940 Suhrawardy had ardently pleaded that "Bengal should be allowed to form its own commonwealth of association with its adjoining states after Indian independence" (Rosser 2004: 15). In a sense, Suhrawardy had been calling for a confederal or federal India.[3] His views were however not incorporated in official Pakistani history after 1947 and instead the ideas and activities of Fazlul Haq, who switched over to the Muslim League, were recounted extensively. In general East Bengal's "cultural longevity or its contributions to nation building" (Rosser 2004: 15) were absent not only in textbooks of the time but also in speeches.

In Pakistani textbooks there was great remembrance of the Lahore Resolution (also known as the 'Pakistan Resolution') of 1940 during which the view was expressed that there were "two nations known as Hindus and Muslims" (Mahajan 1970: 233) and during which Jinnah who presided over the Lahore Session of the All-India Muslim League, declared, to quote him at length:

> If the British Government are really in earnest and sincere to secure peace and happiness of the people

of this subcontinent, the only course open to us all is to allow the major nations separate homelands by dividing India into autonomous national States. There is no reason why the States should be antagonistic to each other. On the other hand, the rivalry and the natural desire and efforts on the part of the one to dominate the social order and establish political supremacy over the other in the government of the country will disappear. It will lead more towards natural goodwill by international pacts between them, and they can live in complete harmony with their neighbours. This will lead further to a friendly settlement all the more easily with regard to minorities by reciprocal arrangements and adjustments between Muslim India and Hindu India, which will far more adequately and effectively safeguard the rights and interests of Muslims and various other minorities (Mahajan 1970: 237).

Related to this Krishna Kumar (2001: 199) analyzed:

> Every Pakistani textbook virtually stops the narrative flow in order to celebrate the Lahore Resolution. We hear about its historic significance before we are given its content and an elaborate comment on its spirit. Just as Indian textbooks specify the Gawalia Tank Maidan as the venue of Gandhi's 8 August speech, Pakistani texts name Minto Park (now Iqbal Park where the Minar-e-Pakistan stands) as the venue where the Lahore Resolution stands like a commanding peak in the landscape of the early 1940s in Pakistani textbooks just as the Quit India movement does in the Indian textbooks. This basic difference is indicative of the rival landscapes in which the last phase of the freedom movement unfolds in the two sets of school textbooks.

This absence of Bengal in public memory and in the rhetoric of nation building, and therefore the existence of mental borders that separated East and West Pakistan, was also evident from political decisions taken at the time. One of the most important that caused numerous violent protests by East Bengalis through the years 1948-1971 was the "Urdu Only" policy declared by the "Father of Pakistan", M.A. Jinnah, which effectively meant the announcement that "Bengali was of secondary importance, even though more than half of the citizens in United Pakistan spoke Bengali as their native tongue" (Rosser 2004: 8).

Therefore, not only was Bengali and in fact were Bengalis forgotten in the grand-narratives of the nation but if Bengali were remembered, they were represented as marginalized 'minorities', as the 'semi-alien others' who if not 'voluntarily assimilating' could be subject to "purification" or even "elimination" (Cf. Houtum and Naerssen 2002: 126). This is in particular clear when Pakistani accounts of the 1965 and 1971 wars with India are examined. Clearly in these narratives Pakistanis are the '(suffering) heroes' and Indians 'violent villains' with Bengalis depicted as 'possible' and 'real' 'traitors' endangering the 'idea of Pakistan' (Cf. Adhikari 2000: 87).

Challenging the Mental Borders of the Pakistani Nation-State: Muslim Bengalis

The first partition of Bengal had taken place in 1905 and had resulted into the creation of a separate Muslim dominated province. In 1906, important Bengali Muslim leaders established the All India Muslim League in Dhaka and lent their support to the partition of Bengal on religious lines as decided by the British Government. Under the pressure of high-caste Bengali Hindus however, the British rulers annulled this partition in 1911 (Das 1991: 25). Ironically however, though Muslim leaders of Bengal later on also proposed the so-called two-nation theory, they had vehemently tried to avoid the partition of Bengal in 1947 in particular as they feared it would involve the loss of Kolkata (Ahmed 2004: 120 note 119). Alternatives were formulated such as a plan for a United Bengal as a third independent nation along with India and Pakistan (Ahmed 2004: 280-287). When these Bengali Muslim leaders finally lost the battle for Kolkata and became part of a truncated Bengal, they nevertheless rejoiced as partition was seen as a new beginning of a better future for the Bengali Muslims. Though the trauma of the communal violence of those days remained alive in their minds, partition was, as shown in Chapter 3, basically remembered as a first and necessary step in the process of nation building.

After 1947 a period had started which would last for twenty-four years during which these Bengali Muslims perceived the mental borders that alienated them from the nation. Initially, they accepted these borders and tried to (voluntary) assimilate, but when they increasingly realized the power of these borders that remained excluding them, they started rejecting these borders, posing alternatives that finally caused a change the geographical borders that circumscribed a United Pakistan.

Before independence, the leaders of the Bengali Muslims generally were landlords or Calcutta-based urban cosmopolitans, who were either non-vernacular or bilingual. But in the years following independence, pre-existing factional groups and new social forces gave rise to a Bengali counter-elite, which was mostly vernacular and regional (Adhikari 2000: 81). Initially, they tried at more effective participation at the centre and thus worked within space the mental borders of Pakistani nationalism had provided them. Yet, increasingly and cumulating during India-Pakistan war of 1965, the difference in mental outlook between the 'dissident political leaders' of East Pakistan and the guardians of the Pakistani nation-state became clear. For one, these East Pakistani Muslims "did not share the passionate anti-Indian and anti-Hindu feelings of the principally non-Bengali Pakistan establishment", which was in particular clear during the so-called Kashmir dispute (Adhikari 2000: 85).

Slowly, therefore these Bengali leaders started doubting as well as challenging the mental borders that formed the ideological basis of Pakistan and in Pakistan's east wing a "secular, territorial Bengal nationalism" (Adhikari 2000: 86) emerged as an answer to this decades-long marginalization. This weakened the national bond between East and West Pakistan and finally led to the change in geographical borders as well. This new ideology, which later on became the rhetoric of the new nation-state Bangladesh with its new mental borders, as discussed in Chapter 3, can be found in newspapers, journals and pamphlets of this period, now available in the libraries in Dhaka.[4]

Thus, though Pakistan had been established on behalf of Muslim Punjabis, Sindhis, Pashtuns and Baluchs in its western part and Bengalis in its eastern part, not all Pakistanis experienced the geographical boundaries that circumscribed the nation-state as 'lines of security'. Right from the beginning, Bengali Muslims in East Pakistan realized that in reality the mode of conceptualizing the nation, the 'Two-Nation-Theory' as well its cognate mental borders did exclude them historically, politically, economically and socio-culturally from the nation and state. If not excluded, they were made 'minorities' in these disseminated state-owned television, radio, and state textbooks narratives. In 1955, Sheikh Mujibur Rahman, at the time student leader of the East Pakistani political party the Awami League[5] and who later became known as Bangabandhu (friend of Bengal),[6] for instance sensed this possibility of 'official forgetting' and vented in a speech in the Constituent Assembly:

Sir, you will see that they want to place the word 'East Pakistan' instead of 'East Bengal'. We have demanded so many times that you should make it Bengal

(Pakistan). The word 'Bengal' has a history, has a tradition of its own. You change it only after the people have been consulted (quoted in Fazal 2004: 282).

The rhetoric of Islamic unity that was employed by guardians of the nation-state, these Bengali Muslims increasingly perceived, proved thus a bundle of narratives that divided West Pakistanis from East Pakistanis and were used in the post-independence period to deny the validity of claims and demands of the less powerful citizens such as Bengalis and also Sindhis, Pathans and Baluchis, for their recognition of their distinct identity and needs. Initially reacting to perceived inequalities by trying to accommodate within the nation-state, a quest for an "intrinsically secular 'Bengali' concept" had started among these Bengali Muslims. They formulated narratives through which they did not seek to remove the 'proof' of the differences in aims, aspirations, perspective and awareness between "the Bengali of West Bengal and the Bengali of Bangladesh" from Bengali 'mass memory', but through which they nevertheless conveyed that they "refused to bifurcate the common history" of the United Bengal that preceded 1947 (Cf. Dasgupta, 2002: 22).

During this early phase of protest against the existing mental borders, the so-called language movement in 1952 was started during which both Bengali Muslim and Bengali Hindus in East Pakistan demanded that Bengali should become a national language (Umar 2000). Later on Bengali Muslims proceeded to the demand for more autonomy and independence from West Pakistan (Samad 1995) and finally their protest cumulated in the extremely violent liberation war of 1971 (Mascarenhas 1986). During this process, these Bengali Muslim leaders not only challenged the mental borders set by the leaders in Karachi and which separated them from (West) Bengal in India, they also formulated new borders that united them with other Bengalis and separated them from the West Pakistanis. In their new and alternative concept of 'the nation', the common cultural heritage between the two Bengali communities in West and East Bengal was not forgotten and served in fact to root them in an East Pakistan separated from West Pakistan. The Pakistani leaders in Karachi in particular rejected the struggle that established Bengali as one of the state-language. The move was perceived as a threat to the mental borders that sustained Pakistan as Bengali was one of the cultural links between East Pakistan and West Bengal in India (Pakistan's main enemy). Making Bengali the first language in East Bengal thus meant a progressive transgression of the internal borders set by these (self-appointed) Pakistani guardians of the nation-state.

These Bengali Muslims accepted partition however though they also remembered their traumatic experiences as could be perceived from writings of Abu Rushd and Dilara Hashem (*Hong Kong Standard*, 14-04, 1999). Yet, they also saw in partition an opportunity for a new beginning, the building of a new nation, a third nation. These Bengalis had soon found themselves alienated from West Pakistan and their answer to the by the Pakistani leaders enforced mental borders that placed these Bengali Muslims at the margins or even outside the nation, was the birth of 'Bengali nationalism', which would root them in the soil and which borders should provide them economic, social-cultural, religious and economic security. Kamruddin Ahmad, one such Bengali Muslim looked in 1967 back to the year 1947 and remembered that 'Independence' had,

> Brought a new consciousness among the younger generation of boys and girls of eastern Bengal. Unlike the older generation of Muslims who lived in an abstract world, these young people have found concrete and solid ground under their feet. They love their native land, its clouds and sunshine, its air and water, its

language and literature, its music and dance, its society and people. They are really at home in their native land. The older generation of Muslims denied everything they received from the soil. They liked to feel that their forefathers had all migrated from Arabia or some other Muslim countries of western Asia, that they had come here as conquerors and never felt at home in Bengal (Ahmad 1967: 197).

These Bengali Muslims thus embarked on a project that formulated narratives that would create feelings of historical, intellectual, cultural and even religious 'superiority' among the masses in Bengal and which would root them in Bengal and finally would legitimize their demand for a separate 'homeland'. It was during the 1965 Pakistan-India war that these Bengali Muslims realized that they would never be equally assimilated in a United Pakistan and that, though numerically superior, they remained in fact to be treated as (inferior) minorities, exploited denounced and degraded intellectually, religiously, socio-culturally as well as economically. As Adhikari accounts:

The war of 1965 deeply affected the attitudes of the Bengali intelligentsia. It may be worth connecting the 1965 war with earlier and later transformation in the thoughts of the Bengali intellectuals, particularly the economists of East Pakistan. The newspapers, journals and pamphlets of this period, now available in the libraries in Dhaka, would reveal how far the 1965 war gave a fillip to the lack of confidence about East Pakistan and the latter's inability to give economic help. It is in this sphere that the phenomenon of internal colonialism needs to be investigated.

These Bengali Muslims had thus joined Muslims in West Pakistan in the "geo-politics of place-making" (Chaturvedi 2002: 149). Yet, in their cognitive map of 'Bengali nationalism' they replaced 'India' and 'Pakistan' as the two opposed and self-contained communities as found in the 'idea of Pakistan' by the categories

'Pakistan' and 'Bengal' and incorporated these mental borders in their 'idea of Bengal'. The new mental borders as embodied in their narratives of the (third) nation were initially translated in Mujib's six-point demand named *Amader bachar dabi* (Our Right to Live), which concentrated on regional autonomy, land reform, nationalization of industries and removal of other social-economic and political inequalities between East and West Pakistanis (Cf. Ahmed 1996: 222). This finally culminated in narratives, as illustrated in the next chapter, formulated to 'proof' that these Bengalis constituted a nation in itself.

References

1. Pakistan signed the Universal Declaration of Human Rights in 1948 (Ahmed 1999: 120).

2. Novels written between 1947 and 1971 by Bengali writers in East Pakistan, "reflect the West Pakistani and international exploitation of East Bengal". See: www.banglapedia.org/HT/N_0213.HTM.

3. Related to these views of Suhrawardy I have, during the summer of 2000, found excellent archive material in the Hartley Library (University of Southampton, United Kingdom) while doing fieldwork for a by IDPAD supported project. This library contains the official papers and correspondence of Lord Mountbatten successively as the last Viceroy of India, and after the transfer of power to India and Pakistan on 14 August 1947, the first Governor General of India in 1947-1948 (MB1/D). Among others it contains Partition Council Papers (July 1947), Papers in Bengal (March-May 1947, June-July 1947 and August 1947-March 1948). It also preserves the file: 'Bengal: Memorandum of the Calcutta District Muslim League to the Bengal Boundary Commission (D114) (July 1947). Of great interest here are the files (D251-253) containing newspaper articles about India and Pakistan, correspondence with the British Broadcasting Corporation, statements to the Press, etc. (May 1947 to April 1948) and the file (D 257), 'The future of the Indian provinces after the transfer of power, including

proposal for the transfer and the reaction of the Muslim League'. From this archive material we get an excellent view of historical narratives that were completely absent after 1947 and not used for nation building in either Pakistan or India. Though, as will be shown some of these narratives were retold by Bengali Muslims after 1947 and incorporated in their rhetoric of Bengali nationalism, some have been completely 'forgotten' by nation builders in India, Pakistan and Bangladesh alike.

4. This "Bengali nationalistic fervor" found its reflection in writings of important journalists, such as, Tafazaal Hossain Manik Mia and cultural ideologues, historians and literary persons such as Shahidullah, Azizur Rahman Mallik, Munir Chowdhury, Salahuddin Ahmed, Anisuzzaman and Abdul Karim who all contributed to the "growth of a sense of a Bengali Muslim identity" (Adhikari 2000: 89). In Chapter 3, I argue that nation builders marginalized or even suppressed such alternative cognitive maps once Bangladesh had been established, even though in this instance members of the so-called majority community projected them.

5. This party was founded by Hussein Shaheed Suhrawardy the, ex-chief minister of United Bengal. Suhrawardy had been banned from entering Pakistan in its early years and after he did so he founded the Awami ('People's') (Muslim) League Party in 1949, of which Mujibur Rahman became the secretary general. The party was founded as an alternative to the Muslim League popular in West Pakistan. The party developed little in West Pakistan but formed along with the Krishak Sramik Party and some smaller parties united in the United Front of 1954, the strongest party in East Pakistan, which won the legislative election in East Bengal (later called East Pakistan) from the Muslim League (Cf. Baxter and Rahman 2004: 64).

6. Mujibur Rahman was a political figure in East Pakistan who was elected prime minister of United Pakistan in December 1970 but was instead arrested by the Pakistani Army on March 25, 1971.

3

The Working of Mental Borders in Bangladesh

The Idea of Bangladesh

Though there had been different and alternative visions of 'Muslim nationalism' and partition during colonial rule (Cf. Metcalf 2004: 173-189), Pakistani leaders selected the so-called Two-Nation Theory as the organizing principle and the raison d'être of the nation-state after 1947. Based on the idea that Hindus and Muslims constitute two separate nations (Cf. Aziz 1987: 46-47) this theory clearly excluded the idea of a third nation for Muslims as it recognized Muslims as "a distinct political entity" (Datta 2004: 4330). East Pakistanis contested these borders of the Pakistani nation-state, first the mental and finally the physical. The final 'rebellion' of 'the Bengalis of the East' against 'non-Bengalis' (Cf. Datta 2004: 20) lasted nine months and ended with the establishment of new geographical borders that outlined the nation-state of Bangladesh. During this nine month period the mental borders of the West-Pakistanis had successfully been changed but at the costs of tremendous numbers of deaths, which the new government of Bangladesh estimated to be around three million.[1] Besides, this Liberation War caused the displacement of more than one-third of the 75 million people residing in East Pakistan and nearly 10 million took 'refuge' in India (Kamaluddin 1985: 229).

It was to this devastated place that Sheikh Mujibur Rahman returned after nine-month of solitary confinement in West Bengal. The population of Dhaka was reduced by a third and as the Pakistani Army had killed many of the 'rebellious Bengali nationalists' it was left to only a handful of 'leaders' to develop an 'idea of Bangladesh'. The guardians of the newly established nation-state had not only to begin their task of nation-building in a totally devastated country but also had a legacy of mental borders against which Bengali nationalists had fought combined with the new borders formulated by the 'freedom fighters' that rejected the 'Two-Nation-Theory' and the borders it represented. Instead these freedom fighters had formulated new borders that emphasized the difference between Pakistan and Bangladesh rather than the difference between Bangladesh and India. New narratives were now needed that could replace those that sustained the older mental and geographical borders of the Pakistani nation-state and that could support the birth of the third nation-state Bangladesh. For some time, only narratives that described the "heroic birth of the nation, amidst great suffering and sacrifice" would do. Significantly, the textbooks during this early phase after Independence show that in the 'retelling' of the birth of the nation, it was not August 14, 1947, that signified the beginning of the new nation, but 1971 (Cf. Rosser 2004: 16). The "critical moment" for East Bengal/East Pakistan, now Bangladesh, was the "war of independence" in 1971, and not the 1947 partition. Narratives during the period immediately after 1971 embodied the new mental borders that were developed by Bengali nationalists between 1947 and 1965 and these were used to constitute the idea of Bangladesh.

The most significant border embodied in the idea of Bangladesh was the opposition between Bangladesh and Pakistan. Besides, this difference was described as a difference between a nation-state based of religion (Pakistan) and a nation-state based on ethnicity (Bangladesh). Consequently, in these new narratives, 'Bengali', as Fazal described, "acquired a secular connotation emphasizing the cultural dimension of identity" and Pakistani, on the other hand, implied a continuing belief in the oppressive two-nation theory and in giving primacy to religion subsuming all other identities. The works of Nazrul Islam and Rabindranath Tagore came to be celebrated. Besides, "in place of 'Pakistan *Zindabad*' '*Jai Bangla*' became the nationalist outcry" (Phadnis quoted in Fazal 2004: 284).

The ideological hegemony of the Pakistani nation-state built on the 'Two-Nation Theory' was thus countered by alternative narratives that gave pre-eminence to ties supposedly un-Islamic. Bangabandhu and other new leaders, who belonged to his party the Awami League, subsequently supported a secular state that distanced itself from religion and nationalism was anchored in the Bangla language. The preamble to the new constitution (1972) was pledged on the "high ideals of nationalism, socialism, democracy and secularism" (Kamal 1994: 13-27) and the national edifice of the new state was defined as:

> The unity and solidity of the Bengalee nation, which, deriving its identity from the language and culture, attained sovereign and independent Bangladesh through a united and determined struggle of independence shall be the basis of Bengalee nationalism (Article 9, quoted in Fazal 2004: 292).

Consistent, with it, the 1972 constitution termed the citizens of Bangladesh 'Bengalees' and adopted *Amar Sonar Bangla* as the national anthem of the Republic (Cf. Fazal 2004: 292). The idea of Bangladesh was not based on irreligious fundamentals however and "secularism" did not mean "irreligiousness" (Fazal 2004: 292). Yet, as for the majority of Bangladesh's population (around 99 per cent) Bengali was their mother tongue and as nearly 86 per cent were followers of Islam it seemed that this 'idea of Bangladesh', including its new mental borders that separated Bangladesh from Pakistan rather than from India, would appeal to most of Bangladesh's citizens.

Yet, apart from non-Bengali speaking minorities such as so-called tribals and the Urdu-speaking population, there was another group that felt excluded from the nation. This group of Bengali Muslims had been scornful of the liberation struggle and some of them had even "actively collaborated with the Pakistan army against their co-nationals" (Fazal 2004: 294). Hamza Alavi (1973: 167 and 171) explained:

> There were, therefore, two traditions in the Bengali movement: (1) a petty-bourgeois elitist tradition for those who hoped to rise to senior positions in the bureaucracy or to become members of the newly created business community in Bengal on the strength of governmental financial support and subsidy; and (2) a rural populist tradition that articulated the frustrations and aspirations of the long suffering sections of the extremely poor Bengal peasantry.[2] The two traditions were intertwined but remained distinct. The educated sons of rich peasants had other aspirations than those of the peasantry in general [...] Since the creation of Bangladesh, the confrontation between the elitist element in the Awami League and its populist base has re-emerged on a new level.

These 'petty bourgeois elitists' were therefore more anti-India than anti-Pakistan and launched a campaign for 'Muslim Bengal' and argued for "only Muslims in Bengal to be declared nationals" (Fazal 2004: 294). Though till 1975, when Mujibur and most of his family members were killed and Bangladesh till 1990 was ruled by different military regimes, this alternative cognitive map of Bangladesh was not dominant in the grand-narratives of the nation-state, subsequently, these narratives that were characterized by a distinctly anti-Indian orientation became however more institutionalised. Alternative cognitive maps with other 'inner borders' even those projected by members of the so-called Muslim majority community, were silenced by the new nation-builders in Bangladesh. Thus, as Ahmed (2001: 21) questioned:

> Did the emergence of Bangladesh, ostensibly on the basis of a linguistic-cultural identity, fundamentally transform the orientation and character of the Bengal Muslims? Although, theoretically, it meant greater emphasis on Bengali cultural identity for those in Bangladesh, it is doubtful whether it signified a fundamental break with the earlier trend [during Pakistan days]. Even Bangabandhu Sheikh Mujib (d. 1975), the architect of secular Bangladesh, could not ignore the Islamic content of Bengal Muslim culture and had to make concessions to Islamic symbols and institutions [...] If anything, the independence of Bangladesh has reactivated the debate: 'What are we? Muslims or Bengalis?' The consequent tension is all too real.

After Mujibur's massacre the military that took over mandated that the historical narratives in school textbooks were altered in order to "Islamise and de-Indianise" (Rosser 2004: 17). Yet as Rosser (2004: 17) analysed:

> [...] results of the overhauls of historiography were not as thorough in Bangladesh as compared to Pakistan. In Bangladesh, just the recent events, as narrated in textbooks, were altered to suit the military leaders. The stories of the ancient and medieval periods, as formulated by "Bengalee Nationalist" historians in 1973-1975, were not significantly changed. Alterations in textbooks in Bangladesh were implemented in a more haphazard process than in Pakistan. But eventually, during revisions orchestrated by Gen. Ziaur Rahman in 1977 and Gen. H.M. Ershad in 1984 and 1987, the retelling of the creation of the Bengalee nation shifted its stance. The manipulations of the historical record undertaken by the military rulers of Bangladesh are

a manifestation that will keep recurring as long as the government changes hands between BNP and the Awami League, or perhaps until the nation comes of age in a collective sense of accepting the past.

In 1991 there was a restoration of the democracy in Bangladesh. After long nation-wide demonstrations against General H.M. Ershad during 1989 and 1990, two major political parties in Bangladesh, the Bangladesh Nationalists Party (BNP) and the Awami League agreed on ousting Ershad and holding "free and fair" elections under a "neutral government" (Baxter and Rahman 2004: xvi). From that time onwards till 2005, Awami League rule has been altered by BNP rule during different phases and for various periods. Though the two parties and their members are great rivals and the tussles between them greatly characterise Bangladesh society and are often violent, after 1990 there has not been any significant change in their idea of pre-1971 'Bangladesh' and their cognitive maps, including its borders, are pretty alike. Alternative maps as also projected by some members of the so-called majority community have no place in their maps. O'Connell (2001: 193) explains:

> There were several reasons for doubting that Bengali language and literature, while certainly necessary, would be sufficient as resources to build a cognitively persuasive and emotionally compelling sense of national identity and purpose. One reason was its restricted emotional appeal, another the ambiguity of boundary and content of Bengali literature and Bengali/Bangladeshi national identity being rooted in that literature. A third reason for doubt is perhaps, implied by the first two: a gross underestimation of (or resistance to) other foci of socio-cultural identity, especially varying types of Muslim commitment and identity.

Though the narratives of both parties significantly differ in their views on whoever declared Independence and other post-1971 developments, these 'state-guardians' do not disagree on the date of Bangladesh's birth. For them, 1947 signifies a false dawn and the period between 1947 and 1971, is represented as an interlude during which Bengali Muslims resisted the mental borders imposed upon them by ruling military-bureaucratic oligarchy of West Pakistan. Whereas they markedly differ in terms of emphasis on the common bond among Bengalis on basis of language, culture (Awami League) and Islamic religion (BNP), they do not differ in their narratives that all describe that, "Bangladesh has been created through a bloody liberation war based on the symbol of Bengalee nationality" (Cf. Huq 1984: 63). Yet, as these guardians of the Bangladesh nation-state have, as explained below, till date neglected to retell the partition story of 1947, 'Bengali nationality' had by 1971 already become to mean Bengali Muslim identity with the Bengali Hindus in fact reduced to a 'minority' in narratives told by Muslim Awami Leaguers and to 'non-nationals' by those of BNP-ers. Till date, both categories of nation-builders accept the 'Pakistani' version of partition as far the role of 'Hindus' is concerned. Alternative maps with other borders between the two communities are silenced. What is more, not only were poor scheduled caste Hindus who stayed put after 1947 obliterated from the narratives of the nation, but so were the whole poor peasantry and their armed struggle during the liberation movement. Hamza Alavi (1973: 172) described the situation around 1970-1971:

Whereas the elitist leadership [in East Pakistan] found a safe haven in Calcutta, the populist and Marxist political cadres, who were once isolated, have now established a new relationship with the people in the course of their armed liberation struggle. The organization and strength of the armed resistance were not yet strong enough to overthrow the Pakistani army, but they were growing. Moreover, the position of the Pakistani army was reaching a point of crisis because of the weak economy of West Pakistan and the outbursts of public discontent opened up new prospects for the advance of the liberation forces in Bengal. It was precisely at that moment that the Indians [the Indian army] chose to intervene, so as to forestall the liberation of Bangladesh by popular forces and to install the Awami League elitist leadership in power.

Actually, it was this 'elitist' leadership that created new mental borders, embodied in the idea of Bangladesh. These borders unite Bengali Muslims against Pakistani Muslims but at the same time marginalize or even exclude Bengali Hindus and other poor (Muslim) peasants from the new nation-state.[3] These borders are still at work in contemporary Bangladesh and at times cause severe so-called communal riots too.[4]

Hindus and Partition Narratives of Bengali Muslims

Though 1971 is thus an important year in the grand-narrative of the Bangladesh nation-state as formulated by its leaders, 1947, is not forgotten. Many Bengali Muslims remember 'the partition of Bengal'[5] in 1947 as a turn of fortune as it had meant the end of British rule and the creation of Pakistan. Yet, the narratives are more concerned with the period between 1947 and 1971, as 1947 signified a 'false dawn' for these Bengali Muslims. After 1947, these Bengali Muslims try to show that the borders are not between India and Pakistan but between West Pakistan and East Pakistan and these narratives are typically written with these latter borders in mind. Had 'Hindus' and 'the British' dominated in the narratives of these Bengali Muslims before 1947, afterwards, their problem concerned West Pakistani domination. Significantly, narratives concerning this period, incorporated in the rhetoric of the Awami League, which generally emphasizes its 'secular' leanings as well as those of the BNP, do not include Bengali Hindus. As reflected in speeches of politicians, officials but also in work by fiction writers,[6] poets, and also found in other written material, Hindus are not part of the 'majority' of East Pakistanis after 1947. By implication, Jinnah and his 'Two-Nation Theory' were thus not fully rejected as after all Jinnah roused Muslims political identity and announced a better future. Rewritten textbooks in Bangladesh in 1973, feel however disappointed as Jinnah never really considered East Bengal as part of his "Home for Muslims in the Subcontinent" (Rosser 2004: 39). Jinnah had also enacted policies, these textbooks state, that were detrimental to the interest of the eastern wing. The Muslim Bengali grand-narrative of the nation-state therefore criticizes but does not eradicate Jinnah's two-nation theory (Cf. Rosser 2004: 39).

Though fiction demonstrates that the traumatic aspects of the partition of 1947 were not forgotten,[7] many Bengali Muslims also remembered 1947 as the beginning of a better future. Bengali nationalists had already started incorporating a more regional focus in the Pakistani discourses about 'Pakistan's' ancient period, the medieval period and especially the colonial period. Within a year after independence this had materialised in a new set of Bangladeshi textbooks that had been completely rewritten. In these textbooks as Rosser (2004: 38) analysed:

> The point of view was distinctly Bengali-world events unfolded as they impacted the geographical area of the world now known as Bangladesh. Thus, the Aryans are discussed as noble invaders, whose Rishis brought Sanskritic culture to the subcontinent and hence, the Bengali language. However, the discourse stressed that Bengalis had historically resisted "Aryanisation" and had retained a distinct identity. This historical autonomy facilitated the eventual emergence of Bangladesh as a modern nation state.

These guardians of the new Bangladesh nation-state thus imagined an 'isolationalist Bangladeshi identity and nationalism', one that excluded Hindus for instance as, according to them, 'Bangladesh' seemed to have been the result of the efforts of Bengali Muslims only. Narratives that supported such a view were reproduced in textbooks and through speeches with the hope that they would unite the majority of Bengali Muslims, by imagining the 'inalienable Islamic character of Bangladesh', and in this way these guardians of the new nation hoped to protect the state from its downfall. Clearly, the mental borders here are not any longer those supported by the West-Pakistanis but new ones that separate Bengali Muslims from Pakistani Muslims. Bengali Hindus are excluded however from this idea of the nation. These narratives remain dominant after 1990 as well. Through these narratives, Bengali Muslims remember that partition has liberated them ('we') from the Bengali Hindus ('they') who had exploited them for centuries. Though some narratives regret that Suhrawardy's plan of a United Bengal was "quashed by opposition from the Congress under the leadership of Nehru" (Ahmed 2004: 5), partition, at least, had caused the out-migration of an enormous number of Hindu upper-castes and classes who had acted as a 'majority' in a region where Muslims outnumbered Hindus. Thus, "For too many if not most of the Muslims of East Pakistan, 1947", Dipesh Chakrabarty argued, "was not only about partition, it was also about freedom, from both the British and Hindu ruling classes" (Chakrabarty 1996: 2143).

Of course, this quest for freedom had begun long before 1947 when Bengali Muslim leaders including a youthful Sheikh Mujibur Rahman who later would become Bangladesh's first President had struggled for independence from the British rule. Nevertheless, in 1947 not only did the British leave East Bengal but so did a great number of Hindus too. Partition narratives remind Bengali Muslims of this exodus, which implies their own rooting. Indeed, since 1971, nation builders in Bangladesh refute the mental borders of the Pakistani nation builders that were intended to unite West and East Pakistani Muslims as "we" on the basis of a common religion. Instead, these Bengali Muslims try to forge unity among themselves on the basis of region, language, ethnicity, class and religion and thereby not only draw a line between themselves and Pakistanis but also effectively between Hindu Bengalis and Muslim Bengalis. Clearly, if not totally excluded from the new nation, Hindu Bengalis are excluded from the majority and rendered a 'minority'. These new narratives were and are used by Bengali Muslims not only in their demand for their own nation-state but also during the process of nation building that started after 1971. Actually, nation builders after 1971 feel that, "if there had been no two-nation theory, there would not have been Pakistan in the first place and if there had been no failure in the working out of that theory, Bangladesh would not have come into existence" (Ahmed 2004: 6).[8] These Bengali Muslims had thus proceeded by accommodating the two-nation theory in the new narratives of the third nation-state as reflected in narratives of pre-1947 East Bengal.

These narratives reflect the apprehension among Bengali Muslims of Bengali (upper-caste) Hindu domination as it had existed before 1947 and which only ended with the partition. They describe how Bengali Muslims had earlier been Buddhists and had later converted to Hinduism. The "rigid caste system" that prevailed among the Hindus is emphasized in these narratives. It is also narrated that as a large number among these Hindus belonged to the scheduled castes, they wanted to escape from the rigidity and oppression of the caste system of Hinduism and converted to Islam. These narratives thus correspond with what H. Beverley wrote in 1872 that,

The existence of Muhammadans of Eastern in Bengal is not due so much to the introduction of Mughal blood into the country as to the conversion of the former inhabitants for whom a rigid system of caste discipline rendered Hinduism intolerable.[9]

The impression one gets from these narratives is that the lower castes among the Hindus all voluntarily converted to Islam as this "could offer to this people a hope and status denied to them in the Hindu system" (Spear quoted in Ahmed, 2004: 46 note 30). Some narratives also recount that this "conversion to Islam to the religion of rulers [...] gave protection and respectability to Scheduled Castes" (Chitkara 1997: 66). Others narratives recount that, "Islam has gained its greatest and most lasting missionary triumphs in times and places in which its political power has been weakened as in Southern India and Eastern Bengal" (Arnold 1974: 263). In short, it is narrated as reflected in history textbooks written after 1971 (Rosser 2004), how gradually many scheduled caste Hindus converted to Islam. The rest of the Hindus who did not convert are labeled as 'upper-caste exploiters'.

In other words, lower caste Hindus all become Muslims and gradually vanish from these accounts and what remains are the upper-caste Hindus. Narratives proceed to depict these higher caste Bengali Hindus in East Bengal before 1947 as a relatively small Hindu elite in East Bengal (the *bhadralok*) who, along with the British, acted as a dominating minority exploiting the impoverished Muslim masses (Ahmed 2004: 83-89). Besides, these Hindus are not only described as rich moneylenders, *zamindars* (semi-feudal landlords), who exploited the poor Muslims, but also as 'outsiders' from West Bengal who only hoped for the submission of (local) Muslims to Hindus'.[10] Increasingly, these narratives continue to explain, these two groups grew apart and formed separate entities in socio-cultural, political and economic fields with the Hindu elite exploiting the Muslim masses in East Bengal. Clearly, at this momentum the two-nation theory is incorporated in these narratives and new mental borders that divide

Hindu Bengalis from Muslim Bengali are included. We hear the resonance of Jinnah's 1940 speech:

> It is extremely difficult to appreciate why our Hindu friends fail to understand the real nature of Islam and Hinduism [...] The Hindus and Muslims belong to two different civilizations which are based mainly on conflicting ideas and conceptions. Their aspects on life and of life are different. It is quite clear that Hindus and Mussalmans derive their inspiration from different sources of history. They have different epics, their heroes are different, and different episodes. Very often the hero of one is foe of the other and, likewise, their victories and defeats overlap. To yoke together, two such nations under a single State, one as a numerical minority and the other as a majority, must lead to growing discontent and final destruction of any fabric that may be so built up for the government of such a State (quoted from Mahajan 1970: 237).

These narratives, which separate Hindu and Muslim Bengalis and make the former a 'minority' in Bangladesh or exclude them from the nation and relegate them to India, can be found in contemporary textbooks in Bangladesh, but its mental borders are also incorporated in speeches and works of the guardians of the nation-state. H.S. Suhrawardy, for instance, former prime minister of Bengal, who became prime minister of Pakistan and had previously demanded a 'United Bengal', did by the end of his life not doubt that by the turn of the last century, Bengali Muslim and Hindu cultures had become vitally different from each other. He wrote in his memoirs that there "seemed to be ingrained substantial irreconcilable differences between Hindus and Muslims in outlook [...] in customs and practices" (Talukdar 1987: 100). Suhrawardy furthermore wrote that this "minority of rich Hindus" was so unfair to the masses of Muslims that,

> I was forced to the conclusion that the talk of Hindu-Muslim unity was a myth and that the Hindus wanted nothing but complete surrender from the Muslims as

the price of unity [...] It appeared to me that the only hope for Muslims was to stand on their legs and look after their own separate interests if they wanted to survive and progress (Talukdar 1987: 103).[11]

In their narratives concerning the struggle for independence in East Bengal these Bengali Muslims remember that 17 August 1936 proved to be a turning point in the history of the Muslim League in Bengal when Jinnah and his Muslim League as well as the demand for Pakistan had started making headway in East Bengal at the expense of the "Congress *raj*", which was "out to destroy the Moslem resurgence in this country". Ever after this year, the Muslim League was identified with 'Muslims' and Congress with 'Hindus'. Besides East Bengal was labelled as a Muslim dominated region in these narratives. However, Bengali leaders in East Bengal did not propagate at first that the creation of Pakistan should necessarily imply the partition of Bengal. To the contrary, great efforts had been made to keep the two parts of Bengal together. Before the Partition of 1947, there had been two short periods during which East Bengali Muslim leaders struggled for a United Bengal. These narratives ascribed the failure of the last plan of Suhrawardy and Sarat Bose and supported by Jinnah as well as the last Viceroy of British India Lord Mountbatten to Nehru's rejection of the plan. Therefore Bengali Muslim leaders had no other choice than opting for 'partition'. After 1971, Bangabandhu Sheikh Mujibur Rahman felt that "the Bengali Muslim culture had to be preserved against the Hindu cultural influence emanating from Hinduism". He also thought that, "stressing the Islamic identity was a necessary bulwark against being swamped by or emerged into the cultural matrix of West Bengal and, by implication, of India". It was also his assessment that,

Bangladesh should reassert not just its Bengali linguistic and cultural identity but its Bengali Muslim identity as well if the country were not to be swamped by identification with West Bengal and India. He was therefore keen for Bangladesh to be acknowledged as an important Muslim country of South Asia (Franda 1982: 224-225 and 157-158).

These narratives thus explain how and that Islam and Hinduism in Bengal are two separate religions. The rigid caste system prevalent among the Bengali Hindus is remembered as, "a direct negation of nationalism, equality, democracy and all the noble ideas that Islam stands for".[12] Narratives further indicate that when these upper-caste Hindus finally realized Muslims would neither give up their political aspirations nor Bengali-Islamic values and traditions, they opted out of the proposed United Bengali Nation and instead they preferred partition of the territory. What follows are the narratives of the flows of Hindus out of East Bengal to India and similar flows of Muslims from India direction East Bengal. From that time onwards histories on the position of Hindus in Bangladesh link them with this mass exodus and with communal riots, in other words with partition. As a result, these Hindus stopped acting as a majority and became labelled as a minority in East Bengal. These 'minority Hindus' who usually had made a living from non-agricultural professions had now lost their privileged socio-economic status as upper-caste groups and as a result and in anticipation of better economic opportunities, they left for India (Cf. Haque 1995: 195). Guha (1959: viii) in an in-depth anthropological study concluded that,

> The Muslim League state policy in East Pakistan elevated Muslims into professional managerial class and deprived the Hindus [...] What really, however, compelled them to evacuate was not so much the insecurity of life and property, and inability to get redress against unprovoked attacks, but a sense of complete frustration in preserving the cherished values of life deeply embedded in their personality and which constitute their ego-wants.

In short, these narratives concerning Bengali Hindus which have become part of the grand-narrative of the Bangladesh nation-state as espoused by Bengali Muslims concern, by and large, the lives of upper caste or upper class Hindus who ever after the loss of the throne of Bengal in 1757 by Nawab Sirajuddaulah, along with the British rulers dominated the Bengali Muslims. The role of the Bengali Hindus residing in East Bengal during this period is described as one of deceiving 'Mother Bengal' (Bengal-*Mata*). Besides, as the Bengali Hindus opted for the partition of Bengal in 1947, they 'logically' became the citizens of India. Though the majority of the people of Bangladesh are Muslims, the nation-state still needs this rhetoric in order to preserve their distinct Muslim culture and identity while simultaneously wanting to preserve their rich Bengali cultural heritage and ethnicity. In other words, in order to forge the nation Bangladeshi Muslim leaders think that,

> It is crucial to the future to maintain the distinction between Bangladesh's culture, way of life, and religion and similar cultures found on the other side of the Indian border in West Bengal (Franda 1982: 145).

Hindus as a Minority and Outsiders

To a great extend narratives describing the exodus of Hindus from East Bengal towards West Bengal correspondent with reality. Besides, scholars have suggested that, and corresponding the mental borders that were and are enacted, Hindus in Pakistan were marginalized and "became hostages to politics of the dominant society and the state" (Guhathakurta 2002: 72). Later on, "Pakistan army was deliberately resorting to expulsion of [the] Hindu population as part of its policy" (Kamaluddin 1985: 230). Importantly, though the new constitution of Bangladesh in 1972 laid down the principle of "secularism" as one of the basic tenants of statehood, "the sense of alienation" (Guhathakurta 2002: 74) deepened and outflows continued. The decline of the Hindu population in East Bengal is indeed great.

According to the Census of 1941, the last census before the 1947 partition, the Hindu population in East Bengal was at that time 28 per cent and immediately after partition it came down to 25 per cent and according to the 1991 Census, Hindus number 12.5 million and represent 10.5 per cent of the total population (Tajuddin 1999: 107).

Yet, while these flows are huge and still continue, there are many Hindus in Bangladesh who have 'stayed put' or 'were left behind' (Sinha-Kerkhoff 2003: 27-44). These Hindus are mostly not the upper-caste and rich Hindus who had been, according to the rhetoric of the Bangladesh nation, dominant in every walk of life, like trade, commerce, administrative services and professions. These latter Hindus, indeed, had mostly migrated to newly established India. Crucially, of the Hindus who now reside in Bangladesh only a very few belong to the upper-castes and most of them identify as so-called scheduled castes. Besides, even those who identify as upper-castes rarely hold positions of dominance in contemporary Bangladeshi society. Today the socio-economic differences between the Muslim and the Hindu communities, in particular in rural areas, are "much less marked than it was earlier" (Samad 1999: 76).

Nevertheless, in the narratives that sustain the Bangladesh nation-state these Hindus are omitted in those that describe post-1947 'Bangladesh'. At the time of partition in 1947 Hindus are supposed to have left the 'nation'. Those 'few' that remained were separated from the majority of Bengali Muslims and labelled as a 'minority' (Iman Ali 1992: 234) What is more, ever after 1971, the invisible, and not so invisible, mental borders embodied in the 'idea of Bangladesh', do not only marginalize, or 'colonize', the remaining Hindu citizens of the country but also, and regularly so, denationalize them and threaten to expel these Hindus. Meghna Guhathakurta (2002: 79) describes in detail how these "discriminatory practices" adversely affect the "security both physical and material', the "business", "employment and education" as well as the "identity" of Hindus in Bangladesh. Though some of this "discrimination" is even institutionalized in laws, politics and textbooks, as will be illustrated in Chapter 4, mental borders that divide Muslim Bengalis from Hindu Bengalis in Bangladesh, mostly manifest themselves, "in tenacious, largely unconscious stereotypes and cultural fantasies" (Cash and Schwab 2004: 133), which impact today's negotiations between people in Bangladesh who come from opposite sides of the religious divide. Whereas, in day-to-day life these Hindus and Muslims share more than they differ (Cf. *The Milli Gazette*, 16-30 September 2004), this 'inter-faith' harmony is at times rudely disturbed by the enactment of the partition rhetoric embodied in the idea of Bangladesh.

In particular after 1990, the mental borders that separate and antagonize Bengali Muslims from Bengali Hindus are enacted again and again amidst relatively poor and sometimes landless cultivators, potters, weavers, peasants, fishermen, school and college teachers, musicians, priests, village doctors, union chairmen, milkmen, writers, clerks, lawyers, share-croppers, shopkeepers and other small businessmen, librarians, and social workers. When we did our field-work, in villages in Bangladesh in 2002, we were told that though Muslims lived separate from the Hindus in different parts of the village or even in altogether different villages, Muslim peasants always had come to the *pandals* of the Hindus during *Durga Puja* and also that Hindus celebrated *Eid* along with Muslims. Besides, we were told that in Dhaka, Bangladesh's capital, *Paila Baisakh*, was observed "as a common festival of all Bengalis irrespective of their religions". Yet, our Hindu informants told, "this year it is different". We indeed attended a *Ram Lila* function in a Hindu dominated village where Muslims had been invited but the atmosphere was extremely tense. Later on, I was told, some Muslims had attacked Hindus on their return to their own village. Though the motive seemed to have been robbery, Hindus the next morning told me that these kind of attacks on Hindus are more frequent now than in the past as "we are easy targets as the police does nothing". They also added that, "they [Muslims] treat us differently, they even speak to us differently".

One can therefore argue that the boundaries embodied in state supported partition rhetoric are not only reflected in state-supported literature and historiography in contemporary Bangladesh but can also be discovered in the language people speak and if Wittgenstein is right these boundaries of people's language then create the boundaries of their world, which expands to the unconscious, making it accessible to communication and communal exchange (Cf. Cash and Schwab 2004: 134). In other words, this state supported rhetoric allows some people if 'need' requires to, at the one hand, identify as 'majority' and at the other hand label and 'colonize' 'others' as 'minorities'. Bangladeshi researcher Meghna Guhathakurata of Dhaka University (*The Times of India*, November 2, 2002) commented that,

> The minority-bashing was part of the reactionary degeneration of the country's politics. The Islamisation of politic and public life had already made minorities marginal. Terror is playing an increasing role in politics and social intimidation is part of the power structure. Political elites based in Dhaka behave like absentee landlords. They use their hirelings to plunder underdogs to oil their election machinery and maintain their post-poll fiefdoms. Minorities are the softest targets.

Partition rhetoric was in particular enacted during so-called communal or anti-Hindu riots.[13] In December 1992 for instance such riots took place in the aftermath of the Babri Masjid demolition in India where a mosque was demolished by a group of so-called fundamentalist Hindus.[14] I here quote two parts of a narrative of a

Hindu victim interviewed by Sultana Nahar (1994: 55-56) and translated from Bengali by Guhathakurta (2002: 80) as they provide an excellent illustration of the presence and working of such mental borders among Hindus in Bangladesh ever after 1947:

After October 1990, I had gradually started loosing my sense of self-respect. All around me I heard slogans such as 'Malaoon' (derogatory term for Hindus), 'leave the country'. If Hindus want to remain alive then they must leave Bangla etc. They made me feel as if I was born as one of the lowest subject on earth. I have no right to live in this country and if I do so, I will have to remain only at the mercy of others [...] It is true that the 1990 communal attacks were the first of its kind since the riots of 1964, but it is also true that the flame of communalism had never really been fully vanquished even in the secular independent Bangladesh and there are isolated instances of disharmony. Many Hindu homes had to bear its brunt of it so much so that they had even to flee the country.

Clearly, predominately scheduled caste Hindus live under the weight of these narratives that are included in rhetoric of the nation-state and which are occasionally institutionalised and embodied in laws and the constitution as well. These narratives are used by Bengali Muslim guardians of the nation-state to maintain unity among themselves and cast these scheduled castes as 'upper-caste Hindus' with pasts as 'outsiders', 'exploiters' and who are about to 'crush' the rich culture of the Bengali Muslims of Bangladesh unless they are excluded from the nation and re-rooted to West Bengal where they actually belong. These mental borders cause these Hindus to feel 'homeless at home' and turn them into 'internal displaced people' in a 'majoritarian democracy' (Cf. Guhathakurta and Begum 2005: 175-213). Whereas this state-rhetoric and its mental borders therefore securely 'root' and therefore 'include' the majority of the Bengali Muslims in the nation-state, they simultaneously place Hindus outside the nation and often out of the state as well. This state-rhetoric therefore works as a kind of unwritten social rules, an unwritten law that tries to keep Hindus in their place, either as 'minority' or if necessary, can be used to relocate them. In this way, the nation-state hopes to survive.

Yet, not all guardians of the nation-state subscribe to this rhetoric. Besides, not always and everywhere are these mental borders enacted. Subhoranjan Dasgupta argued, for instance, that in the newly created nation-state some members of the majority Bengali Muslims (or Muslim Bengalis or Bangladeshi Muslims), "fully returned to its secular Bengali roots". As an example he quoted the "great novelist Akhtaruzzaman Elias" who wrote that, "The two communities, Hindu and Muslim could well maintain their differences. But why did this lead to the division of the Bengali people? Partition was an unmitigated disaster" (Dasgupta 2002: 22). Similarly, Badruddin Umar (2000) described the emergence of Bangladesh in 1971 as "the return of the Muslim Bengali to its secular Bengali roots" (*musalmander swadeshe pratyabartan*). In 2001, an "independent body of leading Bangladeshi intellectuals was established called PIC that condemned efforts by fellow Bangladeshis to "destroy the minorities' sense of belonging so that they are forced to flee the country". PIC conducted a detailed inquiry into the "persecution of minorities after the 1 October 2001 parliamentary elections in which the Bangladesh Nationalist Party and Jamat-e-Islami combine came to power". PIC blames the "ruling alliance for unleashing planned and systematic attacks to attain far reaching objectives such as the "cutting off of the minorities from the social and political mainstream by destroying the unique concept of pluralism and unity-in-diversity that is carefully nurtured for ages as part of Bengali culture and society". Its report states that:

The main purpose of minority persecution is to create and consolidate communalism as a political weapon which would help strengthen and spread religion-based communal politics in the country [...] the immediate objective is to create a fear psychosis so that the minorities would not vote and flee their homes (*Muslim India*, 248-250, vol. 21, nos. 8-10, August-October 2003: 985).

Such groups and individuals did and do not only reject the mental borders as embodied in the narratives of Pakistan and which were used to unite East Pakistanis and West Pakistanis in the "one nation-one state" rhetoric (Fazal 2004: 275), but also reject the mental borders that are embodied in the idea of Bangladesh and which separate the 'Hindu Bengali minority' from the 'Muslim Bengali majority', marginalize the former and exclude them from the nation-state. Though, many Bangladeshi state-guardians do not recognize the existence of these borders and they point out to formal laws and the constitution that guarantees the inclusion and well being of all Bangladeshis. The principal secretary of the Khaleda Zia government, Kamal Siddiqui, who head a committee of secretaries to probe into alleged atrocities committed against Hindus denied for instance the effects of such mental borders and stated that there had, "no persecution taken place of any kind because there is no minority or majority community in Bangladesh. All are Bangladeshis" (*Muslim India*, 248-250, vol. 21, nos. 8-10 (August-October) 2003: 985).

Yet, repeated amendments in the constitution of Bangladesh after 1971 show not only that these mental borders do their work but also marginalize Hindus and potentially can help to expel Hindu Bengalis from Bangladesh. During the military regimes of General Ziaur Rehman (1975-1981) the principle of secularism was scrapped and the Islamic phrase, "*Bismillahir Rahmanir Rahim*" (in the name of Allah, the Beneficent, and the Merciful) was inserted into the constitution (Samad 1999: 81). Besides, in 1975, Islam was declared a state religion (Samad 1999: 81). What is more, there are regular reports of "ethnic cleansing in Bangladesh". Rahul Gupta (*Muslim India*, 253, vol. 22, no. 2 (January) 2004: 71) reports, for instance:

> Ethnic cleansing of minorities in Bangladesh (them East Pakistan) started in 1947. Over half-a-century has passed with no end in sight. Minorities in Bangladesh, including women and children were subjected to extreme brutality and torture following the last National Election in Bangladesh held in October 2001, forcing many families to migrate out of their "Homeland of generations" for physical safety.

Others report on 'discriminatory practices' against Bengali Hindus in Bangladesh. Rabindra Ghosh reports (*Muslim India*, 252, vol. 21, nos. 12 (December) 2003: 1235):

> I have just come from Nowbabganj upazilla, about 150 km from Dhaka town. Over 100 Hindu families living there had to approach the officer of Nowbabganj to complain that they had been tortured and oppressed by some terrorists from the ruling BNP. The Hindu families, they alleged, had already been forced to pay more than Tk 3,00,000 in *jizia* tax and more was being demanded. Instead of giving them a sympathetic hearing, the officer-in charge, Nowabganj, snatched away their banner and refused to return it. He also threatened to file cases against the complaining families. I met the police officer and other law enforcing agencies and talked with the victims. The Hindu families said that they want to leave the country due to torture and repression.

Though Bangladesh guardians of the state remain promising inclusion of all citizens in the nation-state, Hindus, and increasingly so, feel insecure in their homeland. The borders of the nation-state do not protect them. Some even want "our names struck off the voters list because the state won't protect us". They ask: "why are we deprived of our rights despite constitutional sanctions?" (*Muslim India*, 248-250, vol. 21, nos. 8-10 (August-October) 2003: 986). The reason has been explained here as the workings on mental borders as embodied in partition rhetoric that forms the base-line of the Bangladesh nation-state and which can escape constitutional sanctions as after 1947 in the encounter between religious communities, these borders have become part of "cultural stereotypes, fantasies, projections and modes of othering" and of 'emotions' (Cf. Bhargava 2000: 199), or of what we can call the "cultural unconscious" (Cf. Cash and Schwab 2004: 133).

Some authors have argued that, "questioning on the decrease or increase of the percentage of any religious group of people is useless as people are exercising migration driven economy". Abdullah (*News from Bangladesh*, August 7, 2005)[15] for instance argued that, "a chunk of the Hindus of Bangladesh is living in the U.S.A. [and India] because they found better lives as the Muslims of Bangladesh who migrated to the U.S.A. do". I do not deny that Muslims migrate too and to India as well.[16] Yet, this chapter has shown that mental borders in Bangladesh do clearly alienate Hindus more than Muslims. Besides, there are new laws enacted after 1974 that clearly discriminate against Hindus (Barkat, Zaman, Rahman and Poddar 1997 and Barkat 2000). Yet, more importantly, there are 'unwritten laws' at work in Bangladesh that cause 'low intensity violence' (Samad 1999: 87-91) against Bengali Hindus ever since Bangladesh was established. These 'laws' embodied in the nation-state's rhetoric can be used at any moment by any state guardian to 'unify' the country by bordering and exclusion of the 'others'. In the next Chapter I show that this indeed does not mean that this is the (only) reason for Hindu migration or that all Hindus have migrated or are planning to migrate. I argue however that this partition rhetoric has triggered off "counter voices" among this Hindu 'minority' (Cf. Samaddar 2003: 33). In the next Chapter I give a say to Hindus who stayed put and want to stay put but for whom mental borders incorporated in state rhetoric make it difficult to do so. Though this rhetoric declares them indeed 'outsiders' and 'migrants', as will be shown, these Hindus have their own 'counter-narratives' defined by me as 'stories of independence' (rather then partition stories) with their own and alternative mental borders, which rather than causing migration root them and allow them to remain in the country they were born in.

References

1. See for more figures: "Case Study: Genocide in Bangladesh": http: //www.gendercide.org/case_Bangladesh.html

2. The Bangladeshi author Akhtaruzzaman Elias in his novel *Chilekothar Sepai* (Soldier of the Attic) depicts the pre-1971 mass movement amongst these poor Hindu and Muslim peasants. In an interview Elias condemned the partition of Bengal in unequivocal terms: "My father, like many other members of the educated Muslim middle class of that time, earnestly wanted that Muslim boys and girls should keep pace with their Hindu counterparts that they live with equal dignity. But, let us not forget, these Muslim boys and girls belonged to a particular class, to the Muslim middle class. It also needs to be underlined that only the progress of this middle class was aspired for. But the movement they unleashed in order to fulfill this aspiration simply cannot be approved. The partition of 1947 was so catastrophic, so deplorable, to heartrending and meaningless that we are realizing it more every day" (in: Subhoranjan Dasgupta, 'History's creative counterpart' on: www.india-seminar.com/2002/510/ 510%20subhoranjan%20dasgupta.htm).

3. See, for instance, Syed Waliullah (1922-1971) novel *Lalsalu* (1948) in which he describes the exploitation of Bengali (Hindu and Muslim villagers). In fact, with about 90 per cent of the people of East Pakistan living in villages and depending on an agricultural economy, the general theme of novels was based on village life.

4. Bangladesh witnessed severe communal riots after a caretaker government was installed on 15 July 2001 in the run up to the general election. In October 2001, the Bangladesh Nationalist Party (BNP) came to lead a coalition government with as partner the Jamaat-e-Islami. There have been many reports in Bangladesh of violence against mostly the Hindu minority, who were 'uprooted' and 'tortured' after the BNP had assumed power. See for instance, *Dhaka Courier* (26 October 2001: 12-14) or *News and Views* (20 October 20, 2001: 17-22). Bangladeshi Ministers as well as the Prime Minister of Bangladesh dismissed such reports of atrocity as untrue however and as politically motivated. The vernacular daily *Janakantha* reported that in one instance, persons (all Hindus) of a village were told by Muslims to leave their houses and 'return to India' (30 October 2001).

5. Note the significance of the fact that the discourse of these Bengali Muslims concerns the partition of Bengal, i.e. not the partition of the whole of British India or *Bharat* (i.e. including the partition of Punjab).

6. Novels such as Abul Fazl's *Ranga Prabhat* (Red Dawn) or Abu Rushd's *Nongor* (Anchor) greet the establishment of the "Muslim homeland" in 1947 but show that the partition "was used to establish the authority of the Muslim middle and upper middle classes who were no less apathetic than the Hindus towards the exploited belonging to the Muslim community". Partition was seen by them, Subhoranjan Dasgupta writes, as "historically incorrect" (Rafiuddin Ahmed) or as "false promise" but these writers identify Hindus as exploiters (at times along with elite Muslims) and never as part of the 'exploited'. An exception is Elias who saw partition "as a calculated betrayal of the exploited, irrespective of their religious identity, on both sides" (www.india seminar.com/ 2002/510 510% 20 subhoranjan % 20 dasgupta.htm).

7. See Bagchi and Dasgupta (2003: 261-268) for an extensive bibliography of short stories, films, poems, memoirs, plays and novels on the 1947 partition, displacement, memory and Hindu-Muslims relations in East Bengal.

8. Salahuddin Ahmed (2004: 17-19) also quoted Basant Chatterjee's *Inside Bangladesh Today: An Eye Witness Account* (New Delhi, 1973: 155) who wrote that, "[N]o person in Bangladesh today can dare to assert from the public platform that what was done in 1947 was wrong, for the people know that had Pakistan not been created then Bangladesh too would not have come into existence".

9. Report on the Census of Bengal, (Calcutta: Secretariat Press, 1872: 132).

10. Dixit (1999: 280) argues that such narratives help Bengali Muslims at present to dissociate themselves not only from 'Hindu Bengalis' but also from West Bengal: "Cultural and social memories of Bengali Hindu domination of Muslim Bengalis results in this deeply desire for difference and distance from West Bengal. So, the insistence of Islamic identity of Bangladesh should be acknowledged as logical".

11. Nirad C. Chaudhuri in his *The Autobiography of an Unknown Indian* (New York: Macmillan, 1951: 226-227) described how such narratives that alienated the two religious communities were also espoused by upper-caste Hindus at the time: "The new Indian culture of the nineteenth century built a perimeter of its own and put specifically Muslim influences and aspirations beyond the pale. In relation to it the Muslims stood outside as an external proletariat, and if the Muslims wanted to come into its world they could come only after giving up all their Islamic values and traditions".

12. Resolution of the Muslim League Legislators' Convention held on 9 April 1946. Quoted in: Sherwani (1969: 97).

13. These communal riots are sometimes defined as "ethnic riots" as they involve 'othering' by sending people out of the nation-state. This, according to Gupta for instance, does not happen during "communal movements" (Cf. Gupta 2002: 4619-4620). See for such violence, for instance, a speech by Sitangshu Guha at the 9th Session of the UNHR Sub-Commission's Working Group on Minorities at the UN office in Geneva from 12-16th May 2003 in *Muslim India*, 251, vol. 21, no. 11

(November 2003): 1144. See also: Nurul Kabir 'Living with Terror. Minorities in Bangladesh', in: *Communalism Combat*, September 2004: 8-16 and Datta (2004: 83-94).

14. Believing this controversy to be well known to my readership, I provide no further details here. Those who need more information may consult Peter van der Veer's *Religious Nationalism: Hindus* and *Muslims in India* (Berkeley: University of California Press).

15. Available on: http://www.bangladesh-web.com/news/view.php? hid Date = 2005/08-07 & hid Type = OPT & hid Record = 0(170)55259.

16. Such Muslims who migrated to India are often called 'infiltrators' in the Indian nationalist discourse (i.e. partition rhetoric), whereas Hindus are welcomed through a discourse of 'homecoming'. In Bangladesh this kind of Muslim migration to India is often denied to take place at all (Cf. Van Schendel 2005: 191-209).

4

Living with the Burden of Other People's History in Bangladesh

Those Who Stayed Put: Suffering Hindus and Out of History

In October 2001, citizens in Bangladesh voted the Bangladesh Nationalist Party (BNP) to power and along with the Islamic Party Jamaat-e-Islami (the Islam Unity Council) became part of the cabinet. Consequently, various media disseminated messages about "The Oppressed Minorities", "Destruction of Temples in Bangladesh, the enforcement of "a medieval anti-Hindu tax, Jizya", rapes of Hindu women, killings of Hindus, human right violations of Hindus and about the "mass exodus of Hindus to India" (e.g. *Mayer Dak*, 15 April 2002). The "proliferation of Islamic fundamentalism" in Bangladesh is given as the main reason for this process of "ethnic cleansing". Sandip Roy[1] reported, for instance, on 20 November 2001:

> The festival of the Goddess Durga in October is normally the high point of the Bengali Hindu cultural calendar. But this year, for thousands of Hindu families in Bangladesh there was no festival and no rejoicing.

Instead, gangs of Islamic extremists torched their homes, raped women, poisoned ponds and attacked temples.

Indeed, the scale of violence, which affects some four million Hindus in Bangladesh, seemed to have gone up after the October 2001 elections. Yet, when we look into reports on the position of Hindus before October 2001, when the Awami League was in power, Hindus in Bangladesh did not seem to have had reasons to feel more secure in their country of birth. Though the Awami League is said to "traditionally" be perceived "sympathetic towards Hindus", the 'exodus' of Hindus to India has never stopped after partition. Awami League or BNP Hindus, it appears, remain being marginalized and even 'expelled' from the nation-state since 1947. Besides, those who protest are 'silenced' by state supported partition rhetoric.[2] Their stories framed by a 'history' that silences their voices, many of these Hindus have indeed chosen to leave. One of them, now living outside Bangladesh wrote:

> Growing up in Bangladesh as a "*Malowan*", I have experienced the very face of first hand discrimination by our fellow tolerant Bangladeshi Muslims in almost every step of my daily life. I have seen in pain how my Dad had to retire from the Government Service being in the same position for 15 years. It was very tormenting for his kids to see him sharing his pain to his wife about how he had to respect someone as his superior who was supposed to be much junior to him in the professional chain of hierarchy. Living in a big city Dhaka, we were immuned from much of the physical part of the torture, but we knew about lot of physical crimes committed on my relatives living in villages. Gradually, lot of these people left their dear homeland in silence. I remember talking to a Hindu priest who once explained how his neighbours who would come to eat Prasad from his temple participated in destroying his little temple! I still remember seeing thousands of raged people marching towards Dhakeshwari Temple with sticks and other ammunitions and my mother pushing us inside to hide in the bedroom not to be

seen by the marchers and my father desperately looking for keys to lock the house from inside. I was lucky to leave Dhaka but my poor family still live in despair and insecure in a different safer neighbourhood in Dhaka.

However, the interviews we conducted in Bangladesh proved that many of these 'suffering Hindus' not only did not leave but also, as will be illustrated in this chapter, escaped the "prison guards" (Cf. Samaddar 2003: 32) constituted by partition narratives and told us other 'accounts of independence'. Importantly however, though the percentage of Hindus in Bangladesh has indeed decreased ever after 1947, those Hindus who were "left behind" or "stayed put"[3] were not these upper-caste and rich Hindus who had been dominant in every walk-of-life, like trade, commerce, administrative services and professions. In a "Statement of Non-Muslim members of the Central Legislative from [undivided] Bengal",[4] Pandit Lakshmi Kanta Maitra mentioned that, "The second objection to the proposed creation of a new province is that it will "leave the Hindu Minority of East Bengal to a dire fate". Many also stated that in case partition of Bengal would take place, upper as well as "Scheduled Castes" would both leave East Bengal. The Viceroy of India wrote in a letter to Sir F.J. Burrows on 6 May 1947:[5]

You will recall that at a meeting on 1st May you expressed the view that Liaquat's claim, that the majority of Scheduled Castes in Bengal would choose independence rather than partition, was wishful thinking. This view seems to be confirmed by a conversation, which I had at a garden party here on 3rd May with two Scheduled Caste representatives to the Constituent Assembly from Bengal. They claimed to represent the views of the Scheduled Castes in Bengal and warned me against Mandal who they thought had been misleading me. They added categorically that the Scheduled Castes on no account wanted separation from the Caste Hindus and were determined not to be left under "the brutal oppression and domination" of the

Muslims. They firmly demanded partition. I asked what would happen to the Scheduled Castes in eastern Bengal. They replied that they themselves lived in Eastern Bengal but did not intend to stay there and they suggested that all the seven million Scheduled Castes in eastern Bengal should be moved to western Bengal.

The Bengali Muslim leader Liaquat Ali Khan had however another opinion about the fate of Scheduled Caste Hindus after partition. An extract from a meeting on 21 April 1947 of the Viceroy of India[6] concerning democratic approaches for the future of the provinces of India included a discussion on matters related to "Scheduled Castes". It was stated that His Excellency the Viceroy asked Mr. Liaquat Ali Khan whether he thought the Scheduled Castes would have the least idea what they were voting about. Mr. Liaquat Ali Khan replied that, "the issue would be quite clear to them— the choice between oppression under the caste Hindus and freedom under the Muslims. He added that he considered the Viceroy's responsibility to give them every chance to escape from the domination of the caste Hindus was very great". Till partition, it remained therefore unclear whether the Scheduled Caste in East Bengal would stay put yet many did.

Crucially, of the Hindus who now reside in Bangladesh only a very few belong to the upper-castes and most of them identify as so-called scheduled castes. Besides, even those who identify as upper-castes rarely hold positions of dominance in contemporary Bangladeshi society. In fact, in contemporary Bangladesh the division between upper-castes and lower-castes is blurred and "the caste-oriented professional boundaries are undergoing a change" (Guharhakurta and Begum 2005: 195).[7] Today the socio-economic differences between the Muslim and the Hindu communities, in particular in rural areas, are "much less marked than it was earlier" (Samad 1999: 76). (Cf. Ali 1992). Yet, most studies on these scheduled caste Hindus describe them as a "minority", separated from the Muslim majority and suffering. Nevertheless, officially, Meghna Guhathakurta (2004) writes:

> Despite the fact that there exists a whole range of minorities in Bangladesh, especially religious, the Constitution of Bangladesh does not distinguish these groups from the majority population [...] Article 6(2) states that the citizens of Bangladesh be known as Bangladeshis. There is no specific reference to the recognition [...] Article 27 states that all citizens are equal before law and are entitled to protection of law. Article 28(1) says that the state shall not discriminate against any citizens on basis of religion, race, caste, sex or place of birth. However political realities have proved otherwise.

In the previous chapter, I have shown that "political realities" are thus contradictory and differ from laws that are designed to guarantee 'equality'. Though, the Bangladeshi nation-makers do not officially recognize the existence of 'minorities', in narratives people are not only labelled as such but fieldwork shows that there is in reality also a part of the population that identifies as a 'suffering minority'. I have argued that this contradiction can be explained by the existence of a cognitive map in the mind of nation-builders in Bangladesh that does recognize and even force upon borders that separate the majority Muslims from the minority Hindus. Actually I showed that there are other forces at work than just laws and the constitution in Bangladesh. Mental borders divide these Hindus, as a 'minority' from the majority and make them suffer too. Whether during phases of "Banglee nationalism", "Bangladeshi nationalism" or "Islamic nationalism" (Samad 1998), the state-rhetoric is enacted again and again amidst these relatively poor and sometimes landless cultivators, potters, weavers, peasants, fishermen, school- and college teachers, musicians, priests, village doctors, union chairmen, milkmen, writers, clerks, lawyers, share-croppers, shopkeepers and other small businessmen, librarians, and social workers. What is more, these scheduled caste Hindus do not only suffer, as these narratives detail, they are also removed from history. In other words, the narratives teach us that either Hindus are a suffering minority or they have left (for India). In general, however, these scheduled castes are absent from the nation's rhetoric.

History textbooks used in Bangladesh's schools narrate that most of the Bengali Muslims had earlier been Buddhists and had later converted to Hinduism. The "rigid caste system" that prevailed among the Hindus is emphasized in these narratives. It is also narrated that as a large number among these Hindus belonged to the scheduled castes, they wanted to escape from the rigidity and oppression of the caste system of Hinduism and converted to Islam (Cf. Rosser 2004). H. Beverley is quoted who wrote in 1872 that,

> The existence of Mohammedans of Eastern in Bengal is not due so much to the introduction of Mughal blood into the country as to the conversion of the former inhabitants for whom a rigid system of caste discipline rendered Hinduism intolerable.[8]

The impression one gets from these narratives is that the lower castes among the Hindus all voluntarily converted to Islam as this "could offer to this people a hope and status denied to them in the Hindu system" (Spear 1955: 46 note 30). Some narratives also recount that this "conversion to Islam to the religion of rulers [...] gave protection and respectability to Scheduled Castes" (Chitkara 1997: 66). Thus these narratives explain that 'most' Scheduled Castes converted to Islam and the remaining few were 'suffering'. Mohammad Abdullah (*News from Bangladesh*, August 9, 2005) argues that conversion is also one of the reasons for the slow disappearance of Scheduled Castes even after 1971:

> Another important aspect of the demography is that a vast population getting converted to Islam periodically. This is quite common for the Scheduled

Caste Hindus to get converted to Islam in Bangladesh. I have seen this in the city of Dacca in 1960s and they changed their names. Also they got married to the Muslims. Inter-religious marriage was common during Pakistan era and even now. This is one of the reasons for decreasing the percentage of the Hindus in Bangladesh.

These narratives suggest that most Scheduled Castes have converted to Islam and that the 'majority' among the Hindus in East Bengal were upper-caste Hindus who are depicted not only as rich moneylenders and *zamindars* (semi-feudal landlords), who exploited the poor Muslims, but also as "outsiders" from West Bengal who "only hoped for the submission of (local) Muslims to Hindus". Mohammad Abdullah (*News from Bangladesh*, August 9, 2005) writes for instance that even before the 1947 partition was finalized:

> The Hindus of Bangladesh did not want to stay with the Muslims even though Bengal remained undivided. Thus, no Hindu supported for united Bengal. These Hindus wanted Hindu majority Indian domination by hook or by crook. Openly they expressed their mind too. Syama Prasad Mukerjee offered to take back the Muslims as the Scheduled Caste after conversion process. If refused the conversion process then the Muslims would be drowned in the River Burhiganga first, and then the remaining will be thrown away to the Bay of Bengal [...] [Syma Prasad Mukerjee's] utterance was tough and also posed to eliminate the Muslims from the Hindu Audhyushito (dominated) *Bangla-Bhashabhasi Anchal* (Bengali-speaking territory) on several occasions thereafter at various places within undivided Bengal.

Increasingly, these narratives continue to explain, these two groups grew apart and formed separate entities in socio-cultural, political and economic fields with the Hindu elite exploiting the Muslim masses in

East Bengal (Cf. Ahmed 1981). Such narratives are included in partition rhetoric of the nation-state, which explain why Bengali Muslims had to put a stop to this injustice. Naturally, these upper-caste Hindus left after partition and the Bengali Muslims got their 'freedom' (Cf. Ahmad 1982).[9] What happened to the Scheduled Castes remains unwritten or they are said to have converted to Islam. Scheduled Caste Hindus who stayed put thus are burdened with this state-rhetoric with mental borders that separate them as 'the others' from the 'majority of Muslims' (Cf. Chaturvedi 2002: 149-159) and has the following features:

1. It highlights a religious identity of Hindus in Bangladesh that threatens to supersede all other identities whether based on class, gender, ethnicity, regional background, nationality or any combination of these.

2. It presents Hindus in Bangladesh as 'exploiters'. Hindus are never portrayed as 'locals' in peaceful coexistence with other 'locals' or as 'locals' in binary opposition to 'outsiders'.

3. It depicts Hindus as 'outsiders' and as 'the other' instead of 'we' and forces Hindus in Bangladesh to identify with the (alleged) deeds of Hindus in pre-1947.

4. It makes Hindus 'minorities' by separating them from the 'majority' Muslims. It never unites them with other citizens in Bangladesh as Bangladeshis.

5. It does not recognise that Hindus in Bangladesh have any other pasts than those of the upper-caste Hindus who were dislocated after 1947 and left for India. These pasts relate to uprooting rather than rooting in the nation.

Relocating Scheduled Caste Hindus to Bangladesh

Yet, not all Hindus left and got uprooted like for instance Tathagata Roy narrates (2002). What is more, not all selves were suppressed and narratives silenced by the enactment of above described partition rhetoric with its mental borders. In fact, many we interviewed provided alternative narratives of partition; in fact stories of independence that brought the scheduled caste Hindus back in history and thus in Bangladesh. We interviewed around eighty people in the rural and urban regions of Sylhet,[10] Dhaka, Bagerhat, Pirojpur, Faridpur, Khustia, Khulna[11] and Rajshahi. These areas house relatively large Hindu populations and have preserved many Hindu structures.[12] The people we interviewed all identified as Hindus and many were believers in Vaishnavism (Nicholas 2001: 52-71) and others were *sudras*. They worshipped among others the God Krshna, his beloved Radha and Goddesses Durga and Kali but also Lakshmi and Saraswati. Most of them (around 80%) said they were scheduled castes such as *mahishyas, pods, kaibartas, rajbansis, jaliahs, haris, rishis, jalo das and also namasudras*. We also interviewed *brahmins, kayasthas* and *kaishabs*. Yet caste, they felt, was not much of consequence for them as "we all are poor". Besides in Bangladesh, unlike in India, there is no reservation for such "*malauns*"[13] like them. Actually, rather than caste, they identified as a kind of a class of 'dalits' (without however using this nomenclature, Cf. Satyani 2005) in the sense that even those labelled and identified as 'poor upper-caste Hindus' were taken in. Besides, they often did not separate between themselves from other 'lower-class Muslims'. In that sense they severely challenged the borders set by the state. Their voices concerning the meaning and effect of partition are completely absent in above-described partition rhetoric. In this chapter we bring them back in Bangladesh by presenting their own stories.

One of the most puzzling findings of our oral history project in Bangladesh was the frequently returning opinion of the Hindus we interviewed that "things had been better during Pakistan times" and that only after the dismemberment of Pakistan "things became really difficult for us". I could not rhyme this with my readings of the period between 1947 and 1971, which clearly showed the workings of mental borders that drove Hindus out of the country. I found a few memoirs of scheduled caste politicians narrating their lives and that of other Hindus "who stayed put" after 1947. These narratives illustrate that due to the continuous enactment of the partition rhetoric ever after 1947, these Hindus had not only resigned from their posts but had also opted out of the nation. J.N. Mandal, for instance, wrote a multi-page letter of resignation in October 9, 1950 addressed to the Prime Minister of Pakistan in which he detailed how not only upper-caste Hindus had been forced to leave the country of their birth but also how "the backward Hindu masses of East Bengal" had been tortured and persecuted by an "anti-Hindu policy". He wrote that these scheduled castes never "received a fair deal" and he recollected incidences during which "brutal atrocities were committed on local *Namasudras*" and during which Hindu shops and houses had been looted and their owners killed. According to him the "Delhi Pact" that should have stopped the exodus was not carried out with "earnest desire" and there was actually a [unwritten] plan, "to squeeze Hindus out of the Province". According to Mandal, there was not only a "boycott by the Muslims of Hindu lawyers, medical practitioners, shopkeepers, traders and merchants" but also "interference in matters educational" and "methods adopted by the Educational authority for Islamisation frightened the teaching staff of secondary schools and colleges out of their old familiar moorings". Besides, Mandal added, "almost all the priests who used to worship the household deities at Hindu houses" and "artisans who made images of gods and goddesses" had all left. He narrated "the abduction and rape of caste Hindu girls" and "even few depressed class girls who live in rural areas with their parents are not even spared by Muslim *goondas*". As a "matter of fact", Mandal concluded "there is no operation of law, justice or fair-play in Pakistan, so far as Hindus are concerned" and:

> I shall not be unjustified in stating that Hindus of Pakistan have to all intensions and purposes been rendered 'Stateless' in their own houses. They have no other fault than that they profess Hindu religion. Declarations are being repeatedly made by Muslim League leaders that Pakistan is and shall be an Islamic State. Islam is being offered as the sovereign remedy for all earthly evils. In the ruthless dialectics of capitalism and socialism you present the exhilarating democratic synthesis of Islamic equality and fraternity. In that grand setting of the *Shariat* Muslims alone are rulers while Hindus and other minorities are jimmies who are entitled to protection at a price, and you know more than anybody else, Mr. Prime Minister, what that price is. After anxious and prolonged thought I have come to the conclusion that Pakistan is no place for Hindus to live in and that their future is darkened by the ominous shadow of conversion or liquidation. The bulk of the upper class Hindus and politically conscious scheduled castes have left East Bengal. These Hindus who will continue to stay in the accursed province and for that matter in Pakistan will, I am afraid, by gradual stages and in a planned manner be either converted to Islam or completely exterminated (Kabir 1980: 131-152)

In other words, as Mandal's memoirs illustrate, the position of scheduled caste Hindus in East Pakistan was affected by the workings of mental borders that 'squeezed' them out of the country. In a Memorandum submitted before the Prime Minister of Pakistan in 1950, five Hindu members of the opposition party in

East Bengal recounted in similar vein how "the ill-fated minority community here" was "inexorably faced with a grim prospect of virtual extinction". They further stated that after having witnessed severe communal riots:

> We are meeting you to-day under lingering shadow of an unprecedented and sweeping orgy of communal disturbances and carnage of recent occurrence, the dreadful enormity and experience of which far surpass those of the hectic days of the Holocausts of 1946 [...] The way in which the occurrences took shape with unmistakable political manipulation and bearings and the manner in which administrative authorities generally handled the situation have naturally given rise to an almost irremovable apprehension in the minds of the most miserably plighted minorities in general that something equally or more terrible may happen every moment. Their sense of security thus stands completely shattered. In the midst of this all-encompassing gloom and sufferings, they see no ray of hope as to the protection of their life, honour, religion and property (Kabir 1980: 106).

Considering the above it came therefore as an enormous surprise to hear our informants' statements about the time they had lived under the Pakistani flag. Listening to their narratives however, I started understanding why they had considered life in Pakistan to be better than in Bangladesh. In Pakistan, as will be demonstrated below, these Bengali Hindus identified Pakistanis and other 'outsiders' as the main 'trouble-makers'. They had indeed faced problems but they felt that they had shared these problems with other 'downtrodden peasants' like them. They therefore struggled along with them for a better deal from the Pakistani state. It was this belief in a common struggle and common interests between Hindu and Muslim Bengalis that enabled them to stay put while others around them all left. In other words, these scheduled caste narratives fundamentally reject the mental borders designed by the Pakistani guardian of the nation-state to divide Hindus from Muslims. What is more, in these narratives these Hindus claim 'unity' with all other East Pakistanis.

In 1950, during a meeting of the Scheduled Caste Federation in Dacca, some of these scheduled caste Hindus had demanded their recruitment in the Government services. Yet, that year had just followed an India-Pakistani war and consequently witnessed huge communal riots during which partition rhetoric had been enacted and Hindus had been told its 'lessons'. In a letter on their behalf addressed to Liaquat Ali Khan the then Prime Minister of Pakistan, a scheduled caste leader of the time wrote that "to their utter misfortune" Scheduled Caste Hindus had realized,

That those demands are not yet met with, though they are co-operating unreservedly with the Muslim League and the Pakistan Government. They [i.e. Scheduled Castes] are the real Nationals of Pakistan and they are born and brought up in this country so they cannot think it otherwise but their beloved Mother Land Pakistan. Still they feel helpless and insecure of their lives and properties now due to the recent disturbances in the Province [...] In view of the gloomy international atmosphere and the suspicious activities of some of their neighbours at this stage of their State, they are ready to undergo any sufferings and sacrifices for the defense of the Pakistan State (Home Political Department. Dacca: vol. 54, 1950).

These scheduled caste Hindus realized however that they were in the same boat as the Muslim Bengalis and they, along with them, knew that in order to get real 'freedom' they had to fight for an independent 'Bangladesh'. They therefore waited for the take-off of the new nation, which indeed came in 1971 and which promised them equality as Bengalis. Serajul Islam Choudhury (2002: 135) remembered:

After independence creatively seemed to be at the stage of a take-off. There was great enthusiasm everywhere. Farmers returned to their fields, workers to their factories and students to their institutions. People volunteered in building bridges, setting up schools, particularly colleges, and helped each other in mending the breaches. What could have been a tragedy promised to be an epic, because of the hope and confidence people had gained in themselves. Foreign aid seemed to be unnecessary and irrelevant. The state was on its own. Signboards on shops and streets written in Bengali letters announcing Bengali names were more than objects; they were testament to a revitalisation and an arrival.

When Bangladesh got her constitution in 1972 it was mentioned in Article 6(2) that, "The citizens of Bangladesh shall be known as Bangladeshis" (Ziring 1992: 151). It therefore came as a complete surprise to me that over and over again interviewed Hindus (upper and lower caste alike) complained that all sorts of problems arose for them only after their return to a liberated Bangladesh. True, they had faced difficult times in Pakistan too, in particular during so-called communal riots, but somehow things seem to have become much more difficult after 1971. In fact, for the Hindus we interviewed it seemed, 'Liberation' meant a slow but steady exit. These Hindus told us they had expected a lot from the new nation but very soon had started to feel "alienated" in the nation, which did not seem to want or need their help in its (re-) construction. After the establishment of Bangladesh it became increasingly difficult to accept, these Hindus narrated, the unwritten laws according to which they were supposed to live. Partition rhetoric after 1971 taught these Hindus that they had no right to protest (as they had to pay the price of partition). Partition narratives explained with whom the real power now lay [with the Bengali Muslims] and silenced the powerless. After 1971 these Hindus had hoped, things would change. The Hindus we interviewed seemed to have expected that now that, as Narindranath Sarkar,[14] one upper-caste Hindu with some land narrated, "we had our own country", we thought we will get a fair treatment. He remembered:

I went to India in 1971. That was my first and last time. In 1947 a riot had taken place but I did not go to India. Again, in 1956 a riot took place but I stayed put though my elder uncle left Bangladesh because he thought it was not safe anymore for us, Hindus, to stay here. He returned however as in India he had not a single relative and he faced many problems as a result and though he had applied for land there, the Government of India did not allot any. When I went in 1971 to India with my whole family, most of the other people in this village including Muslims also came along with us. There was a lot of stabbing going on that time and some villagers got injured too so we all had to leave. We returned after a nine months stay in a refugee camp there. We wanted to return as we felt that Bangladesh is the place of our birth so we had to return home. Besides, by that time, we had got our own country. We had received that news through the radio and believed it. We had taken only a few belongings with us to India and had left our cattle and other things behind. We had no time to ask anybody to look after our property. As we returned we found our home destroyed and cattle and goods stolen. The local Muslims did not return our property but Government helped us to some extend. We started working in other peoples' fields and after great struggle we bought all things back that we had lost.

However, things did not become better for Hindus like him in independent Bangladesh and Sarkar further remembered:

I think that we were better of under the Pakistan Government. Actually, things changed a lot here in the village during that time. Our landlord had been the poet Rabindranath Tagore. These landlords used to collect taxes during the rainy season. In 1947 these landlords left and settled down in India. The land, which we used to cultivate, became ours. We captured it. In 1947 most of the upper caste Hindus like me left so our population became very less. We were therefore forced to interact with lower-castes and slowly we build up a very good relation with each other. Since we all belong to the minority group it is better to have a good relation between lower and upper castes. Now, also due to increased education among the lower castes, any type of caste discrimination has stopped and we eat together which before 1947 we never used to do. Besides, during the Pakistani regime we also developed very close relations with Muslims here in our village. When I was a child, Hindus did not visit Muslim houses but after 1947 we started visiting each other frequently. Muslims loved to celebrate Durga Puja with us too and we went to their houses when they had a function. But nowadays everything is different. Muslims are not seen here during Durga Puja anymore and if they come it is just to keep an eye on us. Under Bangladesh Government we are not in a better position. I like liberation but we did not get any of its fruits. Now life is full of problems here. In fact, it is much worse than before. Local leaders are all the time extracting money from us and if we do not want to give it, they take it by force or create even more problems. During the Pakistani regime the locals never tortured us. We cannot get Government jobs because if we write our Hindu names they say no. We also do not succeed in business as too much of money is taken from us. That is why we are cultivators. But now they want our land and there is too much of corruption going on here. Two of my children have been kidnapped because the law and order situation in so bad. The Muslims think they can do everything to us and that we will not protest. They do not like us.

Analysing their narrations, I realized that the most disheartening experience seems to have been the fact that after 1971 they were not treated at par with the Bengali Muslims though living along with them in the same cities and villages for centuries and under more or less equal conditions of exploitation. In fact, it seems they had expected the nation to take them in but partition rhetoric remained excluding them from it[15] and some of those we interviewed were made to feel like foreigners in their own country. In short, these narratives illustrated that while the nation-state constructed a self in Bangladesh with the help of partition rhetoric, Hindus who stayed put were made homeless. Or rather, they were told that their home was India as that was where all Hindus had migrated to and that is where they should go to as well. Hindus who stayed put were made to feel that they had stayed back (as suffering minorities) and had become the 'other' of the nation. Though these Hindus were all Bangladeshi by birth, citizenship and legality, partition rhetoric now labelled them Hindus and Hindus only. Legal rights in such a social context were and are of little use. To the contrary, partition rhetoric self-censures Hindus, as they believe that they, as a minority, cannot challenge majority rulings. Besides, the majority use partition rhetoric to accelerate this process of 'minoritization' (Bajpai 1999: 220-242). It forces Hindus to leave or sell their land and other property, forbids them to withdraw substantial amounts of money in cash from commercial banks, excludes them from any sensitive positions and various civil and military jobs and excludes them from business and trade, bank loans and credit (Bhowmick and Dhar 1998). In other words, the continuation of the enactment of partition rhetoric among these Hindus has caused that their dreams of liberation have turned into nightmares.[16] As a result, the place these Hindus knew as their home became 'enemy land'[17] and a foreign country and many among them indeed started hoping that in India they would get a better deal (Cf. Samad 1998).

Challenging the Mental Borders of the Partition Rhetoric: Narratives of Rooting with Different Selves

Partition rhetoric in Bangladesh underlines displacement and uprooting of those who migrated [Hindus] as well as of those Hindus who were uprooted without physical movement. As shown partition rhetoric also denies Hindus "access to various communities" (Chandhoke 1997: 272-304). Accordingly, they were Hindus and Hindus only. We have illustrated that many Hindus indeed suffered under the burden of this rhetoric. Yet, not all Scheduled Castes have left and many we interviewed are trying to stay put. What is more, the stories they narrated to us, radically differed from those incorporated in the state rhetoric. In fact, in order to stay put, they challenged the mental borders embodied in it. The narratives we collected thus concern "the alienation of the inner self and the renegotiation of identity within a radically altered milieu" (Chakrabarty 2003: 105 and Cf. Rahman 1996: 299-315). Bidyut Chakrabarty (2003: 76) explains,

> Critical in these narratives was not so much the event of Partition, but 'the impingement of its consequences on the consciousness of the individual: a defining moment that forces him/her to realize the pastness of the past and the presence of the here and now'. The individual found himself/herself rootless and homeless, a refugee 'who has to strive to relocate his/her identity in a radically different present, which paradoxically enough, is shaped, influenced and conditioned by the very past which is irrecoverable'.

Yet, our informants though going through moments of confusion whenever partition rhetoric was enacted in their lives which indeed temporarily and mentally displaced them, they also recovered and came out with stories in which they rooted themselves in Bangladesh's past, present and future. According to Sultana Nahar the only scholar that I am aware of who has also tried to compare the situation of the two religious minorities in their respective countries (Nahar 1994), there were two categories of Hindus "who never leave their motherland". In her book on the position of the Hindu minority in Bangladesh she stated that,

In the first category fall the hard-core patriots. Whatever may be the sufferings, the harassment or tortures, the lack of gainful occupation, they shall never flee to India. The poor and uneducated people like peasants, fishermen, cobblers and watermen come under the second category. They have no means to migrate or have no relatives in India to initially support them. They cling to the soil of their birth (Nahar 1998: 15).

We found not only many of these "hard-core patriots" but located them also among these "poor and uneducated people". They clang to the soil not because they were left behind but because they had opted to stay put. We should not forget that these scheduled caste Hindus who stayed put were often economically and socially at par with the masses of the poor and often landless Muslim cultivators in rural areas. Narratives sometimes emphasized such bonds that existed between these Bengali Muslims and these scheduled castes. Some scholars have also commented on the "hybrid culture these two religious communities had created" and argued that "Hinduism and Islam are like two curries spread on a plate of rice – it is impossible for them not to blend together" (Hartmann and Boyce 1983: 214). Indeed, even though scholars found that even before 1947 tensions had existed between the *namasudras* and Muslims,[18] many of the Hindus we interviewed emphasised that actually there was not much difference between the two communities in terms of class background and history and that tensions were caused by competition due to sameness rather than difference.[19] In such situations partition rhetoric could be used by the majority to expel the 'minority Hindus' from their lands.

Many also narrated that, in the past, they had visited each other's festivals and celebrations and had shared food. The fact that Muslim Bengalis and Hindu Bengalis also shared a common language and a history of common struggle against 'outsider Muslims' was also frequently highlighted to illustrate commonality rather than difference between the two religious groups.

These Hindus reiterated for instance the bond they had shared with Bengali Muslims in particular during the days of the so-called language movement. In short, apparently, religion had been only an "essence of the distinction" and not the "essence of the community" as partition rhetoric likes to have it. Judging from the narratives told by our informants generally therefore, the "bonds of region, class, caste, gender, ethnicity, language or nationality" had always been much stronger than the "bonds of religion" (Cf. Ghosh 1998: 232).

Partition rhetoric denies these Hindus a place in the Bangladeshi nation (and the state) and subsequently makes them feel like outsiders or even refugees who have only India to 'go back' to and where they can find a home. Yet all Hindus we interviewed had "opted" (Cf. Van Schendel and Zürcher 2001: 1-13) for Bangladesh and expressed a strong sense of national identity. Indeed many of them had left their houses temporarily during the extreme violence that constituted the Bangladesh liberation war, but had returned with hopes. Though most of them returned only to find their houses burnt, (scarce) possessions looted, land occupied or crops stolen, theirs were nevertheless stories of "people fighting to cope, to survive and build anew" (Pandey 2001: 187). Some had witnessed extreme violence and had been unable to trace members left behind or just found a sari of a sister who had been left behind hanging in a tree.[20] Nevertheless, they narrated that they had come home and they pitied those who they had left behind in India. Besides, the new secular constitution of Bangladesh was considered the fruit of their struggle and a bandage with which they could cover their wounds. The future looked bright once again. Haldar is a cultivator in Khustia, who narrated that though in his village only Hindus lived,

We had good relations with Muslims living in neighbouring villages. We used to attend each other's festivals and come over to each other's houses. We all ate fish, meat, chicken, vegetables but the only thing we did not take was beef. Actually, we all got our land here after the landlords left during 1947 when India and Pakistan were created. Many landlords gifted the land to local people here when they left. Some also sold the land and even poor people could buy some, as during that time the land was very cheap. We bought the land in small quantity like two to three *katha*. We all [Hindus and Muslims] have equal quantity of land and cultivate it. The only difference between Hindus and Muslims is that generally Muslims marry more than once.

Haldar recounted however those problems had started in 1964 when "we were harassed in a different way". Yet it was only after 1971 that Haldar finally realised the full impact of partition:

That time we were very afraid because many people had been killed. We faced problems in 1971 not in 1947. The landlords shifted to India in 1947 and never came back. We also went to India in 1971 and stayed in Malda District in West Bengal for nine months. We returned because we had land and houses here. Besides, our economical condition was very bad in India and how could we leave our motherland? Nobody likes to leave one's native country? When we returned, our land had been captured and Muslims were cultivating our land. But they returned our land and most of our goods that had been looted. We felt good in Bangladesh in comparison to India. Yet, Muslims asked me: "Why have you returned?" I replied: "We are now all Bangladeshis and now we will live together". But they replied that, "if you will live here all your prestige and moral values will be destroyed. This is not a place for you to live in".

Haldar had concluded: During the British period we could buy things very cheap and now things have become very costly that is a major difference. But the British had to go and we were free. But if partition had not have taken place than religion would not have been such a big thing. After all, we all are cultivators.

For Mala from Dhaka things had changed after 1992 only. It was only then that she realized the impact of partition. During that time in India the destruction of the Babri Masjid in Ayodhya in India had repercussions in many places in Bangladesh too. Mala told me about her past friendships with Muslim girls of her age. She actually felt that the position of Muslim women was somewhat better as 'they are allowed divorce'. She always had been very close with her friends:

> We used to put *bindhi* and we dressed up in the same fashion. All that has changed now. After this Babri thing, they [Muslim women] have started dressing up differently. Not only that, one of my very close friends, she is a Muslim, told me that my mother is an Indian freak as she wears *sindoor* and *shakas*. I felt very hurt. What India has to do with all that? She is a Hindu that's all. All married Hindu women wear these things!

Saha could clearly visualise what had happened to him after he experienced a riot during 1962 in Rajshahi District: he had been made a 'minority' and endangered too. It had been during his matriculation exam that he had been advised to go home immediately as some people expected problems. On his way home he saw people bringing their womenfolk to safer places and others painting their houses with mud. People told him that looting was going on and that several houses had been set on fire. He also came across a Kali temple where Muslims had shouted '*Allah O Akbar*' ('Allah is Great') and Hindu women and men had been running away like mad. Some persons had stopped him on his way however and had asked him whether he was a Hindu or Muslim. He had answered that he was a Muslim. They however refuted this and remarked that his whole behaviour showed he was a Hindu. Yet their attention had been diverted as they saw some

Hindu women approaching and he managed to escape. When he had finally reached his parental home, he saw that people of the village were extremely afraid and they talked about Muslims coming to attack houses of Hindus. Saha recalled:

I became desperate when I saw all these people running away. I did not know what to do. At that moment an unknown person came from Tanzimpur. He was surprised to see that I had not run away. He told me to come along with him and he said that Muslims would give me shelter. But then something very strange happened to me. I suddenly ran away one side and that other person the other side. At that time it was impossible to know who your friend was and who your enemy so I ran away.

But Saha's story did not finish here: I reached a nearby village and a person approached me with the intention to kill me. At that time I had a bamboo stick in my hand and I started beating him till he fell down. But he rose again and cried: '*O re baba re*' ('Oh, oh!') and I realised he was a Hindu. Then I also realised I knew him. I carried him on my shoulders and kept him for shelter in a Muslim house. I am talking about Pakistan time. That time there were very kind Muslims and Muslims who were real villains.

Hindus in Bangladesh we interviewed were indeed not satisfied with being grouped on the basis of religion only. Haldar from Kamargah sighted.

Some land of people was confiscated under the Vested Property Act but why to mind? Already the river took so much of our land. Some people have gone to India. Yet, we have no relatives there and no land. What can we do there? Muslims here also suffer. We all [Hindus and Muslims] used to go for fishing too yet there is no water in the ponds anymore so what can we do? Government should do something for us because we are illiterate and backward.

In Bangladesh, Hindus feel not necessarily a bond with Hindus in India because they share a common religion. In fact some feel threatened by the way certain Hindus in India present their cause. Ghosh, a lawyer in Dhaka complained:

They [Hindus in India] think they help us. Not at all! They only create problems for us here in Bangladesh. You listen to this. Recently, there appeared something very bad on the Internet. He might have had good intentions, I do not doubt that but you see they do not understand our struggle. This fellow writes that we are exploited and repressed etc. He wants Hindus to take up arms and fight for a separate homeland for Hindus here within Bangladesh! We are already Bangladeshis. We have our homeland and struggled a lot to get this along with the Bengali Muslims. What we now need is our rightful place as citizens in this country of ours.

Bela from Khustia does also not identify much with Hindus in India:

I hope you do not mind me saying this. Yet, I do not like India very much. They think they are superior to us in particular the Bengalis there. They all think we are from lower caste background and look down upon us. Besides, Indians still expect us to thank them for their contribution during the war. In 1971, we all fled to India. We received rice. Yet, we did not have land there so we returned. One of my brothers died in India. When we returned from there, everything here was looted and destroyed. Our land was captured and we had to start all over again. But I love this country. I am born on its soil. Those who migrated say they are secure there but why than do they keep on crying? We are all Hindus yes, but I feel very different from them. They cannot understand our sufferings.

Rahul, a student in Rajshahi University would like to study in India as he feels his chances in Bangladesh are limited not for him as a Hindu but for all young people without connections:

> Our parents have struggled and died for this country. We are all Bangladeshis. We speak the same language. Bangladesh is a poor country so we all suffer and the Government is corrupt so what can we do? On the campus there is also a lot of politics going on. If India really wants to help us they should provide scholarships. If I can study there I can return to my country and do something. Instead of helping however, Indians have created many problems for us. Whenever there is a riot in India, we suffer here. Unnecessarily, they divide us.

In short, as these narratives evidence Hindus in Bangladesh have thus become "minorities by force" (Kabir 1980: 9-11) and suffer due to the workings of the partition rhetoric. Yet we also have seen that our informants reject the process of minoritisation (Cf. Gupta 1995: 2207) caused by this enactment of partition rhetoric and which only weakens their position as minorities. They do not identify themselves as victimized monoliths on the basis of religion (Cf. Salat 1998: 188) as the partition rhetoric labels them. They do also not act as exclusive communal factions but rather as "composite pressure and interest-oriented groups, which can involve a multi-communal composition" (Khan 2001: 54-78). They realise that religion despite being significant in its own way does not provide the basic ingredients of socio-political cohesion. Instead, they know that the one and only factor that remains resolute and indissoluble is that of 'citizenship'.

Since Pakistan days they know that it is only by protecting the dignity of the individual as a citizen that one can mitigate the harshness of minoritisation that takes place during the process of partition. The lessons they learnt then still hold in present-day Bangladesh. By way of conclusion I therefore quote a letter addressed to the Prime Minister of Pakistan and written by a group of mostly scheduled castes after they witnessed "everywhere severe rioting and disturbances" in 1950 (Home Political Department Dacca 1951, Vol. 54):

> The minorities in East Bengal cannot feel a sense of security unless the majority community as a whole are made to believe that the minorities are the citizens of the State as much as the majorities are and are entitled to the same privileges and protection of law with equal rights. But the constant propaganda that the State is an Islamic State encourages and generates a belief in the minds of the ordinary Muslims that non-Muslims have no place in the State except perhaps as subservient people and are not entitled to any rights in the State. The idea that the minorities are "jimmies" must not be allowed to grow in any section of the people and must by all means be discountenanced.

Therefore, these scheduled castes did not always identify as 'Hindus' as this would mean the acceptance of a past they did not consider theirs. Besides, they aimed at acceptance within the nation and its state and therefore rejected the boundaries that separated them from the 'Muslims'. (Upper-caste) Hindus did either leave for India or demanded another partition. These upper-caste Hindus had demanded a separate secular state. Dr. Subodh Mitra in his speech during a public meeting under the auspices of the Council for the Protection of the Rights of Minorities held on August 26, 1949 in Dacca reminded his "fellow Hindus" that "East Bengal Hindus took a leading part in the struggle for freedom of India. They were also responsible for annulling the partition of Bengal" [in 1911], and Mitra therefore, "urged upon all East Bengal men to unite and make every sacrifice to attend the objective of partition of East Bengal" and asked also the "people of West Bengal to assist their brethren in distress in East Bengal". This was, according to these upper-caste Bengali Hindus, "the only escape for Minorities in East Bengal from the tyranny of the Muslim League Government" (Home Political Department Dacca 1949, Vol. 50).[21]

At the same time, members of the East Bengal Scheduled Castes Federation felt "proud and honored to have the Prime Minister in their midst" as it gave them an "opportunity for the exchange of their thoughts and views on some of the problems of the day for the Scheduled Castes arisen from the recent disturbances in the Province of East Bengal". These Scheduled Castes therefore asked the "Quaid-E-Azam" [Liaquat Ali Khan] to bring his "Noble Mission" of "live and let others live" to "a successful end". They also asked for "equal rights of citizenship and universal brotherhood to all Pakistan National irrespective of caste and creeds". They assured the Prime Minister of their full cooperation with the Government and the Muslim League and emphasized that they were "the real Nationals of Pakistan". They were "born and brought up in this country" so they could not think it otherwise than that Pakistan was their "beloved Mother- land". Yet still they felt "helpless and insecure of their lives and properties now". They however understood that things were difficult for the state in "view of the gloomy international atmosphere and suspicious activities" of some of their neighbours. These scheduled castes wanted to help in the nation building process and wrote that, "at this stage of their State", they were, "ready to undergo any sufferings and sacrifices for the defense of the Pakistan State" (Home Political Department Dacca, 1950, Vol. 54).[22]

References

1. Various web sides report on these "Attacks on members of the Hindu minority" in Bangladesh. See, for instance, the Pacific News Service, PNS (IMDiversity.com): "Attacks on Hindus in Bangladesh Raise Fears of Talibanization" (Sandip Roy, November 20, 2001).

2. This refers, for instance, to the arrest of Shahriar Kabir, a prominent journalist and writer in Bangladesh on 22 November 2001. The explanation the government gave for his detention

was that Kabir was involved in "tarnishing the image of Bangladesh and of the government in the outside world". Kabir, a Muslim Bengali, who was investigating the situation of Hindus after the alleged attacks on them, had sent "a chilling message to human rights defenders in Bangladesh and throughout the world" (Bangladesh Attacks on members of the Hindu minority.htm). Kabir had clearly challenged mental borders in Bangladesh that the government sought to sustain.

3. According to the 1991 census, there are about 11.2 million Hindus in Bangladesh, comprising 10.5 per cent of the population (Baxter and Rahman 2004: 111).

4. File: MB1/D111/8. (1947). This file is available in the Hartley Library (University Southampton, UK) (Mountbatten papers).

5. File: MB1/D115/10 (Mountbatten papers).

6. File: MB1/D119/16 (Mountbatten papers).

7. Guhathakurta and Begum (2005: 195) describe: "Previously, many of these communities were looked down upon as their work was not considered clean by upper caste Hindus. But currently many of these professions, which have proved to be lucrative, are being taken over by peasants and landless labourers outside the traditional caste boundaries. The injection of the cash economy, therefore, is eroding traditional caste boundaries".

8. See also: Report on the Census of Bengal (Calcutta: Secretariat Press, 1872): 132.

9. Baxter and Rahman (2004: 111) argue that, "it is clear that the two major out-migrations of Hindus, in early 1950s and in 1971, were comprised primarily of caste Hindus".

10. A Sylhet Referendum was held in 1947, in the Sylhet district of Assam to determine whether that district would go to India or Pakistan in the partition. The district did vote to go to Pakistan.

11. With the local government reorganization during the Ershad regime, the former Khulna district was divided into the Khulna, Bagerhat, and Satkhira districts and Khulna is also the third largest city in Bangladesh.

12. The regions (former districts) with the highest ratio of Hindus in the 1981 census (comparable data for 1991 and 2001 are not yet available) were Khulna (27.2 per cent), Dinajpur (21.9 per cent), Jessore (19.6 per cent), Faridpur (18.8 per cent), and Sylhet (18.0 per cent).

13. Bengali Muslims label Hindus as *malaun* or *kafir*. See also File: MB1/D108/43 (Mountbatten papers).

14. Informant interviewed in Khustia in December 2001. Age: 60.

15. For these Hindus therefore the process of partition started immediately after 1947 in East Bengal and lasts until date in Bangladesh. Though it is perceivable in day-to-day business, the enactment of partition rhetoric becomes in particular visible during the so-called communal riots that are reported to have taken place ever after 1947. Some however do deny the existence of these atrocities whereas others argue that these are not "riots" but should be called "pogroms". The Hindus we interviewed were scattered all over Bangladesh and in some areas there seemed to have been more communal tension than in others. Most of our informants contended that, "recently things have become very difficult for us". See also for instance, *Bangladesh Hindu Boudda Christian Oikya Parishad, Communal Persecution and Representation in Bangladesh. Some Facts* (Dhaka: BHBCOP, 1993); A.J. Kamra, The *Prolonged Partition and Its Pogroms. Testimonies on Violence against Hindus in East Bengal* 1946-64 (New Delhi: Voice of India: 2000); S. Guha, *Non-Muslims Behind the Curtain of East Pakistan* (Calcutta: Gobardhan Press, n.d.); P.C. Lahiri, *India Partitioned and Minorities in Pakistan* (Calcutta: Writers' Forum, 1964) and Ain o Salish Kendro (ASK), *Human Rights in Bangladesh* (Dhaka: The University Press Limited, 1999).

16. On the 9th of June 2002, the Bangladesh *Bouddha Christian Oikya Parishad* observed Black Day all over the country and demanded the restoration of the 1972 Constitution that enshrined secularism. Speakers at the rally said that secularism was one of the objectives of the Liberation War. They also condemned what they called continued communal riots in

the country, in http://independent-bangladesh.com/new/jun/10/10062002mt.htm#A11.

17. This happened also literally through the continuance of the so-called Enemy Property Act of 1965 under the name "Vested Property Act" in independent Bangladesh. This Act, Guhathakurta (2004: 6) alleges, "has been responsible for a systematic and pervasive eviction of Hindus from their land and a resultant exodus to India".

18. Mrinal Kumar Basu (1995: 163) wrote that in 1911 serious riots had occurred in villages in Khulna and Jessore and the first reported riot already in 1889. He concluded however that, "these riots demonstrate the lack of racial animosity between the two religious communities" but, "were primarily the outcome of a fierce competition between the Namasudras and the local Muslims whose illiteracy, turbulence and lack of sophistication found expression in occasional riots. The majority Muslims who composed the bulk of the peasantry felt their existence threatened whenever the compact Namasudra posed a challenge. The competition between these two communities coupled with their dislike for caste Hindus in the background of the British policy of wooing the Muslims reached new heights during the anti-partition agitation". See also Das (1991).

19. My argument here is that ever after 1947 but in particular during the last couple of years, poor Muslims in rural Bangladesh can use the state-sanctioned partition rhetoric to serve their own interests whereas it silences the poor and not so poor Hindus in the area. Though at times this Muslim and Hindu peasantry use bonds of class to get their piece of cake, the unwritten laws embodied in partition rhetoric work in favor of Muslims in situations of fierce socio economic competition between them and the scheduled castes. For a similar argument though differently styled see: Roy 1994: 193.

20. This refers to a short story entitled "Roots" by Syeda Farida Rahman, in Zaman (2000: 124-129).

21. This report was printed in *The Nation*, 29 August 1949.

22. Home Political Department (Dacca, 1950), Vol. 54.

5

The Working of Mental Borders in India

The Idea of India and Muslims as Minorities

On the night of 14 August, 1947, when India was declared an independent nation, Jawaharlal Nehru India's first Prime Minister addressed the members of the Constituent Assembly with the words:

> Long years ago we made a tryst with destiny, and now the time comes when we shall redeem our pledge, not wholly or in full measure, but very substantially. At the stroke of the midnight hour, when the world sleeps, India will awake to life and freedom. A moment comes, which comes but rarely in history, when we step out from the old to the new, when an age ends, and when the soul of a nation, long suspended, finds utterance. It is fitting that at this solemn moment we take the pledge of dedication to the service of India and her people and to the still larger cause of humanity (Mahajan 1970: 86).

Nehru,[1] and for that matter the majority of Congress politicians who became the claimants, makers and managers of the Indian nation-state, not unaware about the 'losses' caused by partition, had accepted partition as a single, definitive act, a clean-cut vivisection that was executed in a single stroke (Cf. Chatterji 1999). For M.K. Gandhi ('Gandhiji') known as the father of the nation, partition had been so unacceptable that he turned against the newly constituted state in independent India. Javeed Alam (2002: 96) commented:

> Gandhi refused to acknowledge the legitimacy of the power of this state, and took up cudgels on behalf of society against the state. He went on protest *padyatras*, undertook a 'fast unto death', and demonstrated his dismay in many other ways [...] In doing so he was raising a fundamental question: where should the final authority to determine the destiny of society reside? Can the state, a coercive institution, take over the voice of society? [Italics added].

Instead Nehru, though he had not seen the final map of the India he was going to rule, when by 17 August 1947, Sir Cyril Radcliffe announced his Boundary Awards, made an appeal to the Indian electorate on the eve of the first general election in India after 1947. In this appeal he and other Congress members provided a kind of "post-facto justification" of partition. To quote from Mushirul Hasan (2002: 213-214), they argued that, "the price of freedom was Partition". The Congress and its leaders resisted the idea of partition till the last moment. Yet after 1947 the leaders thought

> *a strong and stable Central Government could be established by peaceful means only through Partition... It should not be forgotten that without Partition there might have been no transfer of power at all, or the whole of India might have been involved in a civil war the consequences of which would have been infinitely more tragic than the sad events of the latter half of 1947.*

Most leaders of the time, including Nehru, thus accepted partition as an event, gruesome indeed, but a necessary evil without which the nation-state would not have come about. Yet, they recognized that a 'process of healing' (Cf. Chatterji 1999) was needed to overcome the 'event' of partition. Actually, after the Simla Conference in 1945, the "war of position", as Gurharpal Singh (1997)[2] wrote had changed in a "war of manoeuvre", which became a "fight for incumbency [...] in which the objectives of political elites with reference to future career calculations in terms of territory, mobilisable resources, demographic strength and ideological formulas becomes explicit". This ultimately climaxed in the decision of Congress as well as Muslim League leaders to agree to partition and after 1947, "the clash of visions that had led to the partition were now established as hegemonic beliefs supported by a coalition of interests who had most to gain from state contraction" (Singh 1997). Yet, though Nehru and other Congress leaders had thus accepted "state contraction", facing the situation after 1947 in particular in Kashmir, they were worried about further 'contractions' and "in a way the partition of India strengthened the sanctity of the borders of the newly created states" (Singh 1997). The protection of these geographical borders required mental borders however that legitimated and protected the former. In 1950 a national constitution was designed and so the long journey of nation building started.

Nehru and other leaders thus accepted that the price of independence was state-contraction (i.e. partition) and what was now needed was a protection of the borders of this new nation-state, which was only possible if simultaneously borders of the mind did their work. Hence the nation-state was based on this partition whatever the 'voice of society'. What is more, he and other nationalist leaders started influencing this voice. Though for Nehru and other leaders the partition was initially seen as a sad 'event', in the wake of mass uprooting and extreme violence this 'optimistic' idea got challenged very soon. These nation-builders realized that this juxtaposition of partition-independence would always cast a shadow over the memory of 1947 as the year in which India got freedom. Partition was not an event but a process and these leaders realized that this "operation did not cure wounds or solved conflicts". In fact, it became the main factor defining state rhetoric:

the country had to be protected against further 'partitions'. Scholar Samaddar (2003: 25 and 35 note 6) therefore regrets that,

> Even perceptive observers miss the role of 1947 in the development of Indian geopolitical thinking–an event that marked the shift of the nation from marking out a cultural region/area to a geopolitical area as its natural habitat.

Facing communal carnage, problems in Kashmir, a war with Pakistan and problems of integrating some of the so-called princely state in the Indian nation-state, Nehru defended India's borders with 'guarded optimistic secularism'.[3] It was this, he presumed, that would protect the newly born India (and an unclean birth indeed Nehru agreed) from further partition. This secularism was thus born out of fear (pessimism) (for disintegration) mixed with confidence (optimism) in integration. Regarding Nehru's pessimism, Khilnani (2002: 4799) explains:

> For anyone of Nehru's historical intelligence, one clear lesson of the Partition of India was to drive home the in-eliminable force of religion in Indian society, its deeprootedness –something that Nehru already had learned at the individual level through his engagement with Tagore and Gandhi, as well as with colleagues like Maulana Azad and Rajaji. Nehru's views about religion and the state were not based on a prospective optimism about the evanescence of religion, but rather on a retrospective, historically based pessimism about its persistence – and the dangers this posed if it should ever be linked to that most powerful modern form of instrumental reason, the state.

Yet, Nehru also was optimistic in the sense that he believed in a concept of 'secularism' that could once and for all chase away the 'danger'. I here argue that this pessimism-optimism contradiction fundamentally impacted not only Nehru's concept of 'secularism', but in fact his whole cognitive map and therefore his views and decisions regarding 'minorities' and communal relations. As Singh (1997) wrote for instance:

> Legitimizing Indian presence in Kashmir, the Congress fanned a curious double-speak, which held India's secularism would be threatened if Kashmir left the Indian Union. The observe, that if India's secularism was so strong the right of provinces to self-determination should be entertained, was insidiously made a political non-issue, supporting the inference that the forced inclusion of Kashmir symbolized a tokenist secularism, and an instrumentalist ideology.

During his years as prime minister (1950 to 1964), Nehru and other Congress leaders decided they had to transform India from a highly feudal, hierarchical, caste ridden and communal society to a secular democracy. For this these leaders needed narratives that took 1947 as the great momentum on which the darkness of before was replaced by hope after 1947. The constitution of India was based on this 'forced' hope, not on ground realities, and on a rhetoric (at times called the Nehruvian vision) that embodied an 'emancipatory and egalitarian vision'. As Bhargava (2000: 199) explained:

> Let me return to Indian historiography. Why did Hindu leaders not see that two cultural communities can live together in a single state? The simple strategic rational explanation is that they cynically constructed an ideology of Hindu-Muslim brotherhood in the service of their desire for a unified nation-state. The more complex strategic explanation is that their passionate desire for a unified nation prevented them from acknowledging the growing estrangement. Passion affected their desire for national unity, and this intense desire induced a false belief of lasting warmth between Hindus and Muslims. In other words, this was a classic case of wish fulfillment. When something is desired strongly, it is seen to exist before it actually does; the

very passion that induced the slogan of Hindu-Muslim unity also obscured the lack of amity in their relations.

Consequently, the partition rhetoric determined the idea of India: India was born out of partition and had received independence only after facing tremendous (territorial and otherwise) losses. To be sure, further separation had therefore to be avoided and the present boundaries had to be protected if not expanded. What is more, 'Indians' should adhere to this idea of India, the new rulers ruled. Refusing to or even countenancing the possibility that "different people with varying 'national composition' could have different notions of what it means to be an Indian" (Alam 2002: 102), Nehru and other leaders chose for a monolithic idea of India that imposed nationalism and national unity on diversity (Alam 2002: 101). Actually, as Samaddar (2004: 25 and 35 note 6) argued this idea created "majoritarian states that may be referred to as 'ethnocracies' in which ethnic and religious conflicts only increased". This influenced the discursive regime that constitutes 'Indians' as political and psychological subjects. Those who accepted this idea of India would be included into the nation-state and those who threatened the 'unity and integrity of the country' were 'silenced' and made to accept it or otherwise excluded.

Among India's constitution's concerns were the so-called minorities. Though the word 'minority' was not defined in this or any other constitutional documents, the constitution of India, unlike that of Bangladesh, nevertheless refers to 'minorities' and speaks of those based on religion and language. Its preamble declares the State to be 'secular' and all citizens of India are secured 'liberty of thought, expression, belief, faith and worship', as well as, 'equality of status and of opportunity'. In other words, the constitution ensures 'equality of free citizenship' and though the term 'secularism' was inserted in the preamble of the Indian Constitution only in 1976 (42nd amendment), "the intention of the founding fathers to build a secular state in India", says scholar Partha Pratim Basu (2001: 272), "was never in doubt". Yet, the gloom of partition did make these leaders add some other acts however. The country had been partitioned in the name of religion and, as Chandhoke (2002: 213) argued,

> Therefore, while the members of the Constituent Assembly agreed that the rights of the minorities to their cultures should be protected, they also believed that minorities had no claim to political rights either in the form of reservations in legislatures or separate electorates. Separate electorates had, after all, reaped a bitter harvest [...] These members had felt that in the light of the changed political conditions (Partition) [....] it was not considered desirable that minorities [read Muslims] should have reserved seats in the legislatures. This, it was said, could lead to further separatism; it also conflicted with the ideal of a secular democratic state.

In other words, the new nation-state was founded on the rhetoric that India should not commit the mistakes that it had made in the past. Noorani (2003: 9) contended that,

> To not a few, partition was the culmination of a process, which began with separate electorates and took in its train various charters of demands like Jinnah's famous fourteen points. Any expression of Muslims' grievances or of Muslims' identity reminded them of that and caused disquiet.

"History", Nehru had said, "had proved that separate electorates had inflicted great damage to the country" (Chandhoke 2002: 214). Yet, though Nehru and other leaders had decided on 'no reservations for minorities' in order "to remove every barrier which separates them [italics added] in the political domain so that they may develop and we may all work together", partition created "its own political reverberations (Cf. Chandhoke 2002: 215). It created mental borders that separated the 'majority' from the 'minority' ('Muslims') and linked the latter to a partition history that should not be repeated. "Now", Chandhoke wrote (2002: 215), "the need was to consolidate what had been left of the nation; the need was to prevent any move that might lead to further separatism". Nag (2001: 4756) remarked:

An interesting feature of this story of nation formation and displacement was that a massive number of people who were Indian by birth, citizenship and legality, were now being counted by two new categories– as Muslims and Hindus (or non-Muslims for Hindus, Sikhs and Christians taken together) in official records.

In February 1948, a special sub-committee of Patel, Nehru, Prasad, K.M. Munshi and Ambedkar was formed on "minority problems affecting East Punjab and West Bengal, which rejected the demand for a separate electorate since such demands "disrupted the whole conception of the secular state which is to be the basis of out new Constitution". In moving his report of a May 11 meeting in the Constituent Assembly on May 25, 1949, Patel exhorted everyone, "to forget that there is anything like majority or minority in this country and that in India there is only one community" (Jha 2002: 3179). Yet, ironically, the steps taken to avoid 'further separatism', mostly but not always unwillingly and unconsciously, enacted borders on the minds of the 'majority' as well as the 'minority'. This was the unplanned outcome of nation making in partition and Nehru's concept of "secularism seemed too weak to counter communalism" (Kumar 2000: 2734).

Yet, whereas in Bangladesh, as shown in previous chapters, this 'forged unity' was institutionalized and the very existence of 'minorities' was denied, in India 'secularism' was proposed in particular to include minorities in the main stream. India, which had as its main aim to avoid 'further partition', explicitly rejected the 'Two-nation theory' that had, in their view, brought about Pakistan and India's leaders placed 'secularism' against 'communalism'. Nehru (Jha 2002: 3179) felt:

I think that doing away with this reservation business is not only a good thing in itself, good for all concerned, more especially for the minorities, but psychologically too it is a very good move for the nation and the world. It shows that we are really sincere about this business of having a secular democracy.

Though Nehru was most likely indeed sincere and certainly optimistic regarding his hope for secularism to work, in practice there was no 'one community', but a 'majority community' that wanted the 'minority community' to join the 'main stream', the secular democracy based on partition. Underlying the constitution was a mental border that divided the 'Hindu majority' from the 'Muslim minority'. Partition thus made 'Muslims' special 'minorities' among whom the 'bad ones' had left for Pakistan and the 'good ones' (Cf. Mamdani 2004) had stayed back and should be helped to become part of the mainstream. If not they would pose a danger for the nation-state and its geographical borders.

In other words, the idea of India was based on a by partition inspired idea of secularism, which as we will see fundamentally influenced state-supported narratives after 1947. When India became a separate nation-state in 1947, the leaders were confronted with a exceptional diversity and complexity that had to be, unnaturally, simplified conceptually in this 'idea of India' (Cf. Alam 2002: 95), which manifested itself in tenacious, largely unconscious stereotypes and cultural myths, which continue to impact contemporary's negotiations between people who are placed on opposite sides of the divide (Cf. Cash and Schwab 2004: 133). Moreover, partition made 'Muslims' special 'minorities' who from 1947 onwards and separated from the 'majority', were linked to the dark history of partition and now should have "trust in the majority" (Chandhoke 2002) who would help 'them' to 'develop and work together'. Besides, as the human rights activist and editor of "Communalism Combat", Teesta Setalvad argued in the newsletter for *Human Rights for the poorest* (14 April, 2003),

> The trauma and memories [of Partition] still gnaw within the collective psyche, non-catharsised. That is why each and every post-partition on the Indian side witnesses this subterranean dialogue tacitly played out by many, even if they are not in the majority, that since it was the Muslim who was responsible for the Partition, it is the Indian Muslims who have stayed behind who 'must pay the price'.

This partition rhetoric with these borders of the mind that constituted the idea of India not only impacted the way in which the constitution and other laws were formulated in India but is also embodied in official state reports and in school textbooks (Kumar 2001). What is more it, and increasingly so during the 1990s, was translated in slogans uttered by non-Congress leaders too who used this idea of India not to 'forcefully' include the religious minorities such as 'Muslims' in the 'mainstream' but rather to exclude them from the nation-state. Therefore, the kind of secularism as advanced by leaders such as Nehru, could and wholly unintended, as Chatterjee (quoted in Basu 2001: 272) warned in somewhat different context easily be "hijacked" by so-called Hindu fundamentalists, or any other group in India that is 'in need', for their own "narrow, sectarian political profit". In the name of this idea of India, and thus using the ideological resources of a secular state born out of partition, they could advance a "national culture, a homogenized content to the notion of citizenship" against people who do not conform to their version of 'national culture', which "does not augur well for communal peace and harmony in the country" (Cf. Basu 2001: 273). These rhetorical politics remain regulating inter-religious relations in India till date.

Living under the Burden of Partition Rhetoric: Muslims in Jharkhand

To recapitulate: when India became a separate nation-state in 1947, the leaders were confronted with an exceptional diversity and complexity and took upon them "the burden of making a multi-religious society work and convert that burden into a blessing" (Iyer 1996: 2037). These leaders absolutely and explicitly declined to accept the two-nation theory embodied in Pakistan's state rhetoric. Instead, they chose 'secularism' that was, unnaturally, simplified conceptually in the 'idea of India' (Cf. Alam 2002: 95), which was based on mental borders, i.e. tenacious, largely unconscious stereotypes and cultural myths about partition and which continue to impact contemporary's negotiations between people who are placed on opposite sides of the divide (Cf. Cash and Schwab 2004: 133). One way to access these "largely unconscious stereotypes and cultural myths" that underlies the 'idea of India' is to look at the narratives people use and what they reveal between the lines, so to speak. It was from the narratives of Muslims in Jharkhand that we discovered the existence of dividing markers, here defined as mental borders, in the minds of 'others', in the case of Jharkhand these were defined as, besides 'Hindus' also as the (Hinduized, Christian or *sarna*) tribals, known as *adivasis*. They revealed cultural stereotyping and modes of othering as perceived by our informants at times on a daily basis but also enacted suddenly and temporarily. Our informants also disclosed that these rhetorical politics remain regulating inter-religious relations even in present-day Jharkhand and they, as a result, 'suffer'.

To be precise: Jharkhand is not a partitioned society at least not permanently. Despite the fact that that the area that now comprises Jharkhand is often thought of as a 'tribal' region, its social structure has undergone tremendous change over the last century and particularly during the last 40 to 50 years. In many areas (especially Ranchi, Hazaribagh and Palamau districts), the ethnic make-up of the population has become substantially less *adivasi*-dominated and the region as a whole now has a tribal population of around 30 per cent. As a result, few villages nowadays conform well to a model of a single tribe settlement and most have at least a few caste Hindu, Scheduled Caste (SC), Backward Caste (BC) or Muslim villagers (Corbridge; Jewitt and Kumar 2004: 156-157). Besides, whereas other states in India, including Bihar, have witnessed periods of severe communal disturbance (Akbar 1988), the region that now comprises Jharkhand has been rather characterized by communal harmony and peaceful interaction between members of different religious communities.[4] Yet, there have been moments of fear and violence during which Muslims who reside in the region, fully realized the impact of partition on their lives. Communal riots in 1964 in rural 'Jharkhand' and the so-called Ranchi riots of 1967 and those in Jamshedpur clearly witnessed the enactment of the partition rhetoric. The riots in Ranchi in 1967 started over the issue of making the second official language in (then) Bihar and ended up with destruction of Muslim workers' colonies where 150 Muslims were killed (Basu 2001: 276). During all these 'riots', as will be illustrated in the next chapter, partition was re-enacted during times when very different issues were at stake. What is more, during an "inter-religious dialogue" taking place during a seminar on "Religious harmony and social cooperation in Jharkhand" in Ranchi in August 2005 (*Hindustan Times* August 29, 2005), a Muslim scholar of Jharkhand, Prof. Shahid Hassan of Ranchi University pointed out that "harmony in Jharkhand society had deteriorated after statehood".

Jharkhand was a part of the state of Bihar until 15 November 2000 when Bihar was divided in two and the new state of Jharkhand came into existence[5]. Bihar had been part of the Bengal Presidency till 1912 (Gordon 1979: 4). We initially asked our informants to speak about how the partition affected the lives of Muslims residing in Jharkhand after 1947. Mentioning the word 'partition' after 2000 caused confusion however as most of the informants thought my inquiry concerned their position after the partition of Bihar and the establishment of Jharkhand. They then informed me that their position had worsened after the establishment of the new state. The disinterest, irritation, sadness and even anger we encountered when we asked people to recount their memories of the 1947 partition was caused by this 'suffering' after 2000, which was I argue the result of the enactment of partition rhetoric in lives of people who felt they "have nothing to do with 1947" and on a more frequent basis than before 2000. Yet, their 'suffering' became only fully comprehensible as I analyzed these peoples' own stories through which these Muslim residents of several places in Jharkhand described the past. Once we stopped referring to 1947 and just asked our informants to tell something about their pasts, vivid descriptions of political and every day life in Jharkhand followed which I define as 'stories of independence' and which demonstrate that these Muslims situate themselves in different and alternative space, time and society with alternative borders while they relate to the set of narratives that I defined as partition rhetoric and which was framed to silence these voices.

These 'counter narratives', as shown in chapter 7, describe such topics as their or their ancestors involvement in India's freedom struggle, their support for Pakistan or for an independent Jharkhand state but also their day-to-day interaction with *adivasis* and other residents in the region and their migration histories to the area. These narratives are extremely diverse and apparently have not much in common. Whereas one of the Muslims we interviewed for instance recounted that Muslims in the state had all supported the Muslim League since they had been "exploited enough" and had needed a state of their own, another would narrate how his grand father had always liked Gandhiji as he "did not want partition". After close scrutiny, I realised however that they had one thing in common as all those we interviewed had mentioned at least at one point during the interview, though variously formulated, that "our pasts are different from theirs".

Later on I understood what they meant by 'our' and 'their past'. Here I explain the latter. In chapter 7 I will illustrate the former and show that these narratives formed counter-narratives with alternative borders different from the mental borders embodied in the partition rhetoric that was enacted in their lives. While talking about 'the past of others' these Muslims referred to the set of narratives that are described in this chapter and constitute state-supported partition rhetoric, with mental borders embodied in the constitution, laws, textbooks and also included in other state-supported narratives. As will be explained, these are the narratives about 'good Muslims' who stayed back and had become 'victims of partition', "the beleaguered and largely poverty-stricken leaderless community, suffering from discrimination and violence of ever-increasing intensity and scale" (Khan 2004: 131) and who had to 'adjust to the new order', were 'leaderless', 'powerless' and 'confused'. These Muslims are tied up however to their religious identity to the exclusion of other identities. There are also narratives about 'bad Muslims', who had demanded partition, who had left or should leave and who were and are in conflict with 'the other', the 'majority' and who form (ed) a threat for the unity of the nation. In short, these narratives link Muslims with the outside, the foreign, the not local, with Pakistan or with Bangladesh, with uprooting rather than rooting and whereas some of these narratives separate 'Muslims' from the 'majority' and define them as 'others', other narratives tend to exclude them from the nation-state. Nag (2001: 4759) explains:

> The journey of the nations thus begins with the construction of 'self'. The basic criterion for such construction is a perceived homogeneity. But the search end up as an exercise in peeling an onion, as such pristine homogeneity proves elusive and the task arduous. Moreover nation building is also a coeval process of majority building so as to ensure that the hegemony of a community is unchallenged. Hence the creation of nations also requires constant shedding of people who do not fit the constructed identity or question the framework. This automatically involves minority persecution, ethnic cleansing, denial of political rights to smaller groups and such forms of atrocities due to which exodus of the persecuted takes place.

The result was that from 1947 onwards, 'Muslims' (as a minority separated from the 'majority') were linked to the dark history of partition and now should have "trust in the majority" (Chandhoke 2002) who would help 'them' to 'develop and work together'. Whereas those who supported Pakistan are grouped as 'bad Muslims', narratives sanction 'acquittal' of the religious minority in India that 'stayed back' as these Muslims are undergoing the 'traumatizing effects' of having been 'left behind' by their 'fellow Muslims' (who left). These Muslims are however urged to behave as 'good Indians', adhere to the 'idea of India' and show commitment to the secular democracy. As rewards they will receive the 'protection' and 'support' of the secular Indian state. In Chapter 7, I illustrate that though our informants in Jharkhand indeed suffered, they neither subscribe to the narratives about the 'good Muslims' nor to those of the "bad Muslims" (Cf. Mamdani 2005). In fact, they had their own narratives, which did not confirm the mental borders embodied in partition rhetoric.

Post-Partition Narratives of the 'Bad' and 'Good' Muslims in Jharkhand

This partition rhetoric is clearly incorporated in post-independence literature on Muslims in Jharkhand with mental borders that in particularly pose the 'Muslim outsider' against the (Hinduised) 'tribal locals'. Post-partition 'historiography' concerning Muslims who lived in the pre-1947 region that now is called Jharkhand is scarce and incomplete. Incomplete as these narratives reflect only the history of some, and leave out the voices of others. Besides, these post-partition narratives are clearly affected by the colonial legacy of dividing the history of the subcontinent into Hindu and Muslim periods and of bifurcating space also on the basis of religion. These narratives describe how during the Early Bengal Sultanate, 1342-ca.1400, Shams al-Din Ilyas Shah (1342-1357), a powerful noble, wrested Bengal free from Delhi's grip and established the first of several dynasties that remained independent from North India for the next two and half centuries. Shams al-Din Ilyas Shah also defeated a host of neighbouring Hindu rajas, among others those of Champaran and Tirhut, now corresponding to modern Bihar (Jha 1988). These narratives authored by Hindus as well as Muslims[6] suggest that the whole of the Chhota Nagpur plateau already known as Jharkhand (or the forest tract), "never was completely subjugated by the Muslims" (Ansari 1964: 59-72) and "remained practically independent throughout the Turko-Afghan rule (1206-1526)" (Roy Choudhury 1957: 66). Other post-partition narratives of the period prior to the arrival of the British typically depict the Jharkhand region as a kind of independent area ruled by tribal kings. The percentage of Muslims in Jharkhand, according to these accounts, was insignificant. Moreover, the few "Mohammedans" who were settled in the state are described in these narratives as "outsiders" and "plunderers" who came "in the train of invaders." Besides, narratives on Muslims in

Jharkhand during British colonial rule also describe 'Muslims' as "foreigners" and as "exploiters" of the "local inhabitants of Chhota Nagpur," the tribals. Though these narratives agree that Jharkhand's population never consisted exclusively of tribals,[7] these narratives depict Jharkhand as a "tribal state" and all non-tribal inhabitants as "*dikus*,"[8] a term the *adivasis* used to describe the so-called non- tribals (Weiner 1978: 179-180). In other words, Muslims and other groups who inhabited the area are not considered to be indigenous people or "sons of the soil" and not even *sadans* defined as "long-settled and mainly agricultural communities" (Corbridge, Jewitt and Kumar 2004). Rather, they are imagined as outsiders and pictured as being antagonistic to the local population of 'tribals' the two defined as somewhat homogeneous and mutually exclusive categories.

In these historical narratives, revolts by tribal groups such as the *mundas, kharias, oraons, hos, santhalis* and *kols* are all described as "tribal rebellion[s] and revolt[s] against the foreign administration," "alien landlords" and "literate persons from Bihar and Bengal". Though the British rulers had selected these landlords from among the local population in the area and had appointed literate persons of the area to help them in ruling, narratives never describe these landlords and literate persons as "locals". Rather, they suggest that these landlords and literate persons were not part of the *adivasi* communities that resided in Jharkhand. Besides, these narratives describe that these landlords and literate persons, among whom there were Muslims too, were (like the British rulers) "ignorant of the languages of the aboriginals of Chhota Nagpur." Narratives conclude that these landlords and literate persons were as much "strangers as the Englishmen" to these tribals. Besides, these "strangers" had disturbed the "original system" of the tribals, which, these narratives emphasize, had come down from "early times" (Verma 1980: 195-196).

At the same time, "tribals" are described as 'locals' being neither Hindus nor Muslims but adhering to their own *Sarna* religion. In this way, these narratives suggest that the population in Jharkhand consisted of 'outsiders' and 'locals' among whom no intermingling had taken place. Clearly, "Muslims' belonged to the former category. In his *An Historical Outline of Pre-British Chhota Nagpur*, first published in 1942 and reprinted after partition, Mangobinda Banerjee (1989: 205 and 217) confirmed the isolation of Jharkhand, stating that we do not possess "any definite proof that Chhota Nagpur was conquered by the Moslems." Banerjee (1989: 201) adds that the "invasion" by an outside ruler upon the borders of Chhota Nagpur,

> May be taken to be an insignificant event in the history of the aborigines of Chhota Nagpur. It produced no effect either on the Chero chiefs, or on the interior of the plateau of Chhota Nagpur, either from the religious or cultural standpoints [...] Chhota Nagpur remained unaffected and unchanged. It continued to live its life of "splendid isolation" [...] Chotanagpur thus enjoyed immunity from Moslem attack for about half a century from 1538 A.D. to 1585 A.D. [...] The Mouhammedan forces, constituting as they did chiefly of cavalry, seem to have been easily beaten back from broken or rocky country, and it will be seen that the mountain loving people of Chhota Nagpur for a long time successfully ousted the attacks of foreigners. Moreover, the religious zeal for the propagation of Islam was by that time considerably cooled down and the religious activities of the Moslems in India had given place to imperialism, territorial expansion and political domination. The days of colonisation, extension of commercial relations or scientific explorations had yet to come. The rugged mountainous country of Chhota Nagpur had nothing to attract the Moslems, except beautiful natural scenery, until the land was known to contain diamonds.

Other narratives recount that "the enormous power of the Mughals [the pre-British Muslim rulers in India] was strictly limited in the hilly tracts of Chhota Nagpur where their orders could not always be easily enforced" (Kumar 1969: 42-44). Though in some narratives it is maintained that Jharkhand's isolation was somewhat broken when it was included in the Subah of Bihar and later, in 1632, given as a *jagir* to the governor of Patna, Banerjee (1989: 215) believed:

> If the Chhota Nagpur chief during the time of Akbar became a malguzar [tributary], it does not appear that the Mohammedans exercised any control over the internal affairs of this plateau. They were satisfied at getting any portion of the stipulated revenue. The only trace of the Mohammedan invasion is the presence of some Moslems, who must have come to this one in the train of invaders and who are now scattered throughout the division.

Yet the number of such Muslim "exploiters" seemed to have been very limited in Jharkhand. Banerjee (1989: 215) concluded for instance that,

> While, therefore we meet with innumerable Mohammedan Zamindars, big and small in the districts of Patna and Gaya, the Chhota Nagpur plateau is conspicuous by the absence of Mohammedan fiefs in this region except in the northern parts of the Palamau district, bordering Bihar, which for a time was brought under the influence of the Mohammedans.

Though these narratives recognize the existence of Muslims in Jharkhand before 1947, they all feel their numbers were and remained quite limited till 1947. Migration from Bihar after partition is most often cited as the reason for the increase and conversion is another factor but one that very few of the historical narratives mention in the case of Jharkhand.[9] Richard Eaton (1997) proposed a 'gradual absorption theory' in the case of East Bengal. His theory that proposes a slow and steady absorption of Muslim culture and religion in East Bengal is also accepted in the case of Bihar. Papiya Ghosh (1998: 229-264) argued for instance that, "It appears that factors other than political power explain the spread of Islam in Bihar from around the twelfth century". She also alleged that in Bihar, "as elsewhere, Muslims comprised local converts largely from the Hindu artisan caste and foreign immigrants". There are no such studies for Jharkhand that appeared in the post-partition period, yet, O'Malley (1910) argued that in the Santhal Parganas in Jharkhand in 1910, "The majority of the Mohammedans are believed to be descendants of low caste converts made during the period of Mughal rule, and many of them can with difficulty be distinguished from the Hinduised aboriginals with whom they live side by side". Again, in 1926 O'Malley (1926) was of the opinion that in Palamau, "Most of the present day Mohammedans are descendants of the converts then made [i.e. during the days of the rule by Mughal emperors], but descendants of the Nawab's family are still to be found at Hussainabad".

In short, post-partition authors present the Jharkhand area (then Chhota Nagpur and part of Bihar) as a tribal region where Muslims and their culture remained separated from that of the 'tribals' and the other way around. This, I would say, is a colonial legacy as in British time such a presentation had become established and is reproduced in partitioned India. Most of the historical accounts on Jharkhand written after 1947 acknowledge that *adivasis* were "much influenced by Hinduism" (Weiner 1978: 155) but they do not mention whether among *adivasis* or Hindus conversions to Islam did take place in the region during the pre-partition days and in all cases it is repeated that the number of Muslims in Jharkhand remained "very limited" till 1947.[10] Besides, as also illustrated above these narratives on Muslims in Jharkhand generally include them in the category of "outsiders" and "exploiters" of the "locals" and "indigenous population" of Jharkhand. In 1986, Niren C. Choudhury and Sharit K. Bhowmik (1986: 323) quoted a passage from a book written in 1864 that concluded for instance that:

> Hinduisation, firstly alienated the tribal raja and his kinsfolk from the rest of the people. Secondly, it brought in an infiltration of non-tribals into the region. The people were known as *dikus* (aliens) by the local tribal population [...] the ruling family encouraged them to take up administrative posts [...] The Nagvanshi rulers introduced the system of granting large portions of land (*jagirs*) which were already being cultivated by the local tribals, to these aliens [...] They encouraged traders, who were Hindus, Muslims and Sikhs [who] obtained farms of villages instead of cash [...] Within a hundred years or so, i.e. during the seventeenth and eighteenth centuries, these petty landlords not only usurped most of the *khunt-katti* villages (original tribal villages based on common ownership of land) but also encouraged other Hindu and Muslim aliens to settle down.[11]

In these narratives therefore Muslims in Jharkhand are never rooted in the soil and so is the case with Hindus for that matter. Yet, though there was 'Hinduization' going on among the tribals no corresponding 'Islamization' took place in the region. Muslims belong to 'the others' (the *dikus*) and are not only separated from the 'locals' but also described as in opposition of these 'locals' and as 'bad exploiters'.

Characteristically, Muslims are all but absent in histories of the freedom movement in Jharkhand when "tribals in the area fought against the Britishers for an independent India". Yet, there is one moment in history where these 'Muslims' and '*adivasis*' are both considered 'bad' and reprimanded in these narratives. Though these two groups are not 'united', or rather their possible union is feared, they both are known for their 'anti-state activities'. These narratives concern the efforts of *adivasis* to establish a separate state, which threatened to erode "the ideological hegemonic beliefs about state size" (Singh 1997) in the view of post-partition India. In these narratives the activities of the *Adivasi Mahasabha* during the 1940s are remembered and in particular the position taken by Jaipal Singh the most important tribal leader around that time is defiled in these narratives. As, during the Second World War, Jaipal Singh offered the, "services of *adivasis* in the cause of democratic rights" and "became ready to supply man power to the British for the struggle" some narratives find this a "prove for the tribal leader's retrograde role that he was playing in the national life" (Sinha 1991: 146). But, it seems, much more than the dislike of these authors for the "loyalist image of Mr. Singh", who happened to be a Christian *adivasi*, their narratives disdain the way in which Jaipal Singh used his platform of the *Adivasi Mahasabha* for his "sinister gain to prevent tribals being enumerated as Hindus and thereby reduce the numerical strength of Hindus so that their political influence ends" (Sinha 1991: 147). Yet, most of all, Jaipal Singh's "greater complicity" with the Muslim League in 1941 was described in these narratives as the real threat to the nation-state. Narratives describe that how in June 1939 the "Star of India" a Muslim voluntary organisation in Jharkhand had, "pledged to work for the separation of Chhota Nagpur". They also recount that the Annual Conference of the *Adivasi Mahasabha* in 1941 invited many of its leaders as well as leaders of the Bihar Muslim League, "to attend the Conference when the tribals were to demand their *Adivasi Pakistan*":

The Annual *Adivasi* Conference was held at Ranchi on the 8th and the 9th of March 1941 and representatives of the Depressed Classes Association and the Bengal

Muslim League were present at the Conference. In his presidential speech Mr. Jaipal Singh repeated his demand for the separation of Chhota Nagpur and pledged full support of the adivasis to the Government in war efforts. His target of attack were the caste Hindus for which they should start a resistance movement. On the other hand his drift towards the Muslim League could very well be found in his words: "I have been invited by the Muslim League of Bengal and the *adivasis* there to make a tour through that province. I have been invited to address a protest meeting at Calcutta Town Hall tomorrow when all the Ministers and eminent leaders of Bengal will be present. I mention this to let the British Government know that we are not alone in our grievances. Let them (Hindus) think that Muslims and *adivasis* are not going to tolerate any *Hindu Raj* for a second. We will fight for our religious integrity and our racial *izzat*.[12]

Narratives detest Jaipal Singh's call to the *adivasis* and in which Jaipal Singh tells his party members that,

> They will have to preach that the *santhals* and *adivasis* should combine and reunite with the Muslims and the League for obtaining their freedom and rights because both of them are beef eaters and as minorities opposed to Hindu domination and both of them demand separation and freedom of Chhota Nagpur and Santhal Parganas just as they demand separation of Pakistan.[13]

Jaipal Singh's other hard work to unite *adivasis* and Muslims and to set them up against the Congress Party and the *Hindu Mahasabha* as well as his preaching that *adivasis* were "not Hindus but a separate nation and the original rulers and masters of India who were ruined and enslaved by the foreign Aryans" are considered to be a sad chapter in the otherwise heroic struggle of *adivasis* for the independence of the country. In post-partition India, such efforts were considered as against the 'national interest of the country' and 'forced inclusion' had to be enacted by the hegemonic belief in 'secularism' and the nation-state had to show that its idea of India was adequately developed to destroy or deflect these movements so effectively that the image of a united (Hindu) India or secular nationalist could itself become hegemonic. Indeed, when partition finally came and Radcliffe awarded Chhota Nagpur to India, *adivasis* were co-opted along with or even as 'Hindus' in the partition narratives and thus again included in the nation-state. Besides, most of these 'Hindu *adivasis*' were praised for their role in the freedom struggle and activities to "partition the country" these narratives teach us, "remained confined to the Muslim Leaguers and the Christian *adivasis*" (Sinha 1991: 155). Jaipal Singh was hooked away from the Muslim League when he was elected to the Constituent Assembly, at Delhi. Narratives describe that as Jaipal "came into contact of the top notch of Indian leadership he opened his eyes and stemmed his turbulence" and "the spell of Nehru and Patel, Ambedkar, etc. made Jaipal an embodiment of national tribal aspiration" and in his presidential speech during the Annual Conference of the *Adivasi Mahasabha* held at Ranchi on 13th April 1947, Jaipal was reported to have said that, although the Muslim League supported the Jharkhand separation movement, the *adivasis*, "will not allow themselves to be mislead by the League as now Jaipal said that he was not in favour of Pakistan" (Sinha 1991: 151-152).

Fortunately for the *adivasis* in Jharkhand therefore, when Bengal was partitioned they proved to have lived on the right sight of the border as post-partition narratives on *adivasis*, do not exclude these (Hinduized) *adivasis* (Weiner 1978) from the nation. To the contrary, contemporary narratives on *adivasis*, describe them as "indigenous people" and a few narratives even narrate with approval how these 'tribals' fought for an autonomous state within the Indian Union ever after 1947 and finally got such a state when Bihar was divided and Jharkhand founded in 2000 (Narayan 1992). Of course, these *adivasis* appeared only 'good' in state-supported narratives as long as their struggle did not challenge, contest and question the idea of India and its mental and international geographical borders. If these *adivasis* did challenge this idea, like in the case of all those labelled as 'minorities', accommodation was needed and if necessary violent control was executed. Between 1947 and 2002, there has been several historical moments during which either the Central Government in Delhi or the Bihar State Government and those who worked on their behalf perceived the nation-state to be in danger due to these efforts of *adivasis*. Many among these nation-builders disliked for instance the efforts among people in Jharkhand to create a separate state by dividing Bihar. Another perceived 'danger' was the spread of 'Christianity' among them and as a reaction some Hindu leaders sought to make Hindus out of *adivasis*.[14] Besides, in order to establish or maintain 'national unity', these guardians of the nation-state also used partition rhetoric that separated the Muslims from these *adivasis* and their common struggle for an independent Jharkhand was either omitted from narratives or depicted, as shown above, as 'anti-national' and reprimanded. In the process, Muslims in Jharkhand were not only separated from the *adivasis* but the relations between these two minority groups in Jharkhand got, at times, severely disturbed as will be illustrated in the next chapter.

Post-partition narratives therefore generally describe Muslims in pre-independence days as 'bad outsiders' often posed against the 'good and Hinduized *adivasi* insiders'.[15] The trend of narrations on the position of Muslims in Jharkhand does change somewhat however in narratives that describe Muslims in Jharkhand after the partition of British India in 1947. For one, their number seems suddenly to have increased tremendously after 1947. Besides, though they remain separated from the Hindus and *adivasis* in these narratives they, after partition, become also 'good

Muslims' who have stayed back after 1947 while their 'fellow Muslims' left and now have to come to terms with 'Partition'. As 'aliens' they are not automatically rooted in Jharkhand but will be accommodated in the nation-state if and when they accept its borders, the mental as well as the geographical. Clearly, mental borders in these narratives function to separate 'Muslims' from non-Muslims and only accommodate Muslims in the nation-state if they behave as 'good Muslims' by supporting the idea of India. Indeed some narratives that describe the situation in Jharkhand after 1947, make 'Muslims who stayed back' visible as the 'other', as enemies (of non-Muslims) who cannot be trusted and should even be excluded from the nation. Old Congress stalwarts such as Sardar Patel believed after 1947 for instance that Muslim officials, even if they had opted for India, were bound to be disloyal and should be dismissed. To Patel the Muslims in India were "hostages to be held as security for the fair treatment of Hindus in Pakistan" and on 15 October 1948, Patel went so far as to advise Nehru to warn Pakistan that if the exodus of Hindus from East Bengal continued, India would send out Muslims from West Bengal in equal numbers (Noorani 2003: 10).

Though these latter narratives therefore can be used to exclude Muslims from the nation-state, narratives also provide space to accommodate them if only these Muslims adhere to the 'idea of India'.[16] Nevertheless, not even these narratives of the 'good Muslims', i.e. those who had opted for India or had voted against partition (the so-called 'nationalist Muslim Biharis), are tales of 'rooting' but rather emphasize the (mental) 'uprooting' of these Muslims who stayed put. Though often labelled as "missing Muslims" (Cf. Banerji 2004) (i.e. missing tales about Muslims who stayed put in India after partition and who as 'good Muslims' had often voted for the Congress party and fought against imperialism) it is at times narrated, though less frequently than tales on the suffering of Hindus, how these Muslims of Bihar who stayed put suffered too after partition but these tales are foremost concerned with their displacement (with or without movement) and with the ways in which Muslims who "were left behind" tried to come to terms with partition (Sajjad 2002: 70-71). They are rarely tales of rooting however. Consider for instance what Dhirendra Vajpeyi (1989: 51-71) wrote about the "predicament" of Muslims who "did not choose to go to Pakistan". Vajpeyi felt they, "were left in the dilemma of the precarious situation" and "leaderless and faced with new pressures in a secular state Muslims found themselves as a minority which lacked political power, was dependent on non-Muslims for its security and survival". They, Vajpeyi continues, moreover faced a "crisis of identity in a secular state", which made them misfits in the secular state as "they want to have their cake and eat it too".

Such narratives do divide Muslims in those who left (the 'bad ones') and those who stayed put (the 'good Muslims') and the later are always seen in the light of the former. Thus, 'good Muslims', from 1947 onwards had to 'prove' they were not 'bad'. That is why some guardians of the nation-state for instance reported that "eminent Muslim citizens" who stayed back in Delhi after 1947, "gave proof of their loyalty to India by wholehearted participation in the Independence Day celebrations" which, it was added proved, that these Muslims, "did not lag behind any community in the expression of joy and thanksgiving on that great and historic occasion" (Ministry of Information and Broadcasting 1948: 42). In other words, Muslims after 1947 in Jharkhand as well as other parts in India, were urged by the 'majority' to remember that,

In 1947, the Muslims of India found themselves leaderless. Those, in whom they had, till the day before, reposed confidence, went to Pakistan. The ones who remained had none of the qualities of Syed Ahmed Khan, Ameer Ali, or Badruddin Tyabji [who were no more] (Noorani 2003: 1).

'Displacement' caused by the enactment of such narratives in Jharkhand, can take multiple forms related to physical movement. Yet, the enactment of state-supported partition rhetoric can also cause internal displacement without having moved physically, i.e. it can cause mental displacement as will be illustrated in Chapter 6. In short, partition rhetoric with these borders of the mind that constituted the idea of India not only impacted the way in which the constitution and other laws were formulated in India but is also embodied in official state reports, in school textbooks (Kumar 2001) and other narratives. What is more it, and increasingly so during the 1990s, was translated in slogans by non-Congress leaders, who became elected nation-builders in Jharkhand[17] and who used this idea of India not to 'forcefully' include the religious minorities such as 'Muslims' in the 'mainstream' but rather and if needed, to exclude them from the nation-state. These rhetorical politics remain regulating inter-religious relations in Jharkhand till date in daily life, during political upheavals and during so-called communal riots as will be illustrated in the next chapter.

References

1. Several monographs all published by Oxford University Press have analyzed several and different aspects of Jawaharlal life and policies. See for instance: Judith M. Brown, *Nehru. A Political Life* (New Delhi: OUP, 2004); S. Gopal and Uma Iyengar (eds), *The Essential Writings of Jawaharlal Nehru*, 2 Volumes (New Delhi: OUP, 2003); S. Gopal, *Jawaharlal Nehru. A Biography* (New Delhi: OUP, 2004). See also: B.R. Nanda, *Three Statesmen. Gokhale, Gandhi and Nehru* (New Delhi: OUP, 2004).

2. This article entitled "The partition of India as state contraction: some unspoken assumptions" appeared in *The Journal of Commonwealth* and *Comparative Politics* and was downloaded from HighBeam Research (unfortunately no further details available).

3. Compare this term with Edward Said's term "pessoptimism" quoted in Samaddar (2003: 24).

4. See, for instance a report on the celebration of Durga Puja in 2005 entitled: "Dussehra a symbol of communal harmony" (*Hindustan Times*, October 10, 2005).

5. See (Prakash 2001) for an overview of the more than hundred yearlong processes during which Jharkhand matured into an independent state.

6. See, for instance, Ansari (1963: 253-260) whose narratives on Muslims in Bihar reflect a similar division of space and time.

7. 'Tribals' in Jharkhand are labelled and identify as *adivasis.*

8. See (Mahato 1994: 51-74) for a discussion of this concept of *diku*.

9. In the case of Bengal Md. Shah Noorur Rahman (2001: 12) alleged that apart from forceful conversions, there also were gradual, peaceful and partial conversions of people to Islam. The area that now comprises Jharkhand is not explicitly mentioned in his analysis however.

10. According to the 1931 census for the whole of Bihar (including present day Jharkhand), Hindus comprised 83 per cent of the population and Muslims 10.1 per cent. Most Muslims lived indeed in the north, totalling 40.5 per cent in Purnea (Bihar); 16.5 per cent in Champaran (Bihar), 11.2 per cent in Bhagalpur (Bihar), and 10 per cent in Patna (Bihar) and Gaya (Bihar). Yet also 10 per cent of Muslims in Hazaribagh (Jharkhand) and the Santhal Parganas (Jharkhand) is mentioned, which cannot be called so limited. The *julahas* (who started identifying as *momins* during the late 1920s)

were the only *biradari* for which statistics were tabulated in the census: they fell just short of 25 per cent of the Muslim population (Ghosh 1998: 231). A good many among them lived in what now constitutes Jharkhand during pre-partition days.

11. The authors had quoted this passage from a book written by Reverend Hoffman in 1864.

12. Jaipal Singh addressed a meeting meant for the "*Adivasi* Women in Ranchi" and organized by Muslim League leaders at Ranchi on 10th March 1941 (Bengal Secret Police Report, 1941) also quoted in Sinha (1991: 147).

13. Bengal Police Secret Report, 1941, also quoted in Sinha (1991: 148).

14 See for more details about this fear for conversion of *adivasis* among Hindus: Barbara Verado, *Rebels and Devotees of Jharkhand: Social, Religious and Political Transformations among the adivasis of Northern India* (Unpublished Ph.D. thesis submitted to the Department of Anthropology, University of London, April 2003).

15. Christian *adivasis* constitute another separate category in these narratives and are frequently marginalized too. They are sometimes depictured as posing a possible threat for the nation-state due to their embracement of a 'foreign religion'. Significantly however if *adivasis* convert to Islam, they stop being labelled as *adivasis*, whereas those who convert to Christianity remain recognized as *adivasis*. This is important as these Christian *adivasis* who constitute another 'minority' in the state, unlike those who convert to Islam, continue being eligible for reserved seats in government supported educational and employment schemes.

16. I therefore agree with Mushirul Hasan who has collected important written narratives of the so-called Congress Muslims in Bihar and elsewhere and stressed that, "Indeed, the part played by those Muslims, who are patronisingly described as, 'Nationalist Muslims' [...], who were eventually let down by the dispirited Congress leadership [...], the Momins in

Bihar, should not be submerged beneath the rationalization of the 'victors'," in Singh (2000: 350). N.P./ 17. The new state was brought into being by the National Democratic Alliance in New Delhi at the behest of its major partner, the Bharatiya Janata Party (BJP) and continues to be the ruling party in Jharkhand. Besides, the Hindu nationalist Rashtriya Swayamsevak Sangh (RSS) is also active in Jharkhand where it enjoys a formidable reputation for providing high quality educational and health care facilities. RSS members also helped to lay the foundation of the rise to power of the BJP in the region in the 1990s (Corbridge, Jewitt, Kumar 2004: 199).

6

Living with the Burden of Other People's History in Jharkhand

Enactment of the Partition Rhetoric during the Daily Round

There is a lack of consensus about the percentage of Muslims that dwell in Jharkhand[1] but Syed Shahabuddin an authority in the field, feels that the Bihar Census of 1991, compiled before the bifurcation of the state and which mentions that Muslims constitute about 14 per cent of the state population, should be accepted for present-day Jharkhand too. Though exact figures are not available and other figures contested, it is not contested that the majority of the Muslims in Jharkhand are *Sunnis* and reside in rural or less urbanised Jharkhand, speak Hindi or the Sadani local dialect (also known as Nagpuri), are relatively poor agriculturists with small plots of lands and who among whom many demand recognition as 'Backward Castes'. Many of them have not received any formal education or are much less educated than Muslims in the urban areas of Jharkhand. These Muslims can thus be described as *ajlaf* and *arzal* though our informants rarely used these terms themselves.[2] According to Syed Shahabuddin this category of "descendants of untouchable and low-caste converts to Islam as well as middle and upper caste converts (Cf. Frøystad 2005:

168) constitute a majority among the Muslims in Jharkhand (*The Milli Gazette*, 1-15 December 2002: 12). This category is posed against the so-called *ashraf* (and this term was used by our informants) such as the *Syeds, Shaikhs, Mughals*, and *Pathans* who claim to descend from the various waves of migrants from Persia and other countries west of the Indian subcontinent and are generally presumed to be wealthier and more educated than the so-called *ajlaf*. Yet, we found relative poverty among them too. Though, they normally communicate in Hindi, many among these *ashraf* know some Urdu (and its script). Though most of them live in the big cities of Jharkhand, some of them possess land and reside in villages and small towns. Besides these Muslims, there is also Bengali speaking Muslims (in particular in the district Pakur near India's border with Bangladesh).

According to the 1931 census (Ghosh 1998: 231), Hindus comprised 83 per cent of the population and Muslims 10.1 per cent. Most Muslims are enumerated as having lived in the northern part (now comprising Bihar), totalling 40.5 per cent in Purnea District (Bihar); 16.5 per cent in Champaran District (Bihar), 11.2 per cent in Bhagalpur District (Bihar), 10 per cent in Patna District (Bihar) and 10 per cent in Gaya District (Bihar). In what now comprises Jharkhand the enumerated percentages were 10 per cent in Hazaribagh District and 10 per cent in the Santhal Parganas. The *julahas* (who identified as momins after the turn of the 19th century and were originally supposed to be all weavers) were the only *biradari* for which statistics were tabulated in the census and they felt just short of 25 per cent of the Muslim population. Many of our informants indeed identified as *momins* or *ansaris* who can be said to belong to the *ajlaf* category of poor weavers and agricultural labourers and in Jharkhand they lived among in particular (Hinduized) *adivasis*.

Though I have not done much field work among *adivasis* and their perception of Muslims, in the past I carried out field work among 'youths' in Ranchi and at times came across *adivasi* youth who told me their opinion of 'Muslims'. These were in general, I would say, 'neutral'. They did neither know much about them or their history nor did they want to know. They mostly felt that these Muslims came "from Bihar" and considered them as outsiders. A few *adivasi* women had however married Muslims and consequently converted and expressed their satisfaction over the fact. These marriages took normally place between *adivasi* women and *ashraf* Muslims and at times were severely criticized by (male) *adivasis* as, they told me, "they only marry our women because they want our lands". There was certainly no idea among these *adivasis* that these Muslims and *adivasis* were ethnically related or that they belonged to the same group and there rather was a feeling of 'us and them'. This feeling was however normally not translated in antagonism. Yet, one (Christian) *adivasi* driver once told me:

> They are very different from us. They do everything the other way around. They read from the right to the left, they talk completely different, they comb their hair the other way around and even tie their shoelaces in the wrong way. Their religion is also completely opposed to ours.

Yet, the scholar Myron Weiner (1978: 179-180) mentioned that during his fieldwork in the late 1960s[3] he had asked an *adivasi* boy to define who were included as "locals" in Jharkhand. The boy had answered:

> First of all the primitive people who have lived here for thousand of years, they are Chhota Nagpuri. Then there are many non-Adivasis who have lived here for centuries – some Rajput *zamindars*, some shopkeepers, quite a few Muslim cultivators [...] if you ask Muslims they will call themselves Chhota Nagpuris [...] we would consider them Chhota Nagpuris.

As said, however, I have not carried out much field work among the *adivasis* regarding their views of dikus (outsiders, non-tribal and often used with the connotation that they are exploitive), though other researchers maintain that Muslims fall in this category and rarely include these Muslims in their descriptions of a 150-year struggle of Jharkhandi ethno-regionalism among these *adivasis* of South Bihar in any other way than as outsiders (or as culprits) The researchers feel that adivasis have.

To restore their economic, political and cultural hegemony over a region where they, the original clearers of the land, have progressively been displaced by non-tribal outsiders: the hated *dikus* of North Bihar and Bengal (Corbridge, Jewitt and Kumar 2004: 19).

Similarly, I have not carried out research among (upper or lower caste) Hindus in Jharkhand with the explicit intension to elucidate their perceptions about Muslims. Since I however live and work in Ranchi the capital of Jharkhand since the last almost fifteen years, I feel that in day-to-day life (upper-caste) Hindus in Jharkhand identify with Muslims in particular with the *ashraf* as 'we all are outsiders' (mostly from Bihar). Besides, in day-to-day life there are cordial and equal relations between these so-called upper-caste Muslims and *marwaris* in the city. Besides, upper-caste Hindus, interact with the *ajlaf*, as they need their services. The interaction between the lower-caste Hindus and *ajlaf* is also often characterised by friendly interaction and at times even based on strong friendships, which also is the case with upper-caste Hindus and *ashraf* Muslims (Cf. Froystad 2005: 159-192). Yet, though in general and day-to-day routine there is no antagonism among Muslim, Hindu and *adivasi* residents in Jharkhand, our Muslim informants perceive however discrimination against them, sometimes on daily basis but more often during times of political upheaval and during so-called communal riots. During these moments, which can last not more than a minute but also extend to days, months and even years, as will be shown in this chapter, partition rhetoric is enacted by these Hindus or *adivasis*, which (temporarily) disturbs the (good) ties that exist between these groups and that previously united them on the basis of class, 'caste', ethnicity, gender or regional identities. This partition rhetoric depicts them not only as "outsiders" (against insiders, at times denoted as Indians at times as *adivasis*) but also at times relegates them outside Jharkhand or even outside India. From the previous two chapters we can deduce that partition rhetoric in Jharkhand has the following characteristic features:

1. Partition rhetoric imposes a religious identity on Muslims in Jharkhand that threatens to supersede all other identities — whether class, gender, ethnicity, regional background, or any combination of these.

2. Partition rhetoric presents 'Muslims' in Jharkhand as "outsiders and conquering outsiders at that."[4] Muslims are never portrayed as locals in peaceful coexistence with other locals or as locals in binary opposition to outsiders.

3. Partition rhetoric depicts Muslims as rulers and forces Muslims in Jharkhand to identify with the (alleged) deeds of Muslims in the area of residence, other areas and even in other countries, in particular, but not only, in Pakistan and Bangladesh.

4. Partition rhetoric makes Muslims in Jharkhand not only 'minorities' but also separates them from other (imagined) minorities such as *adivasis* in the region, who they are supposed to have colonized and exploited. It never unites them with other citizens in Jharkhand as a 'majority' (of Jharkhandis) on ethnic, class or regional basis. Besides, as a 'Muslim minority' they are placed against the 'Hindu majority' of the nation (including the Hinduized tribals).

5. Significantly, partition rhetoric denies that Muslims in Jharkhand have their own pasts that are rooted in a particular regional and class constellation.

Partition rhetoric therefore roots Hindus (with the inclusion of *adivasis* within these religious boundaries) in the territory that now is called India or in Jharkhand as part of India. Muslims are excluded from these narratives of rooting.[5] As the nation was founded on this partition and has become a majoritarian state, the nation building process takes therefore place in "partitioned times" (Samaddar 2003: 21). Ever after 1947, partition rhetoric has become one of the most unifying narratives to keep people together in India, to build up the nation and to legitimate the state. To be precise, every time that the nation-state is thought to be in danger due to wars, civil and political strife, industrialization processes, urbanization processes, sub-nationalism or globalisation processes, partition rhetoric is enacted by the state or by those who act on its behalf in a bit to re-establish unity (amongst the majority). Besides, it also can be, and is used, by those who identify as 'indigenous', 'locals' or 'natives' to exclude 'outsiders' from the territory or positions they desire as this enactment automatically excludes the perceived (religious) minority.

Partition rhetoric, if and when enacted (which in Jharkhand is generally not every day) therefore divides people in Jharkhand into binary-opposed but internally homogeneous communities of 'locals' and 'foreigners' and rather than building up the nation it might therefore actually, if the process is not altered, cause its downfall. In the following I will give some examples of such enactments of partition rhetoric by various (self-appointed) guardians of the nation or the Jharkhand state. This I do not by focusing on these 'enactors' but on those who perceived that this rhetoric was enactment among them sometimes on day-to-day-basis but more often during times of political upheavals and in particular during so-called communal riots. These extracts from our interviews with some of these Muslims in Jharkhand illustrate that in this process of partition, these Muslims feel, and increasingly so, excluded from Jharkhand or even from the nation and therefore suffer as they want to stay put or have no other place to go to.

Let us start with Haji Kurashi[6] a seventy-year old Muslim born in the Kantatoli Colony adjacent to the so-called Bengali refugee Colony in Ranchi where, during the 1950s, the Bihar Government had the Hindus from erstwhile East Bengal rehabilitated. Whereas these two communities had normally shared cordial relations, at times relations between the two communities had been severed however (*Hindustan Standard*, 7 April 1964) and Kurashi felt during those moments "as if we are the outsiders and they are the insiders. In fact they are refugees and I was born here". In fact during this enactment of partition rhetoric these Muslims could feel themselves as 'refugees', mentally displaced if not physically.[7] Kurashi concluded: "Partition has influenced our lives fundamentally. Before partition we did not belong to a minority. There was no fear, no tension. We all belonged to the same community. Now it is different".

Mrs. Khatoon (name changed), an *ashraf* Muslim who lives in a village in Ranchi District and in semi-*purdah* told me the following story:

I do not like the *adivasis* here. They always stare at me when I go out wearing *burqa*. They work in the fields, as they are too poor. I do not have to work outside as my husband can afford to keep me inside. I am happy like this but it is these *adivasis* who make me feel unhappy. Once I went to the local *haat* and overheard some of them giggle. They make me feel like an outsider.

At times this enactment of partition rhetoric is not verbally but expressed in written form such as when this rhetoric is embodied in school textbooks (Cf. Sundar 2004). Activist and scholar Yoginder Sikand in an article on communal stereotypes in Indian text books (*Muslim India*, January-July 2003: 19-20) reports, for instance:

A recent survey of text books undertaken by the Mumbai-based Khoj Project, a non-governmental organisation concerned with the promotion of a secular education system [...] finds that not only in the state-level textbooks prescribed in BJP-ruled states [like Jharkhand] but also in several books recommended by the central ICSE board, negative portrayals of marginalised social groups such as Muslims, Dalits, Shudras and women abound [...] The so-called Muslim period is described in the most lurid terms, and the authors of certain textbooks have not hesitated from hurling all manner of invectives against Islam itself [...] the Muslims are routinely described in the most lurid terms, and the entire baggage of anti-Islamic stereotypes that are a stock-in-trade of the Hindutva propaganda machine is pressed into service for this purpose.

Reza,[8] whose parents reside in Bihar and lives in a hostel for Muslims in Ranchi commented:

During my whole school career I have never read anything positive about Muslims. I attended a Christian school but whereas we performed plays such as Radha and Krishna we never heard anything about Islam. This not only made that my class-fellows never really got to know me but also that I started looking down on myself and other Muslims like me.

Some of our informants also told us they had encountered hostility whenever they cheered for Pakistan during India-Pakistan cricket matches. Related to this, scholar Maurice Zinkin (1991: 273) concluded for instance that the Muslims in India constituted "a complicated case" as, "in the other communities, nobody is quite sure how Indian the Muslims are. One hears, for instance, complaints that they rejoice if Pakistan beats India at cricket, though Muslims have contributed some distinguished members to Indian teams" (related to this see also, Pandey 1999). Masoom who lives in an outskirt of Ranchi in a so-called Muslim *muhalla* defended himself however:

So what if we cheer for the Pakistan team? This does not make us any less Indian. Yes, I do support Pakistan in cricket matches. They are just better players. If the Indian teams plays well I will support them but unfortunately they have of late become horrible players. They have no fighting spirit like the Pakistanis. We can learn a lot from them.

Sultan Ahmad Ansari[9] resident of a village near Ranchi showed me a slip of his friend on which it was written that the latter had been displaced due the construction of a dam in the area where he lived. His friend, who was also present during the interview, had already visited the Government office in Ranchi five times and had submitted an application for compensation. But Sultan Ansari told me:

In fact we were given notice to vacate our homes. No official compensation will be given to us. Muslims who reside in this area are considered outsiders. Only *adivasis* get compensation. They told us in Ranchi that we have come from outside to this area in search for jobs and have therefore no right to stay here.

At times, slightly unexpected actors enacted partition, i.e. Muslims themselves. These latter reminded their "fellow Muslims" that "we have made mistakes in the past" but should now integrate in the "mainstream" and should "forget our shameful past" during which Muslims had supported the two-nation theory, demanded Pakistan and had voted for the Muslim League. Md. Abdul Qaiyum Ansari, the President of the All India Momin Conference as well as Minister in Bihar's Rehabilitation and Welfare Department gave a speech for instance, in which he urged his "fellow Muslims in Bihar (which included Jharkhand at the time) to give up their "communal sentiments" and "accept their Indian nationality and join the Congress without hesitation". Again, in 1952, the same Ansari asked in an article entitled "Our own country" whether Muslims were "anti-nationalists".[10] Muslims in Jharkhand, as will be shown in the next chapter experienced these enactments as a burden of a history that was not theirs and often became angry, sad and surprised when such 'other Muslims' reminded them of 'their pasts'. In fact, the by us interviewed Muslims did often not identify with Muslims in Bihar or other regions or with their histories. Besides, *momins* in Jharkhand did even not always relate to *momins* in Bihar. They therefore distanced themselves from partition rhetoric that was enacted in their lives and narrated their own stories with alternative 'othering' as will be shown in Chapter 7.

Enactment of Partition Rhetoric during Political Upheavals

Around 1947, the first political upheaval was partition itself. When we conducted our interviews, the majority among these Muslims felt that the break-up of the country in 1947 had much less influenced them than Independence had. They remembered 1947 as the year in which "we became liberated". Though some indeed narrated that the "partition of Bengal" had upset them as they had strongly protested against it or as they found themselves at "the wrong side of the border", most interviewed Muslims nevertheless celebrated 15 August 1947 as "India's Independence Day". For many interviewed Muslims who were born (much) after 1947, the date symbolised "our first step in nation building". We learned therefore from our interviews that the event of partition did not constitute a trauma for most of these Muslims in Jharkhand. Yet, the same interviews also taught us that it was the enactment of other people's partition memory ever after 1947 that caused and still causes the burden with which these Muslims have to live. "We all were in festive mood that day", M.D. Musa[11] remembered. He added however that he had felt concerned about what partition would mean in future for Muslims in Jharkhand like himself. Recalling his thoughts during the Independence Day celebrations on Ranchi Hill on 15 August 1947, he told us: "I saw that a snake had come out and I knew no good was to come". Indeed, no good was to come and ever after 1947 during certain political upheavals, partition rhetoric is enacted, which made even those who had considered partition as an (finished) event realize that it rather was a process that continues till date.

In the previous Chapter I explained that Nehru's idea of India was based on partition rhetoric that embodied mental borders, which separated the 'Hindu majority' from the 'Muslim minority'. I here explain that though Nehru's idea of secularism was formulated in order to counter act 'communalism', the narratives embodied in partition rhetoric are continuously and sporadically (mis-) used mostly, but not solely, by those who identify as belonging to the 'Hindu majority' to not only separate Muslims from Hindus but even to expel 'bad Muslims' from the nation. In these acts of violence 'Indian Muslims' are, for instance, made accountable for activities of Muslims in other countries, in particular in Pakistan and Bangladesh, defined as the 'religious homelands' of these Muslims. 'Muslims' in India are distrusted and this distrust gets extended to violence against the community. Immediately after the event of partition some Muslims perceived the reality of partition as a process. Old Congress stalwarts such as Sardar Patel believed after 1947 for instance that Muslim officials, even if they had opted for India, were bound to be disloyal and should be dismissed; and to him the Muslims in India were "hostages to be held as security for the fair treatment of Hindus in Pakistan". On 15 October 1948, Patel went so far as to advise Nehru to warn Pakistan that if the exodus of Hindus from East Bengal continued, India would send out

Muslims from West Bengal in equal numbers (Noorani 2003: 10).

Yet, most of our informants in Jharkhand said that in the beginning just after 1947, "things were quite okay" but that later on "things had become really difficult for them sometimes". This was in particular so, they remembered during the 1960s when so-called communal riots in East Pakistan as well as an India-Pakistan war had rocked civil society elsewhere in India. This was reflected in Jharkhand too and related to this B.N. Azad commented in the *Indian Nation* on 1 April 1964:

> It is unfortunate that the *Hindu Mahasabha* has chosen this occasion to demand the exchange of population between India and Pakistan to solve the problems of the minority in East Pakistan [...] In normal times such solutions are neither practical nor practicable. It could have been greeted academically because in few countries opposition political parties are accustomed to making even impossible demands to embarrass the ruling party. Whether they are right or wrong that is a different matter. In abnormal times, which India is facing today, the proposals, which have the effect of unsettling the nerves of even balanced persons, ought not to be made. *Exchange of population would amount to the reopening of the question of partition and the concept of the two-nation theory.* No one has the right in India to demand Muslims or Hindus to go to another country. Even the Muslim community will not accept it. [Italics added].

Again, during the 1970s, when the establishment of Bangladesh was accompanied by another India-Pakistan war and during which Jharkhand witnessed another series of communal riots in India (one of which in Jamshedpur in 1979 in Jharkhand), interviewed Muslims again recounted that the burden was the enactment of partition rhetoric during these political upheavals. Later on, during the disputes in the 1990s related to the so-called Babri Masjid issue[12] our informants once again felt they were excluded from the nation through the enactment of partition rhetoric. Of late, partition rhetoric has again been enacted in Jharkhand in connection with the establishment of the new state in 2000.[13] The most recent events, during which Muslims in Jharkhand were forced to listen to this rhetoric, concerned the so-called Domicile Policy,[14] the question of job reservations for so-called *dalit* Muslims in Jharkhand, the proposed ban on cow killing and Urdu as the second official language in the state.[15] Remarkably, even events that took place beyond the borders of the nation-state such as several communal riots that rocked civil life in Pakistan and Bangladesh (*Prabhat Khabar*, 16 March 2003) affected the situation Jharkhand. Besides, 'the September 11 attacks' (the World Trade Centre bombing) and global happenings ever after 2001 followed by the terrorist attack on the Indian Parliament in New Delhi affected "Muslims of the Indian sub-continent" (Grare 2002) and also had some negative impact, though limited, on Muslims in Jharkhand who now at times are explicitly and publicly characterised as *jihadis* and enemies of 'Hindus'.[16] Besides, the Home Department move to "identify and deport Bangla settlers" was also reflected on the position of Muslims in Jharkhand (*Hindustan Times*, July 13, 2003), as was the move by the then BJP government in Delhi to "hover over the integrity of the private madrasas across the country" (*Hindustan Times*, 2 June 2003).

As examples, I have here selected the case of the introduction of a so-called Domicile Policy in Jharkhand, which created huge debates all over Jharkhand as to who were the 'real natives' of the state and therefore should get special privileges such as land and other facilities. Whereas, besides Muslims, many Hindus were also outcasted as 'outsiders' during these debates and therefore 'suffered' too, in the case of Muslims, the enactment of partition rhetoric during these debates made any claim to 'indigenousness' invalid in the eyes of the enactors.

During the summer of 2002, the government of Jharkhand, led by the conservative BJP, sought to introduce a policy that was intended to give domicile certificates only to the descendants of persons whose names were included as landholders in a 1932 survey. Those without domicile certificates would be barred from public employment or any other special concessions or benefits in the state. This controversial policy divided the state's population and forced people to prove that they were 'locals' or that others were 'outsiders'.[17] In such an environment, partition rhetoric was implemented by Hindu fundamentalists, as well as by some *adivasis*, to deny Muslims in the state their rights as 'locals'. This policy also polarized the Muslims in the state, pitting supporters against anti-domicile groups. The majority of Muslims in the state identified as *moolvasis*, however, and labelled other Muslims as *bahris* (outsiders). In this way, the domicile policy divided local Muslims into 'Bihari Muslims' and 'Jharkhandi Muslims'. Bihari Muslims, who hailed from the Patna and Gaya districts of Bihar, had come to Ranchi during the 1960s in search of jobs in one of the state capital's newly established industries. They opposed the domicile policy because it meant that they would never receive certificates and would be burdened as a result. Those identifying as 'Jharkhandi Muslims' by contrast, generally supported the policy and they strongly opposed anyone who tried to label Muslims in the state as 'outsiders'.

A.Q. Abdali (*Hindustan Times*, 14 July 2002), for instance, was an ardent supporter of the policy and he disliked the way the BJP tried to, "divide Muslims from *adivasis* by calling us newcomers. Actually, we live here for more than a century". Support for the domicile policy was never unanimous however. Some backward-class Muslims strongly identified as 'locals' but were unsure whether their names were included in the 1932 survey as they were poor. One such Muslim wondered aloud what would happen to those "who have been living in Jharkhand before 1932 but own no land here. In that case, we will be told to leave. *Adivasis* who have no land will not suffer. They are considered the only minority here" (*Hindustan Times*, 14 July 2002).[18] Some organizations that claimed to speak for these "Jharkhandi Muslims" (e.g., the Jharkhand Intellectuals of the Minority Backwards Reformatory Organization [JIMBRO], the Jharkhand Milli Council, the Muslim Morcha, and the Jharkhand Ulema Mushawrati Board) supported the policy. Leaders of these organizations were convinced that most of the Muslims in the state would receive domicile certificates and the accompanying privileges, as they were able to prove that they or their ancestors had settled down in the state long before 1932. One leader estimated that "not more than 5 per cent Muslims of Jharkhand will be negatively affected if 1932 is taken as cut-off year" (*Hindustan Times*, 14 July 2002). Another leader acknowledged that there was "a potential threat" to those or the ancestors of those who were landless during the 1932 survey and he therefore urged that, "the contributions and sacrifices of the original residents of Jharkhand should [also] be taken into account" (*Hindustan Times*, 18 July 2002).

In this environment, it was critically important for "Jharkhandi Muslims" whose names were not included in the 1932 survey to prove that they were 'locals' and, therefore, deserved domicile certificates. Any effort by 'others' to show that they were 'outsiders' was met with counter-arguments in the shape of histories that proved their closeness to *sadans* (i.e., non-*adivasi* Hindus who reside in Jharkhand) and *adivasis* with whom they had been living peacefully long before 1932. Some even identified as *sadans*.

Partition rhetoric, which presents Muslims in Jharkhand as 'outsiders' and in antagonism with the 'locals' (i.e., *adivasis*) was therefore not welcomed by these Muslims in Jharkhand who identified as 'locals' and who looked upon the proposed domicile policy as an effort by the government, "to only uplift the tribals" and exclude Muslims (*Hindustan Times*, 18 July 2002). Qari Jaan Mohammed, chief of the Islami Markaz, a Muslim religious organization with a mass following in the state, supported the domicile policy but disapproved of efforts to enact partition rhetoric among Muslims in Jharkhand. Countering partition rhetoric propagated by 'Bihari Muslims', who narrated their stories of post-Partition migration, as victims, to Jharkhand, he stated that, "Muslims should not isolate themselves from *moolvasis*.[19] The real Muslim population of the state has been living in its villages for centuries. How can neo-Jharkhandi Muslims jeopardize the interests of the sons of the soil for the sake of a few Class III or IV jobs? (*Hindustan Times*, 29 July 2002).

The Enactment of Partition Rhetoric during Communal Riots

After partition, communal riots erupted intermittently in India (Varshney 2002: 104-105). Between 15 August 1947 and January 1948, there was large-scale bloodshed in almost the entire north India. What is more, even after the formulation of India's constitution, communal riots have continued to appear. In the decade between 1950 and 1960, such riots were fewer. But numbers accelerated in the next decade. In 1968 there were 348 such riots. In 1970-71, it created a new trend. In 1969-70, there were three big riots in Ranchi-Hatia, Ahmedabad and Bhiwandi. In 1989 hundreds of lives were lost in a chain of communal riots throughout the country. The devastation had been very severe in 1992 following the demolition of the Babri Masjid (Nag 2001: 4757). The latest in the line were the "post-Godhra riots" in Gujarat (Ahmad 2002).[20] In each of these riots a large number of those killed were Muslims. In Ranchi, for instance, 164 out of the 184 killed were Muslims (Nag 2001: 4757). Besides the deaths, there was after all these riots huge mental displacement as well as migration of people to safer areas and relief camps. Sometimes they moved into a kind of "small ghettos" where they remained staying ever after (Cf. Chatterji 2003). Clearly, Nehru's concept of secularism seems to be too weak to counter 'communalism' as he and other leaders in his time had hoped. Scholars have differently named, analysed and interpreted this kind of violence. They also offer different causal explanations. Roshni Sengupta (2005: 2046) sums up:

> Thus blame for incitement could lie in the persistent hate campaign waged by right wing organisations. The degree of capacity and autonomy vested in a state government also determines its capability to resist a riot situation. Further the degree of communal amity also depends on the bonds of civic engagement and associational activity that exist between communities. While causative factors could differ, it is clear that compulsions of electoral politics and the increasing anonymity and disparity of urban life are playing a greater role in communal conflagrations in post-independent India.

I am not concerned with this violence as such or its causes and effects. My intend is to show that during the riots and independent of the causes of these 'communal riots', which can be political, economic, socio-cultural, ethnic and even religious, enactment of partition takes place during which people for whatever reason, identify as the 'locals' (the 'majority') and label others (in this case 'Muslims') as 'outsiders', 'the others' (the 'minority'). This 'majority' then skilfully manipulates the religious sentiments and cultural ethos of a people ('Muslims') by identifying these aspirations as those of the entire community to which they belong. In this way they somewhat use a "divide and rule policy" that also was adopted by the British in Empire building (Cf. Narayan 2002: 65). Important is to remember that, as explained in Chapter 5, India is born out of partition and that 'Indians' live, in the words in Ranabir Samaddar (2003: 21), "in partitioned times":

> For partition is 'contained' within all dimensions of national politics–in territory, citizenship, bureaucracy, group identity, law, literature, language, and now in history [...] At once an event of the past and a sign of the present time, Partition lives on in post-colonial times to such an extent that we should truly prefer the phrase 'partitioned times' to the more common 'post-colonial times'.

The mental borders embodied in the partition rhetoric that these so-called communal riots or pogroms as some prefer to call them are aberrations. That is not to say however that violence directed against Muslims as a unified religious group does not take place in day-to-day life as it does as shown above. Though, this violence is of a different dimension. Yet, during all these instances of violence, partition rhetoric is enacted in order to separate and unify the two communities on religious basis and to link Muslims to partition. Also, in all these instances Muslims are separated from 'the other' but during communal riots, Muslim indeed pose as the other and thus accept the mental borders embodied in partition rhetoric. They then retaliate as 'Muslims' against the 'other'. At times these Muslims even initiate this enactment by posing as the 'other' demanding for their rights as 'minorities' as embodied in the constitution.

Official reports and scholarly analyses of 'communal riots' in India, mention only a few instances of such violence involving Muslims and non-Muslims (Hindus and *adivasis*) in Jharkhand. Some of them took place in tribal areas without involving *adivasis* but in most of them, *adivasis* were directly involved. Though *adivasis* constitute the majority in a few regions in Jharkhand, officially they are categorized as a minority of 'Scheduled Tribes' (STs). Yet, as shown below, during the enactment of partition rhetoric, these *adivasis* become part of the 'majority', the rooted and the indigenous, posed against the 'Muslim Other'. During these riots, these 'Hindus' see partition as a "vivisection of the limbs of Mother India" that caused "a spiritual and emotional shock to the Hindu consciousness" and was thus "an unforgivable crime on the part of those who demanded it" (Puri 1994: 16).

Our research surfaced several reports and newspaper clippings concerning the communal riots in which the partition rhetoric was enacted in Jharkhand in particular by Hindus and *adivasis* but also by Muslims themselves and during which a "reiteration of the original divide takes place" (Kaul 2001: 19). Those Muslims we interviewed recalled the slogans that were shouted at them during times of communal tensions such as "Hindu, Hindi, Hindustan"[21] and "*Muslim Jao Pakistan. Mussalman ke do asthan: Pakistan ya Kabristhan*" (Muslims: Go to Pakistan. For Muslims there are only two places: Pakistan or the graveyard) (Cf. Pandey 2001: 61). At times, even scholars, while analysing the communal riots that took place in the state, enact partition theory. Jitendra Narayan (1992: 189-190), for instance, concluded from his study of five communal riots in Bihar, including those in Jharkhand that,

> The roots of the problem lie in the past history of the country. From the very beginning when the Muslim invaders set their feet on Indian soil they created a general atmosphere of hatred and hostility against themselves by mercilessly looting properties, destroying important religious places of Hindus and killing numerous innocent lives [...] Even the partition of the country could not remove it. In a society where a particular section of the people is looked upon as the descendants of the foreign invaders and is generally considered hostile to themselves by the other sections of people and such persons look upon an enemy country as their saviour, riots are inevitable.[22]

The "lesson" Narayan (1992: 193) preached is that "Muslims should show they are nationalists and good citizens and should show no sympathy or preference to Pakistan in matters of differences between Pakistan and India". Judging from our interviews, partition rhetoric enacted during so-called communal riots in the state constituted the largest burden for Muslims in Jharkhand. Though Jharkhand has been relatively free from such kind of blatant communal violence, the few incidences that took place were horrifying. Many interviewed Muslims narrated that they had felt the full weight of partition only in 1964, when for the first time after the event of partition in 1947 communal riots had broken out in Ranchi District. I have collected a fast amount of literature on these so-called Ranchi[23] riots of 1964 and riots of 1967 and 1979 in Jamshedpur ranging from newspaper clippings,[24] government reports to academic research papers. Though it is not my intention here to go into the full details of these riots, I want to emphasize that it was the enactment of partition rhetoric either by the "aggressors" or the "victims" that motivated the violence that constituted these riots.[25] Besides, it should be realised that these riots always took place in times and contexts when and where particular people and communities perceived the nation-state to be danger. This danger could be the impending India-Pakistan war, the question of Kashmir, the introduction of Urdu as a second language in Bihar, the losses suffered by the Congress Party in the Centre, the threat of China, communal riots in Bangladesh, the rise of right wing communal parties in Bihar or alternatively the threat of communism in Bihar, the demand for an autonomous Jharkhand State by *adivasis*, or their "mass conversion" to Christianity, to Islam or Hinduism. Whatever incited people to start killing, raping and looting, during all these riots Muslims in Jharkhand were ordained to become linked with partition.

Reporting on the so-called communal riots in the rural areas of Jharkhand's Ranchi District in 1964, the *Ranchi Express* (22 March 1964) reminded its readers for instance that, "Hindus have not forgotten that Muslims were responsible for the partition of the Nation". Similarly, in the "Report of the Indian Commission of Inquiry on Communal Disturbances Ranchi-Hatia" (1968: 70-71), most contributors cited "the partition in 1947" as "the main cause of the communal tension" in Ranchi. The Report urged readers to bear in mind:

1. The reason for Hindu distrust of Muslims, namely, that Muslims betrayed Hindus during the struggle for independence and, as a result, India was partitioned.

2. The treatment of Hindus in Pakistan after Partition.

3. The suspicion of persons of the community having sympathies with or acting as spies for Pakistan showing leanings toward Pakistan during the 1965 Indo-Pakistan War.

A report on the "Communal riots in Ranchi in 1967", published by the Jan Sangh Party,[26] is a good example of how partition rhetoric was enacted in Jharkhand during and just after the riots. This conservative Hindu party addressed Muslims in Ranchi in these words:

That every citizen of India should have equal opportunities and full Justice, regardless of his caste, creed, party or domicile, is a basic principle of the Indian polity. More than that it is the utmost conviction of every Indian nationalist. But nobody should forget that India and Pakistan are two states of what are basically one people. If Hindus are treated as second or third class citizens in Pakistan, there are bound to be unpleasant reactions in India. The Government of India, and especially Indian Muslims must take all steps including a reference to the UN to assure Hindus in Pakistan equal political and human rights. Indian Muslims must be quick to condemn all excesses and injustices against Hindus in Pakistan without any mental reservations. Secondly, the Indian Muslim must not stand apart and away. He must join the main stream of national life to be equal in rights and responsibilities. (*Organiser*, Vol. 22, no. 11 (26 October) 1968: 3).

A pamphlet entitled "Challenge to the Manhood of the New Generation: The Wicked and Fraudulent Plot to Create Yet Another Pakistan within India" also discussed the Ranchi riots in 1967. Its author, Vijay Ranjan, a student member of a Hindu fundamentalist party in Ranchi that was allegedly behind in 1967 riots in Ranchi, asked his "fellow Hindus in Ranchi":

Then what should we do? Should we allow 30 lacs [3 million] votes of 'Pro-Pakistanis' of Bihar to hurt the feelings of 5 crore 20 lacs [52 million] people of the State? Will our land, our nation be again divided in pieces? No more 'Jinnahs' will be allowed to be born in this land again, and the venomous serpent's poisonous tooth will be pulled out and its head will be crushed (Narayan 1992: 209-211).

When asked in 2001 to comment on the riots and communal tensions in Jharkhand during the 1960s, interviewed Muslim politician M.Y. Mirza[27] answered that, "The cause of the riots is Partition" He explicated that before, during, and after communal riots, Muslims in Jharkhand were haunted by a memory that was not their own:

Actually, what happens is this. When during the 1960s some Bihari Muslims wanted Urdu to become the second language in Bihar, many fanatic Hindus protested. You must know that many Muslims had migrated from places like Gaya and Patna in north Bihar in order to get employment in the Heavy Engineering Cooperation (HEC) here in Ranchi. This was disliked by many here. As a result, they started accusing all the Muslims here and even the locals joined, that if they wanted to speak Urdu they better leave for Pakistan.

Abbas Khan[28] complained about the activities of so-called Hindu fundamentalist parties in the region: "They induce *adivasis* to identify as the sons of Hanuman and tell them that we are outsiders." Gulam Rasool[29] had analysed the Ranchi riots of 1967 in this way:

We have always been pro-Congress and *momins* here were anti-Muslim League. But you know what happened in 1967? The Kashmir Vastralaya's owner's sister threw herself on the street and shouted against us, the Muslims. They are Punjabis and refugees. We had nothing to do with partition.

Gulam felt that he had nothing to do with partition, but the processes he defined as the "Hinduization of the *adivasis* here" made him and "Muslims" like him, part of partition. During this process, Hindus who supported Hindutva (Hindu rule) in India tried to make *adivasis* openly identify themselves as Hindus. Gulam concluded: "Very soon a situation will arise here like that which other Muslims faced just after partition. They will decide who outsiders are and who not". Md. Mohinuddin,[30] whose ancestors were tailors and who had come to Hazaribagh in Jharkhand "at least eighty years ago", challenged allegations made by people who were, according to him, influenced by a process that he identified as "saffronization":[31]

In British time there was peace, things were cheap and there was justice. Yet, we were too dependent so they had to go. After independence things became adverse however. In particular after 1964 when riots had taken place in many villages here in the neighbourhood. Peaceful communal life was destroyed. They said we better go to Pakistan. What will I do in Pakistan? But yes, after 1964 people became scared and started living in pockets. Many newspapers at the time stated that riots were due to the arrival of Hindu refugees from East Pakistan. That was nonsense. Politicians antagonized the *adivasis*. We had nothing to do with those people [i.e., these Hindu refugees]. If those people want to live here, okay, but they should adjust and live here peacefully. After the Babri Masjid issue secularism is completely destroyed.

Sultan Ahmed Khan from Daltonganj in Jharkhand[32] told us that,

Most of us came from outside, that is from Bihar. But my family settled here long time ago. I always got jobs as a teacher, also in Hindu schools. I was never discriminated against as a Muslim, but if people behaved uncultured, be they Rajputs or Muslims or Brahmins, I got angry. My father prevented many people from going to Pakistan. I also remember that in the Military Cantonment they were eating beef openly but my father sent a letter to stop all that. These Jan Sangh people were very active during the 1960s and told that Muslims should go to Pakistan. But we are safe here in Jharkhand as this area is not communal. I do not think much about being a Muslim or not. I do not differentiate much but, yes, I am firstly a Muslim and than an Indian. That does not mean I support partition!

Partition rhetoric thus imposes identities and has the power to change or even obliterate identities. Hazi Noor Mohammed from Jamshedpur[33] recalled the time when "Sardarjis and Muslims read Urdu together". But, he told us, after the 1964 riot, "Muslims started living in pockets. Now we live separate from them. They do not know about us nor do we know anything about them. It is just like partition".

Describing the happenings around 1964 in villages near Simdega in Jharkhand, Samrul Haque[34] commented:

Politicians told Hindus that if they killed one Muslim they would get money. They told *santhalis* and *oraons* that they were Hindus too. They built temples. But in fact the BJP unites us [Muslims]. Besides, the relation between Muslims and Christians [also *adivasis*] is now very close. We are both minorities. During riots [the Christians] protect us.

Haque concluded the interview we had with him in the following way: '*To, Pakistan Banna yahan ke Musalmano ke leye zaher hai*' (The establishment of Pakistan was a big curse for Muslims here). The enactment of partition rhetoric during "riot after riot in India" (Akbar 1988) had taught these Muslims in Jharkhand that "staying put" did not mean that all was well. Yet, many learnt this lesson much later than 1947. Some Muslims in Jharkhand were confronted with partition only in 1979, during the communal riots in Jamshedpur, when Bihar military police constables and *havildars* (assistant sub-inspectors of police) broke open the closed doors of Muslim homes, shouting: '*Saala, yahan Pakistan bana raha hai*!' (Damn, you are making Pakistan here!) (Akbar 1988: 28).

Interviewed Muslims explained that at one point in their life (during day-to-day activities, during political upheavals or during and after communal riots), they suddenly became aware of the fact that they were not only grouped by others as a Muslim minority but that this labelling went along with a forced acceptance of a history that many did not recognize as their own. They possessed however, other narratives of independence, which are till date imprisoned by state-supported partition rhetoric.[35] Self-appointed protectors of the state and nation builders have moreover silenced these 'counter-voices' and as Samaddar (2003: 33) remarked:

It is curious that those who should have been most proud of this legacy [alternative narratives of independence] and of the fact that it characterized the times of Partition are, in fact, embarrassed by it and hesitate to accept them as the counter-voices to the process of decolonisation through Partition. And those who speak of the specific experiences of the people during the partition era do not speak of the experiences of their uprisings, their defeat at the hands of the state, the colonial power and the forces soon to assume power. And, expectedly, those obsessed with the search for a history of secularism versus communalism (including the defeat of the former) do not link these events at all; they are an embarrassment to all. It is, however, worthwhile remembering that this exclusionary framing and premature narrative closure were inevitable in the process of Partition and decolonisation itself, in short, the genesis of the nation.

In short, the assiduous enactment of partition rhetoric broke and breaks the hearts of manye mind, as I now shall illustrate.

References

1. Syed Shahabuddin in a rejoinder to one of my reports believed I had put the figure of Muslims in Jharkhand too high and he questioned, "Why this kite-flying to exaggerate the number? It serves no purpose except to raise expectations to the skies, only to dash them down to pieces and plunge the community into a pool of despondency", Syed Shahabuddin, "Jharkhand Muslims," in: *Milli Gazette,* (1-15 December 2002): 12. Related to this see also: Kathinka Sinha-Kerkhoff, "Sadness, fear and hope for Jharkhand Muslims," In: *Milli Gazette,* (16-30 November 2002): 1 and 19. Compare this with Afsar Ali from Jamshedpur who alleged that "Muslims represent 32 per cent out of the 28.4 million population in Jharkhand' (Afsar Ali, "Muslim Contribution to the Formation of Jharkhand State," in: *Milli Gazette,* (16-31 December 2000): 6.

2. Instead of using this categorization, other scholars preferred categorizing some Muslims as "marginal Muslim communities in India" such as the *rangrez, pasi, mirshikars, nut* and *thakurai* (Siddiqui 2004): 91-163.

3. Note that this was after the so-called communal riots during which according to newspaper reports *adivasis* and Muslims

had been entirely antagonized. This was also when 'mass migration' from Muslims of north Bihar (now Bihar) to the industrial belt in South Bihar (now Jharkhand) had just started.

4. Cf. Neera Chandhoke, "Rethinking Rights: A Response to the Needs of a Multi-religious Society," *Social Action*, 47, no. 3 (July-September 1997): 272-304.

5. Pandey (2001: 132) also alleged that after "Partition" those who adhered somewhat loosely to the label of Muslim suddenly had become Muslim only and Pandey added that the whole religious community came to be "suspect".

6. Interviewed in 1999 (during IDPAD fieldwork).

7. In fact I was first prompted to include those who stayed put in my research on the impact of partition, during a previous research that I carried out between 1997 and 2000. Related to that I interviewed Bengali Hindus who had arrived from East Pakistan (present-day Bangladesh) and had been rehabilitated in so-called refugee colonies in Bihar (see Sinha-Kerkhoff 2000). During this research in Bihar a group of people approached me and, identifying as Muslims, they asked me to take their interviews too, as though they had never left their place of birth they said they also felt like 'refugees'. See also in this respect Pandey (1997: 2261) who addressed this problem of the "trauma of moving with nowhere to move". I became even more convinced about the necessity of the inclusion of the alternative 'narratives of partition' by reading Mushirul Hasan (1998: 2667) who wrote though in somewhat different context that, if the "histories of partition are to be rewritten, there are several reasons why we must judiciously draw upon the intellectual resources made available to us by creative writers. They expose the inadequacy of numerous narratives on independence and partition, compel us to explore fresh themes and adopt new approaches that have eluded the grasp of social scientists, and provide the foundation for developing an alternative discourse to the current expositions of a general theory on inter-community relations". Our informants might not have been such "creative writers" but as shown in this book they were certainly "creative story tellers"

who did not only suffer by partition rhetoric that imprisoned them but even challenged the borders embodied in it by the delineation of alternative 'cognitive maps'.

8. Reza (25 years old) identified as a Syed Muslim and was interviewed on 2 August 2005. All informants in Jharkhand will be listed hereafter with the date of interview in brackets followed by age and place of birth, followed by any other information if necessary.

9. Interviewed on 23 December 2000 and aged 72.

10. See for instance: *Hunkar* (in Hindi) (9 November 1947) and *Hunkar* (in Hindi) (4 January 1948). See also: *Sathi* (in Hindi) (September 1952). In these newspapers Muslims asked their fellow Muslims to accept Indian nationality; to accept that the two-nation theory is absolutely wrong; to abandon their struggle against the state and to forget their "shameful pasts".

11. M.D. Musa, 17 April 2001, around 90 years old, born in Munger (Bihar). He identified as *mullick*. On 15 October 1948, Patel went so far as to advise Nehru to warn Pakistan that if the exodus of Hindus from East Bengal continued, India would send out Muslims from West Bengal in equal numbers, in Noorani (2003): 10.

12. On 6 December 1992 crowds of people identifying as Hindus destroyed the Babri Mosque in Ayodhya and claimed it was the birthplace of the God Ram (*Ram Janmabhumi*). These 'Hindus' wanted to establish a temple in place of the destroyed mosque. Extreme violent communal riots sparked off as a result and till date the issue has still not lost its violent repercussions. See for a good discussion on this issue: Sarvepalli Gopal (ed.), *Anatomy of a Confrontation: The Babri Masjid – Ram Janmabhumi Issue* (New Delhi: Penguin, 1991).

13. See related to this issue for instance: *Hindustan Times* (8 June 2003).

14. Related to this see, for instance, S.K. Jamal Safi, "Muslims divided over State domicile policy," in *Hindustan Times*, 14 July 2002.

15. See, for this issue for instance: "Accord Urdu Status of second official language", in: *Hindustan Times* (August 22, 2005); "Muslims to observe Black Day on August 26", in: *Hindustan Times* (August 23, 2005); "Anjuman Tarraqqi-e-Urdu demands restoration of Urdu in Jharkhand", in: *The Milli Gazette* (16-31 March 2005); "Government fanning communal hatred, says Balmuchu", in: *Hindustan Times* (August 23, 2005) and "Enforce Urdu as second official language: AteU, Jharkhand", in: *The Milli Gazette* (1-15 October 2005).

16. See for this issue for instance: "Misconceptions about Muslims have fanned communalism", in *Hindustan Times* (December 8, 2004)

17. Related to this an article by T.K. Oommen makes interesting reading. See: T.K. Oommen, "Insiders and Outsiders in India. Primordial Collectivism and Cultural Pluralism in Nation-building", in: Bidyat Chakrabarty (2003): 231-156.

18. The Jharkhand *Momin Adhikar Manch* (Jharkhand Momin's Right Club) opposed this domicile policy. In the *khatyan* of 1932, they figure as *sheikhs* or *julahas*. Actually, many *momins* are not registered in formal papers as *ansaris* or *momins* but as *sheikhs*, a title bestowed upon them during colonial time. On the basis of this name these *momins* can apply for Backward Caste II certificates yet they demand Backward Caste I (most backward castes) certificates. Instead these *momins* demand a 20% reservation for Muslims in general in order to get more educational facilities and government jobs in the state (*Hindustan*, 15 July, 2002). Shamsher Alam chairman of the *Jharkhand Tanjim*'s protested however that the "present Government policies" were anti-*momin* and framed as "a conspiracy" against them to undermine the socio-economic and educational position of *momins* even further (*Prabhat Khabar*, 5 August 2002).

19. These *sadans* or *moolvasis* comprise several groups among which 'Jharkhandi Muslims'. Some of them are united in the Moolvasi Janandhikar Manch (MJM) and claimed 'domicile certificates' and also demanded that these "moolvasis should get a fair deal in settlement of *haats* and *bazaars*". Its leaders

also complained that the government had given, "settlement rights to *'telis'* and Muslims of Bihar" and thus ignored "the *'telis'* and Muslims from Jharkhand". They demanded that, "a clear policy should be made that *moolvasis* get jobs in their native state" (*The Telegraph*, 26 July 2003).

20. See also for instance: "Genocide. Gujarat 2002", in: *Combat*, year 8, nos. 77-78 (March-April 2002).

21. This was in reaction to the demand of some Muslims in Bihar who wanted Urdu to become the second official language in the State after Hindi, which was severely contested by Hindus in the state. See for instance: "Language Legitimation and Identity: Status of Urdu and Muslims in India Since Independence", in: Yogendra Singh, *Culture Change in India. Identity and Globalization* (Jaipur and New Delhi: Rawat Publications, 2000): 138-177.

22. See also: Jitendra Narayan, "Communal Riots and Administration in Bihar", in A.K. Lal (ed.), *Secularism. Concept and Practice* (New Delhi: Concept Publishing Company, 1998): 80-88.

23. Presently, this is the capital of Jharkhand but during those days it used to be a major town in Bihar.

24. I have analysed Hindi, Urdu and English newspapers that contained columns regarding communal tension in various areas of Jharkhand during in particular 1964, 1967 and 1979, when riots took place in the rural areas near Chaibasa, in Ranchi and in Jamshedpur respectively. Newspaper clippings were taken from the *Amrita Bazar Patrika; Sanmarg; Hindustan Standard; Dawat; Aryawrat; Sanmarg; Ranchi Express; Times of India; Statesman; Indian Nation; New Age* and the *Organiser*.

25. During riots it is often very difficult to establish who is the aggressor and who the victim and in retrospect the aggressor might become the victim and the victim the aggressor.

26. The Jan Sangh Party later became the Bharatiya Janata Party (BJP), which is now the ruling party in Jharkhand and was and is known for its appeal among the Hindu middle classes.

In Jharkhand, it tries in collaboration with the Vishva Hindu Parishad (VHP) and the Rashtriya Swayamsevak Sangh (RSS) to woe to *adivasis* for its programme of *Hindutva* (political Hinduism) (see, for instance: "RSS active in Jharkhand", in: *The Milli Gazette*, 1-15 September 2004). See for the ideology of the BJP in Jharkhand (Jharkhand Pradesh) its web side. See also: Ashutosh Varshney, *Ethnic Conflict and Civic Life. Hindus and Muslims in India* (New Delhi: Oxford University Press, 2002).

27. M.Y Mirza, 14 July 2001, born in 1920 in Ranchi (Jharkhand). He identified as a politician.

28. Abbas Khan, 17 April 2001, 55 years, born in Chaibasa (Jharkhand), name changed on request.

29. Gulam Rasool, 4 November 2000, 72 years, born in Itki (Jharkhand). Identified as "ex-*Pramukh*"(village headman).

30. Md. Mohinuddin, 28 June 2001, born in 1927 in Hazaribagh (Jharkhand). He identified as *idrisi*.

31. Our informants frequently complained of this process defined by them as 'saffronization'. In the context of the state of Gujarat, Lancy Lobo (2002: 4845) called this 'Hindutvisation' where, "Hindutvisation is slightly a different process than Hinduisation. Hindutvisation of *adivasis* [in Gujarat] began in late 1980s. Till then there was Hinduisation, which was a natural, spontaneous process, an outcome of interaction between *adivasis* and the Hindu traders, and later through the Hindu sects. The Sangh Parivar began Hindutvisation of the *adivasis*. This was a planned process. The Sangh Parivar surveyed, selected and targeted villages, planted its men, recruited local people and began its anti-missionary campaigns. They also built their institutions for children. With a view to speedy Hindutvisation they used *Advani's 'rathyatra'*, *'ramshilapujan'* and collection of bricks from *adivasis* for the construction of Ram temple in Ayodhya" [italics added]. In the case of Jharkhand, our interview data, archival sources as well as newspaper reports point to a similar process in Jharkhand already visible during the so-called communal riots in 1964 near Simdega in Jharkhand.

32. Sultan Ahmad Khan, 12 May 2001, 74 years old, born in Arsalhi 65 miles from Daltonganj (Jharkhand). Stated that his father came from Arrah in Bihar and settled in Daltonganj as Revenue Collector during British time.

33. Hazi Noor Mohammed, 29 June 2001, born in 1927 in Jamshedpur (Jharkhand). Identified as *ansari.*

34. Md. Samrul Haque, 7 May 2001, 72 years old, born in Ranchi (Jharkhand). He identified as *iraqi* (those who deal with distilled spirits) but was in cloth business. Opposed to marrying his children in *iraqi* families.

35. In this process certain voices are silenced while only those who separate the 'Muslims' from the 'Hindus' are included in the official narratives. See related to this the move by the RSS to "honour 600 of its veterans" who played a "commendable role in saving thousands of Hindus from the clutches of Muslim goons during the country's Partition in 1947". According to RSS secretary in-charge of north India, Devendra Prasad Gupta, "the idea behind the exercise was to initiate steps to infuse nationalism in young minds to the levels witnessed during Partition days when they protected the Hindu community from Muslim oppression", quoted from: *Hindustan Times* (January 23, 2003).

7

Challenging the Mental Borders of Partition Rhetoric in Jharkhand

Narratives of Rootin Rather than Uprooting

Most narratives of independence do reflect the partition rhetoric as vocalized by (self-appointed and elected) nation builders that is embodied in official reports, laws, most academic research but also in fiction and creative writings on the aftermath of 1947. In other words, these narratives link independence with the losses and the trauma of partition and are rarely about gains. For many, in particular those who were forced to move or stayed back on either side of divided Bengal, Punjab, Assam (and Kashmir) such narratives do indeed reflect their state of minds during the aftermath of partition. In these narratives Muslims who remained in what now had become India, are depicted as people worried about their future as a minority in India, as people who were left behind rather than that they had consciously stayed put and who were confused, had been uprooted without having moved, and as people who felt alienated from the 'others' and whose minds were divided.[1] In short, they were people who "wondered how to overcome the trauma of partition". Ismat Chughtai, an Urdu writer in India, described this state of affairs in the following way:

Those whose bodies were whole had hearts that were splintered. Families were torn apart. One brother was allotted to Hindustan, the other to Pakistan; the mother was in Hindustan, her off-springs were in Pakistan; the husband was in Hindustan, his wife in Pakistan. The bonds of relationship were in tatters, and in the end many souls remained behind in Hindustan while their bodies started off for Pakistan (quoted in: Chakrabarty 2003: 104)

These narratives do indeed also include narratives of Muslims in Bihar, a so-called Muslim minority state, who remained.[2] Likewise, they are depicted as people who had undergone all kind of tribulations such as the so-called Bihar Killings of 1946 (*Amrita Bazar Patrika*, from 30 October 1946 to 8 November 1946).[3] Scholars have labelled these Muslims before 1947 as "*aqliat suba* (minority province) Muslims" (Ghosh 1997: 1-20) and as many of these Muslims left for East Bengal/ Pakistan they were relabelled as "Bihari Muslims", "Stranded Muslims" or "Partition's Biharis" after 1947 (Ghosh 1998: 229-265). Among those Muslims who remained in Bihar after 1947, a few found themselves to be a member of a so-called minority in a state that had been excluded from the map of Pakistan and immediately following partition they wrote a letter to Jinnah in which they stated that, "now that Pakistan has come into being and you are already appointed Governor General of Pakistan, it is obvious that we in India will be without your leadership, guidance, and advice". They asked Jinnah therefore, "Whom shall we look to for such guidance, advice, and aspiration hereafter?" These Muslims also stated that now, "that so many of us will be left behind in India, what should be our attitude towards the majority community from whom we differed so much till lately and towards the government of the country? Have we to change our outlook on life and things like that? In other words how are we to adjust ourselves?" and, "What will be the future of Muslims in India as a minority reduced to a still smaller number and what guarantee is there of their safety and security?" The Quaid-i-Azam answered that these were important questions and that,

> Muslims in India have nothing to be afraid of. They will still be several crores in number. They have made many sacrifices along with Muslims of the majority provinces. It is a result of the sacrifices made by all of them in India that we have been able to achieve Pakistan. While the Musalmans of the majority provinces [who were now included in Pakistan] will be in a position to wield authority and power and mould their destinies according to their genius, the Musalmans in India have yet to go through a number of ordeals, sufferings, and sacrifices. Their future will remain dark for some years to come and thick clouds will be hanging over them (Noorani 2003: 36-37).

Scholars have started collecting the narratives of those who stayed put and often indeed report 'memories of trauma'.[4] Partition is remembered as a national catastrophic event that overshadowed the event of 'independence' and reminds people (Hindus and Muslims) of the price they paid for freedom.[5] In these narratives it is recounted that India not only lost territory due to partition but that it also lost people and wealth. The stories of individuals are narrated, in particular Hindus, who committed suicide and became martyrs, who were killed, raped and abused and of those who were physically displaced and lost their family, property, status, honour and even their motherland. Indeed, these narratives do recognize that Muslims suffered too but are foremost concerned with their (mental) displacement (with or without movement) and with the ways in which Muslims, who 'were left behind' tried to come to terms with 'Partition' (often spelled with capital P). In others words, these scholars as Samaddar (2003: 33) remarked, "are busy looking at the dark side of the independence of the new nation – namely, violence, homelessness, and hatred as the cardinal principle of politics [...]". These stories of independence that link independence with partition are indeed the kind of tales Jinnah must have expected to exist among the Muslims from Bihar who had asked him for advice. They are certainly tales of uprooting, mentally of physically.[6]

When I asked my informants in Jharkhand to tell "their stories of partition", I expected similar stories about the dark side of independence. In fact I, initially, encountered silence. My informants told me that they had nothing to do with partition and so had no tales to tell. Yet, confronted with my pressure on them to tell something about the partition of 1947 and how it had affected their lives as Muslims in Bihar, I unconsciously enacted partition rhetoric, which triggered of not stories that reproduced the mental borders embodied in this rhetoric but narratives of independence with alternative borders of the mind that did not depict these 'Muslims in Bihar' against the other but actually depicted these 'Muslims in Jharkhand' against other 'others', often the 'Muslims of Bihar'. Certainly, these were not stories of uprooting but of rooting. In the encounter between our informants and partition rhetoric enacted by me as researcher and by others in past and present, other memory pieces and narratives were triggered of, which constitute the content of this chapter (see also: Sinha-Kerkhoff 2004d).

Whenever this partition rhetoric was enacted during the interview or in the past, alternative narratives were created. During our interviews we frequently encountered sentences such as, "They went to Pakistan", "They suffered a lot", "It was difficult for them to make a new beginning", "They were other kind of Muslims", "They had wanted to leave but could not go" or "They had a very bad relation with the locals". Clearly, the Muslims we interviewed after the establishment of the new state of Jharkhand not only distanced themselves from the Muslims depicted in the partition narratives but also identified differently, as 'we'. This formed new and imagined ethnic identities with symbolic boundaries that formed the contours of a common Jharkhandi Muslim identity depicted against the 'other Indian Muslims' in Bihar or elsewhere as well as against 'Muslims who had left'. Contrary to expectations, therefore, the experience of discrimination on basis of religion that took place during the enactment of partition rhetoric in their lives, I found that this did not provoke these Muslims in Jharkhand to target the 'others' of partition rhetoric (i.e. the Hindus and adivasis in Jharkand) as a negative group. Instead, many of the by us interviewed Muslims in Jharkhand articulated a 'superiority' over Muslims in Bihar, and in doing so both distanced themselves from what they perceived as 'the burden of partition rhetoric', on the one hand, and asserted their own affinity with the 'other Jharkhandis' in the state, on the other (Cf. Fein 2005: 333).

In other words, among these interviewed Muslims in Jharkhand, minoritization as effected by the enactment of partition rhetoric had not resulted in alienating them from 'the others' or in their complete silencing, or for that matter brought them in the main stream. In fact, these attempts at minoritization of these Muslims in Jharkhand had made them very talkative. Besides, as illustrated in this chapter, our informants conveyed that their narratives were different from those incorporated in state supported partition rhetoric but under the burden of which they were living and which even threatened to 'displace' them. These narratives are indeed different as illustrated in this chapter, as they are not stories of uprooting but of rooting. Yet, as also will be shown the new borders that were incorporated in the narratives of these Muslims could differ and therefore also the basis of unity and the identification of 'the other'.

Changing Definitions of the Other and the Self in Jharkhand

It should be emphasized that I conducted almost all my fieldwork in Jharkhand after the establishment of the new state in 2000 and that in the contemporary power constellation of the new state of Jharkhand it had become extremely important for those who 'have nowhere to go to' to show, by writing their own narratives, that they are 'local'. In such a power constellation, partition rhetoric that depicts Muslims, as 'outsiders' will certainly not be accepted therefore. However, in Jharkhand it has become equally important for others, by writing other histories, to define 'non-Jharkhandis' as 'outsiders' and the chances that partition rhetoric is enacted have increased therefore after the establishment of the new state. Prakash (2001: 99-100; 128 note 11 and 293) argued however that this 'othering' had taken place before the partition of Bihar as well yet that at different times different strategies had been adopted by the Jharkhand leaders and which at times made identities more rigid and at other times allowed for "multiple identities."

Jaipal Singh for instance, who himself identified as a Christian Munda, joined the *Adivasi Mahasabha* in 1939 as President and first claimed to represent "pan-tribal interests". Gradually however, it became a "pan-Chhota Nagpur movement" that also included "non-tribal identities." The *Mahasabha* which demanded separation from Bihar and the establishment of an autonomous state did for some time also receive support from the Muslim League which, in the 1940s, hoped to secure a corridor to connect East and West Pakistan via the tribal areas of south Bihar. Yet, the *Mahasabha* was defeated during the 1946 Constituent Assembly elections in which the Indian National Congress performed well and it also lost the support of the Muslim League. The Government moreover had rejected the demand for a corridor to connect East and West

Pakistan, passing through the tribal areas of Bihar. During the 1950s however, the *Adivasi Mahasabha* realised, "that the support of non-tribal settlers was necessary to achieve the goal of a separate province" and this caused, "the broadening of the social base of the *Mahasabha*" (see also Kuwajima 1998: 202-203). These changes in the attitudes of the potential enactors of partition rhetoric did of course, impact the kind of borders (i.e. the definition of the 'self' and the 'other') Muslims in Jharkhand chose to uphold.

Already under British rule Muslims in Bihar had made differences among and between themselves. In his Presidential speech, Aali Janab Molvi Mohammed Nizamuddin Sb. explained in 1934 during a speech in Gaya (Bihar) for instance why the all India Momin Conference had been founded:

Once the Prophet Mohammed said that all Muslims are brothers from each other and that all Muslims were equal and belong to one community. We live here with four crore of Muslims in India but many groups do not behave properly with us, *momins*. We were mistreated because of our bad economic condition though the prophet had said that we are all equal. There was therefore a need to found the *Jamatul Mominin* to overcome our downtrodden condition so that we will no longer be treated inhumanly by the other Muslim groups who despise us (Ansari 2000: 237-255).

The response of the Conference in Bihar was good and in 1936 local *momin* leaders such as R. Ali and Munsi Mohammad Zahoor organized a big Momin Conference in Ranchi (now Jharkhand's capital), which, "could be called an All-Bihar's Muslim Conference as not only *momins* from Chhota Nagpur participated". Yet, the organization of such a conference was disliked by non-*momins* and in particular by those who supported the Muslim League as they argued that "it divides the Muslims in Bihar". During the meeting in Ranchi in Jharkhand, class and political differences amongst the leaders became visible as the leader from Bihar identified as 'upper-class Muslims' who conveyed during their speeches that they however did, "not at all oppose those who belong to lower class families such as the *julaha, dhunia, butucher* and the *kujra*" [italic added]. Local leader R. Ali from Ranchi said in his speech that he wanted to uplift his fellow *momins*, who were poor weavers, by educating them, by which their condition in the handloom business would improve automatically. But, he complained, "now when we try to remove wrong practices and problems amongst ourselves, some upper class people start to blame us that we are dividing the Muslim community" (Masawat, vol. 3, no. 4, April 1936: 14-17 and 18-25) [in Urdu and translated by Md. Masoom Reza].

From a speech in 1948 delivered in Patna by Abdul Qayum Ansari, Bihar State Minister as well as President of the All India Momin Conference at the time, it becomes evident that immediately after the Partition of 1947, Muslims in Bihar had become even more divided amongst themselves. There were the interests of *momins* who had supported the Muslim League and those who had supported the Congress Party. Besides, it seems *momins* in Jharkhand were united as backward castes *momins* along with other lower castes and classes on a regional basis and the people who, "oppressed us belong to the upper Muslim castes". They had oppressed these, "*momins* and other poor Muslims for centuries because they thought themselves politically and socially superior" as they had been *nawabs*, landlords and other rich and the religious scholars before 1947. The *momins* in Jharkhand said that,

Our enemies were not only the British colonizers but these rich Muslims too. They had started manipulating us with the slogan "Islam in danger" but we remained loyal to the Congress. Patriotism and nationalism is still great among sus and though we, because of communal feelings against us, have abandoned our political aims we now will continue working for the socio-economic betterment of all the backward Muslims here in this area who are victims due to their illiteracy and bad economic as well as social position' (Ansari 2000: 362-385).

Because of these shifting attitudes of 'others' towards Muslims and that of the 'self' among Muslims of Jharkhand historically, our Muslim informants, during their narratives as shown below, therefore also shifted their boundaries at times. Yet, rarely did they accept the boundaries as embodied in partition rhetoric accept and as shown in the previous chapter, sometimes during communal riots where the enactment of partition rhetoric caused a reproduction of the mental borders it embodied resulting in defining of the self as 'Muslim' and the other as 'Hindus' or 'Hinduized adivasis'.

Narratives of Unity and Common Struggle: *Kolha-Jolha Bhai Bhai*

Though most of our informants believed that after 1947, they "stood to reap the fruits of freedom", as one informant told us,[7] these Muslims in Jharkhand sooner or later, as argued before, were confronted with 'truth' as embodied in partition rhetoric that put them in a fix whether to accept these narratives and its borders or to reject them and formulate new narratives with alternative borders. Safirunn Nisha,[8] a vegetable seller from Gumla, had lost her brothers and her father during the communal riots that had spread over the rural areas in Jharkhand in 1964. Her family members had all been killed by *adivasis*. During these riots Muslims in the area, I was told by Muslim survivors during a visit I paid to the area in 2001, had been provoked by *adivasis*. These *adivasis* had said that they had seen a train holding in Jamshedpur that had been full of refugees from East Pakistan who clearly had undergone tremendous torture in the hands of the

Muslim rulers in that country. These *adivasis* therefore had felt that they had no other choice than to defend the honour of their "fellow Christians and Hindus", my Muslim informants told me in 2001. That is why they on one day in 1964, collected all the Muslim children and women of one village and burnt them alive in a nearby mosque. They also looted the village and burnt down the houses. The half burnt mosque can still be witnessed but all women and children died.

Clearly, according to my informants, partition rhetoric had been enacted by these *adivasis* who, on the instigation of fundamentalist Hindus, also identified as Hindus or as Christians and who were asked to expel the 'outsider Muslims' of their village in order to revenge the atrocities that were committed among their 'fellow Hindus' in another country. Jayaprakash Narayan a well-known socialist politician at the time described these communal riots in a letter addressed to the presiding officers of both Houses of Parliament in the following way:

It was during my peace work in Jamshedpur that I read of the Lok Sabha unanimously recommending to the government to enlist world opinion against the atrocities perpetrated on the minorities in East Pakistan. It is but right that members of Parliament should be so concerned over the fate of minorities in a neighbouring nation. But was it not equally right, if not more so, to have shown concern about the fate of the Muslim minority in our own country? [...] I am not writing this in order to make a report to you on the situation in these areas of Bihar and Orissa and the vital steel cities. But I do most earnestly wish to say that India and Indians have no cause to feel smug and complacent or superior and holy. Terrible things have happened, and on a scale that has not been realized by Delhi or the country at large. The tale of provocation caused by refugee trains is only a small part of the full story. There is no doubt in my mind that there was an organization behind these dastardly activities which operated from a common centre, manufactured and spread rumours, planned and financed specific actions, and provided the whole operation with a political and philosophical justification [...] As for the nature of atrocities committed, I do not think there were any holds barred. Every revolting kind of deed was done. The tragedy seen in the mass was terrible enough, but some of the individual cases were fathomless, indeed, in their cruelty and degradation (*Hindustan Times*, 17 April 1964).

Yet, these Muslims did neither remain silent nor did they reproduce partition rhetoric. Instead, this kind of enactment of partition rhetoric often sparked off other tales among Muslims in Jharkhand who had gone through such 'partition'. Above-mentioned Safirunn Nisha was silenced however and said she had "no idea" why her father and brothers had been killed. She added:

I know that Nehruji was still alive. My brothers died that time. Nehruji went to the spot. After that he died, too. I became mad when I heard the news. I did not go there. Bows and arrows killed them. They say it is because we are Muslims. That is not true.

Though Safirunn thus rejected the "truths" embodied in partition rhetoric, she had no alternative narratives to offer however. Like most of the female 'downtrodden' Muslims we interviewed, she had no alternative narrative that could replace the on her imposed partition rhetoric. One Muslim man who requested anonymity and who had lost his own first wife during this incident commented on the incident however:

The *adivasis* had been misguided. You know what really happened? In this particular village we all had quite some land. Jan Sangh people had come and told these innocent *adivasis* that they should kill all the Muslims here and would than be able to grab our land.

They never got our land however. We received compensation from the government to rebuild our houses.

Similarly most men we interviewed possessed alternative narratives that challenged the 'truths' of partition rhetoric and expressed alternative borders where often the Muslims in Jharkhand got united with the *adivasis* against their common 'exploiters'. Bonds of region" seemed stronger in these narratives than "bonds of religion" or even "bonds of *biradari* (i.e. "caste") (Cf. Ghosh 1998: 256). Continuous enactment of partition rhetoric, which defines 'Muslims' as 'foreigners', inspired those Muslims who identified with or even saw themselves as *moolvasis*, to root themselves in the soil of Jharkhand with support of their own narratives. On the one hand, their narratives are separate histories of Muslims in Jharkhand, i.e., separate from those that are included in partition rhetoric, and, on the other hand, these narratives of Muslims we interviewed, pass on a common history of people who resided in Jharkhand, which was expressed by the frequently recited slogan of *kolha-jolha bhai bhai*.[9] This illustrates that rather than any antagonism between Muslims and another important community in the region, the *adivasis* and contrary to what partition rhetoric wants us to believe, there had, according to our informants, been a close interaction between the two communities who had lived together as brothers belonging to the same soil.

That the two communities had lived peacefully together was in particular expressed by interviewed *ansaris* in Jharkhand. Actually, I also found archival sources on *ansaris* in Jharkhand or on *momins* as they had labelled themselves in the past. In these sources they had frequently complained even before 1947, that 'other' Muslims, i.e. non-*momins* had mistreated them. They identified as lower classes or even lower-castes among the Muslims and complained that the rich

Muslims, the upper classes or castes had looked down upon them and had alleged that momins were converted Hindus.[10] These upper class Muslims themselves traced their ancestors to Arabia. Besides, these contemporary sources also provide evidence that there was not always a good relation between *momins* in Bihar and those in Jharkhand. The former wanted to unite all *momins* in India and the latter preferred regional identification and valued their union with the *adivasis* who helped them in their struggle for a separate state. For some time there also seem to have been a discussion among these momins related to their 'Muslim identity'. Some even argued that their habits were very similar to those of the (Hinduised) adivasis. Investigations done by our friend Kurshid[11] highlight the significant role *ansaris* played in the agro-based traditional socio-economic system of the tribal-dominated village communities. "They had come as weavers many generations ago", Kurshid explains, "while maintaining a symbiotic relationship with the tribes" In his paper in Urdu and entitled "History of Muslims in Jharkhand," he elaborates:

Among the *mundas* of Chhota Nagpur there does not appear to be a tradition of weaving cloth either by individual members or families as one can witness among some of the tribes of North East India. They seem to have a clear tradition of recognized weaver castes/classes that they have readily incorporated in the socio-economic life of the village community. Some sources indicate that the *mundas* had a very good relation with the *jolhas* [also spelled *julaha]*, the Muslim weavers. Actually, *mundas* would not weave cloth as this was regarded as one of their accepted social taboos. Another important thing to bear in mind is that the prevailing pattern of land-ownership in the *mundari khuntkatti* system, *jolhas* could not get any land for cultivation, if they desired to do, from the *mundas* without the latter's explicit permission. This was definitely another reason for the weavers' dependence on the *mundas* for their livelihood. From all this we can conclude that the *mundas* and the weavers had a symbiotic relationship, needing one another and one depending on the other.[12]

Yet, Kurshid noted during one of our many informal talks that "now things are changing". He cited the decline of the traditional weaving industry as an example. '*Adivasis* now want readymade cloths,' he said. He further argued that right-wing conservative Hindus parties such as the RSS (*Rashtriya Svayamsevak Sangh*: the National Volunteer Corps) were trying to exploit the situation:

They tell these *adivasis* that we are outsiders and during the 1960s the Jan Sangh told these *adivasis* that we were responsible for the atrocities committed against tribals and Hindus in Bangladesh. When the train carrying a group of these Hindu refugees stopped at Jamshedpur, the problems started. In a village near Simdega fifty Muslim women and children were collected in a small mosque and burnt alive by the *adivasis*. This burnt mosque is still there.

Yet, this burnt mosque is not the only reminder of this tragedy any longer. We now have narratives such as this one written by Kurshid but also above-exposed oral narratives. Besides, these narratives do not solely convey the history of tragedies. These tragedies were actually caused, as explained above, by the enactment of partition rhetoric, which in its turn called forth these other stories. Many of these narratives rejected the truths embodied in partition rhetoric and came up with other truths. Instead of, for instance, a partition rhetoric that narrated the conflicts between Muslims and *adivasis* in Jharkhand we heard stories that emphasized collaboration and harmony and even highlighted the similarities between "Muslims" and the "*adivasis*." Haji Habibullab Sahid[13], ex-assistant commissioner, recalled for instance:

We received land from the Maharaja Chhota Nagpur Nagbansi and he appointed many Muslims. We knew Mundari. We even looked like *adivasis*. Yet, they do not have beards. Actually, we are converted adivasis. We also drank *handiya*, a local alcoholic drink, like the *adivasis*. We did not marry them but they also did observe marriage restrictions. It was the North Biharis who used to deceive the *adivasis*. We formed a small group and worked for Jharkhand already in 1942 and not a single *momin* was pro-Pakistan. I also collaborated with Zahoor Ali of the Jamiyat-ul Momin.

Whereas partition rhetoric emphasized communal differences, Muslims we interviewed thus recalled the close relationships that existed between Muslims and the other important community in the region, the *adivasis*. Md. Yunas Ansari,[14] for example, said that he believed that before 1947, "We did not even do *namaz* [pray] at that time; something that is now considered to be a minimum requirement for Muslims". Mirdaha[15] also spoke of the cordial relationship that he thought had once existed between Muslims, *adivasis* and Hindus in the Jharkhand area:

We were *khans* and the Ratu Maharaja gave us our title. *Mir* means pioneer and *daha* comes from *dehat* that is village. We originated from the Magadh area and were pioneers in this village. The Khan Bahadur Raj family from the Hatma State in Hazaribagh was very close to us. We were also very close to the *adivasis* here. Some *mundas* here even used to be on fast during *Ramzan* just like us. We all spoke Nagpuri.

Yunas Ansari also commented on the "very close relationship" between Muslims and *adivasis*: "We are converted *adivasis*. After conversion we have become *ansaris* and help the people by supplying them cloth. We are like the people who helped the Prophet in Mecca. That time [i.e. before 1947] Muslims here in this area only knew about the festival of *Moharram*. They did no celebrate *Id* or *Bakrid*. Shamima Khatoon Ansari told us that the tribal leader Jaipal Singh had been surprised when a Muslim was once introduced to him as *oraon* and an *adivasi* as *shaikh*. Jaipal Singh, who had fought for an independent state of Jharkhand had then exclaimed, *kolha-jolha bhai bhai*.[16] Md. Mohinuddin,[17] from Chaibasa, did not hide his sympathies for Birsa Munda, the adivasi leader who "struggled for an autonomous region one hundred years ago." "I think Birsa was very good," he declared. "He was a *munda* but he told that Jharkhand will be for all Chhota Nagpur people." Many of the Muslims we interviewed remembered their support for the Jharkhand Movement, which called for the partition of Bihar and the formation a new state named Jharkhand. They recalled their collaboration with *adivasis* in this movement: "Even some educated religious leaders [*ulema*] who were generally not involved in such political issues, had participated in the Jharkhand movement, it was conveyed to me, and Mustaqim Hazi[18] reported that some of them under the leadership of Maulana Ahmad Ali had been demanding such a new state carved out of Bihar."[19] Haji Md. Hanif Ansari, younger brother of Shaikh Mohiuddin, and Md. K. Rahman, a lawyer and son of Shaikh Mohiuddin, both emphasized that Muslims had been involved in the struggle for a new state "right from the beginning" and also that in these efforts they had closely been collaborating with *adivasis*. Ansari explained:

Shaikh Mohiuddin started a movement for Jharkhand in 1937 already. The president of this movement was David Munzni. Yunas Ansari, Mr. Qadir, Bena Puri, and Habibullah Ansari were also involved in this movement, which was parallel to Jaipal Singh who was leader of the *adivasis*. Leading *momins* were involved in the movement and also some *adivasis*. It was separate from the Congress and the Muslim League but we were in close contact with Jaipalji. At the time, the government opposed the division of Bihar and no doubt feared any collaboration between Muslims and *adivasis* in a common struggle.

Indeed, government reports seemed to have downplayed the number and significance of Muslims who had joined the separatist movement. According to a report published just after the 1947 partition the government of India warned for instance of such, in their view, "anti-national activities" and stated that "only a few hundred Muslims" (mostly *momins*) seemed to have joined Mohiuddin's Chhota Nagpur *Momin* Union. The report also mentioned that the movement disintegrated within a year.[20] Yet, the people we interviewed all expressed a spirit of unity and collaboration with 'locals' and their support for the Jharkhand movement. H.H. Rahman,[21] a *shaikh iraqi* told us that Jinnah had never impressed him: "My whole family always mixed with Hindus. The two-nation theory never excited me. I felt a slave under British rule and was overwhelmed by Gandhi. There was no communal tension here". Lastly, Abdul Qadir recounted:

> I liked Congress because it was for simple people like us. I never liked the Muslim League. But Jinnah was not a bad man; he was worked both for the Hindus as well as the Muslims. I think Pakistanis are not good people. I had land here so why should I have gone? Besides, we did not go to Pakistan because our ancestors are buried here. Jaipal Singh was also a good man. He made Jharkhand for all.[22]

Claiming a Separate History: Other Stories of Independence

Significantly, these Muslims in Jharkhand are absent in the narratives of Bihari Muslims that describe the role of Muslims in Bihar in the 'Freedom Movement'.[23] For that matter, they are absent from all accounts on 'India Struggle for Independence' and only appear as Muslims in narratives of partition. Yet, these Muslims in Jharkhand now ask people to pay attention to the role their ancestors played in India's struggle for freedom lest "People forget these great people of Jharkhand" (*Hindustan*, 4 August 2000). After the establishment of a separate Jharkhand state in 2000, these Muslims have formulated a kind of alternative narratives that do reject state-sponsored histories of Indian Muslims depicted as a monolithic and uniform community that is antagonistic to the "other" (as partition rhetoric imagines them). In fact, these Muslims have their own histories (Cf. Singer 1997) and refuse to accept the past of 'others' under which burden they are forced to live.[24] Md. Rafique Ansari,[25] for instance, had heard about the "killings in Bihar" and about "flows of people leaving for Pakistan," but he told us that this was not his past. These were the memories of the "Bihari *sharif*" [elite] [26] and not those of the "*razil* [labourers] Jharkhandis" like himself. He remembered:

> When I was eighteen years old in 1946, there were many riots in Bihar. It was a ghastly scene at the time. Many Muslims were killed and a great number fled to Bengal. In this area it was very peaceful however. Nothing happened here in Hazaribagh. Actually, the lower classes of Muslims never supported Jinnah. Till date, these poor Muslims do not know even to talk about Pakistan. The richer sections were Muslim Leaguers. They mostly lived in Bihar. They shouted: *Le ke rahenge Pakistan. Qaide Azam Zindabad* (Take Pakistan and stay in it. Long lives Jinnah!) Those who left really suffered. At present, Pakistan does not even accept the Bihari Muslims. They differentiate between Sindhis and Punjabis; and in Bangladesh it is the same.

Md. Rafique Ansari's[27] anger was directed against the Muslim League and in particular, against its President:

Mr. Jinnah did not understand politics. He wanted to bring people together in the name of Islam but that was quite impossible. See East Pakistan is only for Bengalis and West Pakistan only for Punjabis. Exchange was also never possible. Jinnah himself was not even a Muslim. He was completely anglicised and did not offer *namaz* [pray] at all. How could he understand the position of Muslims in India? If he had not created Pakistan, there would have been nineteen Muslims as chief ministers ruling here in India. Now we here have the toilet and the house is in Pakistan. This is the division of India.

Imtiaz[28] was very proud of his father, Zahoor Ali, who had, Imtiaz narrated, been involved in India's struggle for independence and who, unlike what partition rhetoric tries to convey, was a Muslim who had never supported the two-nation theory. He said:

We asked him to include his name in the Rajya Sabha or Vidhan Parisad as he had fought the battle of freedom for our country. He remained a loyal and staunch supporter to the Congress Party, which formed a single majority community. He was president of the Ranchi Jamiyat al-Momineen, which was a nationalist organization that had started in 1928.

Insisting that, "we were nationalist Muslims, members of the Momin Conference and had never been pro-Pakistan," Amanat Ali[29] told us:

The Muslim League supporters contended that *momins* were dogs of the Congress. They also told us that we were *kuffar* [plural of *kafir*, non-believer]. Jinnah had told the *adivasis* that they should ask for Adivasistan and he would demand for Pakistan. He had told Jaipal Singh that he himself desired Assam and that he would give Bengal to the *adivasis*. But we were proud of ourselves. The All India Momin Conference condemned even the Congress'[30] decision to support the two-nation theory. Nonetheless, when

Nehru paid a visit here I competed with my school friends over who would touch his feet. We were punished for this in school. The teachers (some of whom were English) did not like us to welcome Nehru. The history of our involvement in the freedom struggle is very old. In 1857 more than 70 per cent of the sepoys who were killed in the movement against the British were *ansaris*. We were called the "bloody *julahas*."[31]

Although he identified himself as "forward Muslim," Gulam Mohinuddin Ahmad[32] declared that the difference lay in the fact that "they were rich and we were poor," and he added that, "only poor people remained in India". Samrul Haque,[33] from Ranchi, was even angry with these "Bihari Muslims," who in his view had been "rich" and part of the sharif. These, 'upper-classes and Patna people went to Pakistan,' he added. Angrily, he said: "We could not even bury our dead bodies in their graveyard (glaveyards). They did also not allow us to pray in their mosques or visit their hotels".

Interviewed Muslims in Jharkhand rarely remembered any relatives or friends who had left for Pakistan. Abdul Hammed Asar[34] told us: "My boss told me once that he would take care of me in Pakistan but I refused to go there. I am born here so I will not go anywhere.' M.D. Musa, a member of the Communist Party, stayed put because he did not want to leave his family. He maintained, in fact that, 'Muslims never did follow Islam. If they had, there would not have been Partition.' Besides, he added, 'I did not like any of the so-called leaders; neither Jinnah nor Gandhi. In fact, the whole idea of migrating appears never to have come to their mind. In addition, partition for those residing in Jharkhand was mixed up with memories of another partition, namely, the battle for a bifurcation of Bihar and the establishment of a new Jharkhand state. Actually, many interviewed Muslims narrated that they had always wanted a separate state and also mentioned that they were "very different from the Biharis". They sometimes felt that they were 'real Jharkhandis'.

At one point even the Muslim League had wanted the partition of Bihar in order to establish in Chhota Nagpur, a separate homeland for the Bihari Muslims so that they would be safe from the Hindu domination in North Bihar. Yet, this is not always what our informants had wanted. We learned from our interviews that staying put had been the first priority for Muslims in Jharkhand. Though Abdul Khalid,[35] a *dafalli*, had opted for the Muslim League and had also supported partition, he had never thought of moving. He had actually guessed that Jharkhand would become part of Pakistan. He recalled:

> In fact my father was known as Pundit Maulvi Abdul Shakoor. He was very gentle, like a cow. That is why one *Marwari* gave him this name. He also wore *dhoti* and *kurta* and was very close to Hindus. Many Hindus actually knew Urdu at that time. We were poor *moolvasis* [people with roots in the area]. I never thought I should go anywhere. But there was this election in 1946 where people had to cast their votes. It was clear to me that time that the Pakistan area would be up to Purulia. So we thought that this area would also go to Pakistan and therefore voted for Pakistan, i.e., for the Muslim League.

The narratives of these Muslims in Jharkhand thus challenged the 'truths' embodied in partition rhetoric and which reproduced the idea that Muslims had all behaved as 'aliens', 'outsiders' and 'enemies' of the 'locals' such as '(Hinduized) *adivasis*'. They also challenged the idea that they, or their ancestors, had all fought for the establishment of Pakistan and the partition of British India. Their narratives in particular challenged those partition narratives enacted by 'others' that described that there had, at all times, been a conflict between the *adivasis* and Muslims in Jharkhand. Living in an environment where these Muslims in Jharkhand may experience discrimination based on religious distinction, these Muslims construct an alternative strategy for coping with boundaries that limit opportunities, in particular those imposed by India's citizenship regime based on partition rhetoric. By distancing themselves from Muslims in Bihar and striving for greater inclusion in Jharkhand, these Muslims feel positive association with *adivasis*. The narratives exposed in this chapter illustrate this process of alternative boundary formation. These alternative narratives of independence therefore not only challenge partition rhetoric and its borders but also offers alternative borders of the mind that could be used to replace the divide between 'Muslims' and 'Hindus' in these partitioned times in India.

References

1. See, for instance: *Dawat* (28 September 2000: 31; 39-41; 47-50 and 53-93) and Qutubuddin Aziz, *Blood and Tears* (Karachi: Publication Division of the United Press of Pakistan, 1974).
2. For a similar tale of the effect of partition on the lives of individual Muslims and their families in Bihar, which caused divided minds see: Abdus Samad, *A Strip of Land two Yards Long* (New Delhi: Sahitya Akademi, 1997). (Translated from Urdu by Jai Ratan). See also: Bhisham Sahni, *Tamas* (New Delhi: Sahitya Akademi, 2001. (Translated from Hindi).
3. It is interesting to mention that after the Great Killings of 1946 in Bihar these Bihari Muslims demanded their own homeland. They therefore supported the Muslim League who had proposed the division of Bihar. The Muslim League urged these Muslims to migrate to the southern part of Bihar and then to establish a separate State for themselves where they would be free from the Hindu *raj*. These Muslims hoped that since, "The districts demanded as a homeland for the Muslims of Bihar form a contiguous area", they, "may form some sort

of union with Chhota Nagpur and Santhal Parganas and make one independent sovereign state" (Ghosh 1998: 232).

4. Yet, scholars also remarked that some narratives do more than solely narrating the trauma caused by the violence that constituted partition. See, for instance, Margit Koves who concluded that, "By countering moralising and sentimentality in their narrative strategies they enabled the reader to deal with and go beyond the paralysing effects of such traumatic experiences", in: Margit Koves, "Telling Stories of Partition and W[illegible]r. Sadat Hasan Manto and Istvan Orkeny, in *Economic and Political Weekly*, Vol. xxxii, no. 33 and 34 (16-23 August 1997): 2147-2153. See also: Gyanendra Pandey, "Community and Violence: Recalling Partition", *Economic and Political Weekly*, Vol. xxxii, no. 32 (9 August 1997): 2037-2045.

5. Most of these narratives describe the lives and experiences of people who resided in the Punjab. Related to this see: Ayesha Jalal, "Nation, Reason and Religion: Punjab's Role in the Partition of India", *Economic and Political Weekly*, Vol. xxxiii, no. 32 (8 August) 1998: 2183-2190. Yet, now narratives are also available that focus, "on the human dimension of the second partition of Bengal (1947) with a clear emphasis on the gender perspective", which fill the "serious gap". See for example, Jasodhara Bagchi and Subhoranjan Dasgupta (eds.) "Porous Borders, Divided Selves", in *Seminar* (Special Issue), 510 (February 2002), 12-93 and also: Dipesh Chakrabarty, "Remembered Villages. Representation of Hindu-Bengali Memories in the Aftermath of the Partition", in *Economic and Political Weekly* (10 August 1996): 2140-2151.

6. For such narratives see for instance, Balraj Puri, "Indian Muslims since Partition", *Economic and Political Weekly* (2 October 1993): 2141-2149; Mushirul Hasan, *Adjustment and Accommodation: Indian Muslims after Partition* (New Delhi: Nehru Memorial Museum and Library, Teen Murti House, 1990); Zafar Imam (ed.), *Muslims in India* (New Delhi: Orient Longman, 1975) and Omar Khalidi, *Indian Muslims Since Independence* (New Delhi: Vikas Publishing House, 1997).

7. Shamima Begum "Ustanijee" (also Shamima Khatoon Ansari), 2 April 2001, aged 64 and born in Itki (Jharkhand). She identified as *ansari*. She is a retired schoolteacher in Urdu and a well-known social worker in the area (see also photo in Sinha-Kerkhoff (2004d).

8. Safirunn Nisha, 17 April 2001, 60 years old, born in Karah (Jharkhand).

9. *Kolas* constitute an *adivasi* group and *jolhas* constitute a Muslim group.

10. We should thus realize that, and contrary to what the partition rhetoric wants us to believe, plurality is what characterizes the Muslims in Jharkhand. Mondal (2003: 4897) who also carried out research among so-called OBC (or dalit) Muslims in India also concluded among others that, "the tendency to represent Muslims as a single, monolithic and homogeneous group in political arenas and academic discourse has no empirical validity".

11. Name changed on request.

12. Translated by Md. Masoom Eza.

13. Haji Habibullah Sahib, 30 March 2001, 73 years old and born in Ranchi (Jharkhand). Identified as *momin*. He played an important role in the Jharkhand Council in Kanke during the first part of the 1940s.

14. Md. Yunas Ansari, 8 April 2001, 81 years old. Had also been involved in the above-mentioned Jharkhand Council, Kanke. He identified as "weaver" (*bunkar*), as "political leader" and also as "agriculturist."

15. Naim Muddin Mirdaha, 27 November 2000, 60 years and born in Beru (Jharkhand). Identified as *khan*.

16. This informant was one of these "exceptional women" who had an interesting story to tell us.

17. Md. Mohinuddin, 28 July 2001, born in 1927 in Hazaribagh (Jharkhand).

18. Md. Mohinuddin, 28 July 2001, born in 1927 in Hazaribagh (Jharkhand).

19. Mustaqim Hazi, 25 December 2000, 70 years and born in Bargain near Ranchi (Jharkhand).

20. File No. 270 (3) 1947 *Political Special (*Patna: Patna State Archives).

21. Hafis Habibur Rahman, 4 April 2001, born in 1934 in Hazaribagh (Jharkhand). Identified as Sayad.

22. Abdul Qadir, 7 December 2000, 72 years and born in Sukerhotoo near Ranchi city (Jharkhand). He identified as *ansari* as "weaver" (*bunkar*) and as "agriculturist."

23. See for instance, Syed Fazle Rab, "The Role of Ulema in Bihar: From Freedom Movement to the Politics of Partition", in: *Indian Journal of Secularism*, Vol.7, no.1 (April-June 2003): 82-109.

24. I have here only exposed oral histories but there are plenty of such recently formulated 'histories' available in written form too in English, Hindi and in Urdu. See, for instance, *Ranchi Express* (3 August 2000) (in Hindi) in which Imtiaz Ali reminds people that his father Late Zahoor Ali tried to involve *momins* in the Jharkhand Movement. He also included an archive photo of some well-known Muslims in Jharkhand who had been Imtiaz alleged, actively involved in the Jharkhand Movement. This photo was reproduced in the *Hindustan* (4 August 2000) (in Hindi) with the heading: 'People forget these great people of Jharkhand'. See also Md. Rafique Ansari's editorial in Urdu in *Farooqui Tanjeem* (3 November 1999) in which he narrated the involvement of *ansaris* in the "struggle for independence". See further Anwar Eraz article entitled "The Jharkhand Movement in Bihar" in: *Ifkar Milli* (in Urdu) (July 2000: 136-140) and Aslam Jamshedpuri's article entitled "Jharkhand Movement and Musalmans" in: *Ifkar Milli* (in Urdu) (July 2000: 140-143). See also another article that appeared in the *Ifkar Milli* (July 2000: 243) on "Jharkhandi freedom-fighter Shaikh Bhikhari". See also: Afsar Ali, "The

Muslim Contribution to the Formation of the Jharkhand State", in: *The Milli Gazette* (16-31 December 2000: 60). Ali narrates in this article that, "Muslims stepped into Jharkhand territory 800 years ago" and that, "Muslims built their first proper mosque in 1661 in Dayoodnagar (Jharkhand) after 450 years of their arrival" and that, later on *madrasas* were set up" and that, "in 1740 it was the first chance when a Muslim known as Hidamatullah Khan was nominated as *jagirdar* of Jalpa in Jharkhand" and finally that the Muslims in Jharkhand had, taken active part in the struggle for Independence as well as in the struggle for a separate state in Jharkhand". See also a souvenir published by the Anjuman Islamia (Ranchi) that was founded by Maulana Abul Azad in 1917. The souvenir discusses the life of "Freedom Fighter" Maulana Abul Kalam Azad whom, "the Muslims of Jharkhand are very proud of", as, "he was from Ranchi and widely respected by Hindus and Muslims alike" and under whose influence, "the Muslims of this region joined the Freedom Movement blindly and instantly". See also another souvenir in Hindi published by the Chhota Nagpur Regional Weaver Society of Ranchi in 1993. This souvenir discusses the life of Haji Abdur Razzaque Ansari (1917-1992) in an article entitled: Ek Bindu Jo Sindhu Ban Gaya (With only one drop of water the whole river Sindhu was created). It describes this founder Chairman of the Chhota Nagpur Regional Handloom Weavers' Co-operative Union as a "prominent Freedom Fighter" as well as a "prominent Momin Leader of the State", who worked for the economic and social emancipation of the weavers community in the Chhota Nagpur region. Lastly, see one article in *The Milli Gazette* (1-15 August 2001: 6) that explains why, "Jharkhandi Muslims should be declared tribals".

25. Md. Rafique Ansari, 4 May 2001, born in 1928 near Hazaribagh. Identified as *shaikh*.

26. *Ashraf* is the plural of *sharif* and Hamza Alavi (2002: 4523n1) writes about these 'elite Muslims': "The Muslim *ashraf* were concentrated in UP and Bihar. With the decay of the pre-colonial state that they dominated (especially in the 18th century) and with the rising power and prosperity of Bengal

under the East India Company (EIC), many Muslim *ashraf* migrated eastwards, and found employment in Murshidabad or with the EIC and settled down in West Bengal. They took with them their languages, Urdu and Persian. There were few Muslim ashraf elsewhere in India, except for Hyderabad under the Nizam".

27. Md. Rafique Ansari, 4 May 2001, born in 1928 in Hazaribagh town (Jharkhand). Identified as "businessman."

28. Imtiaz Ali, 20 December 2000, aged 38 and born in Ranchi city. Identified as *momin* and "businessman."

29. Amanat Ali, 30 November 2000, 72 years old and born in Bundu (Jharkhand). He identified as *momin* and as a "politician by profession."

30. The Momin Conference officially opposed the Muslim League during the 1940s and rejected the latter's 'Islam in Danger agenda'. This Conference wanted to replace this agenda with another one aiming at "correcting the un-Islamic *razil-sharif* (labouring and well-born) divide" (Ghosh 1998: 232).

31. See also the Presidential Address by Amanat Ali during the Chhota Nagpur Santhal Parganas Local Momin Conference on 9 July 1994 entitled "A Big Rally". Venue was the Zeyaull Rahman Ansari Nagpuri Labour Maidan, Sector 4 Bokaro (Jharkhand).

32. Gulam Mohinuddin Ahmad, 4 May 2001, aged between 55 and 60 and born in Hazaribagh (Jharkhand). He said that his forefathers came from Gaya (Bihar).

33. Name changed on request. Interviewed on 1 November 2000. He identified as *ansari* and was aged between 78 and 80.

34. Abdul Hammed Asar, 18 October 2000, aged 76 and born in Ranchi (Jharkhand). Identified as *shaikh iraqi.*

35. Abdul Khalid, 28 July 2001 was born in 1942 in Chaibasa (Jharkhand). It should be realized that Khalid was only four years old in 1946 and might express the opinion his father held around that time and which he later on had adopted as his own. Khalid here gives also the impression that voters

took the elections of 1946 as a voting for or against 'partition'. It should be realised that according in these elections, "the results of which formed the basis for partition, not more than 4 per cent of the Muslim elite decided the fate of the country. Out of 10 per cent that had the right to vote, not more than 60 per cent voted and, out of these 60 per cent, about 40 per cent voted against the Muslim League. Thus, ultimately less than 4 per cent Muslims voted for the partition: 96 per cent of the Muslims had played no role at all in determining the future of India. Either they had no right to vote, or they did not vote, or voted against the Muslim League" (Puniyani 2003: 89). Though, some of our informants said they or their families had voted for the Muslim League (and favoured partition at the time), most of them had never voted either because they were not born at the time or had no voting rights due to poverty or underage.

8

Conclusion: Making an Event out of Partition

Partitioned Countries

The problems of citizens in both the Republic of India as well as in the People's Republic of Bangladesh are manifold. Many of them have started or increased immediately after Sir Cyril Radcliffe, an English barrister who had never even visited South Asia before, drew lines on his map of what till then had been known as British India and part of the British Empire. It has affected "heartlanders" as well as "borderlanders"(Cf. Van Schendel 2005: 377). Clearly, as scholar Willem van Schendel has shown in an extremely thought-provoking study on the Bengal borderlanders, when the Radcliffe line, made public in Delhi on 17 August 1947, turned into "a material reality and a social fact" it hugely impacted "the lives of millions of people today". Now, almost sixty years later, there are border and trade disputes between the two countries and there is conflict related to Ganges River water sharing (*The Economic Times of India*, 23 March 2005), migration (Datta 2004: 122-165), insurgency, the 'infiltrator issue' (Upadhyay 2005), anti-Hindu or anti-Muslim violence, and controversies surrounding gas exports, 'Hindu fundamentalism' in India (Varshney 2002: 70-72) or alternatively 'Islamic fundamentalism in Bangladesh' (Rahim 2001) and 'push back operations' (Ramachandran 2003 and Sen 2003). People contained by the Indo-

Bangladesh border in either country gaze at emaciated rivers or have to cope with floods. They have restricted imports or no buyers for their export. They have minerals but no expertise to exploit them and friends from outside they cannot meet with enemies amongst. They have music but no listeners. Most of these problems and the list is much longer, relate to the particular geographical boundaries of both nations. Rivers stop where they should flow. Goods pile up and do not circulate. Cultures freeze in need of exposure. People are relocated though they desired to stay or see their ways blocked but want to move on. Indeed, the partition of Bengal in 1947 has brought losses for many.[1]

Yet, both countries, and many who live on either side of the border value 1947 and also 'gained', for partition has brought independence too. The year signalled the end of British colonialism and the beginning of new processes of nation building during which partition became looked upon as a necessary evil while the new borders provide many with security, mental as well as physical. The evil lays in the losses. In this book we were concerned, though not solely, with these losses and have described why Hindus in Bangladesh and Muslims in Jharkhand did not gain from partition as both nation-states have turned into partitioned countries that are in fact, ethnic democracies (Peled 2005), majoritarian states or ethnocracies (Samaddar 2003: 25). Other scholars before me have dealt with these losses at great length and described how partition was not only a "political divide, or a division of properties, of assets and liabilities" but also 'divided hearts' (Cf. Van Schendel 2005: 386 note 1). In this study I have shown that partition divides minds till date. State makers in both countries try, and often successfully to attain hegemony (and thus protect the geographical borders that constitute their nation-states) by prescribing mental borders, or an "internally stored cognitive map"[2] to use another frequently used term in border studies. I have illustrated how such state-supported 'internal maps' look(ed) like in the case of

Pakistan, Bangladesh and India and its workings in every-day life of people that live within these states' geographical borders.

In Chapter 2 and 3 I illustrated not only what this 'cognitive map' in Pakistan looked like but also that its borders were contested and finally subverted which also caused the alteration of the very geographical borders that circumscribed the nation-state. Pakistani state-makers had tried to fashion these borders by the implementation of a map in the minds of all Pakistani citizens that was based on a nationalist rhetoric with 'partition' as central organizing principle. In this rhetoric, nation-builders focused on what can be called "Islam in its communal sense" described by Metcalf (2004: 224) as "the place of Pakistan as a homeland and a refuge and as a guarantor of the rights of some fifty million Muslims in India". This was, as shown in Chapter 2, made more poignant by the creation of Pakistani historiography that, Metcalf (2004: 224) explains,

> Reads back into the past the self-conscious religious identity of the present: found heroes in the military conquerors and proponents of legalist, un-eclectic Islam; and generally painted a picture of glory that was to be reclaimed. The anger channelled against India and the pride in a Muslim state was expressed in the 1965 war [...].

Besides Islam, Urdu was chosen as the symbol of excellence of Muslim communal interests and both these markers delineated the mental borders on the cognitive map of the Pakistani state that should have protected its geographical borders (against India). The treatment of Islam by the nation builders had two significant elements. One was the modernist orientation and the other was "the contempt for regional expressions Islam". Indeed as Metcalf (2004: 227) explained, "the particular kind of Islam fostered by the regime was its rejection of regional forms of Islam":

Both Khalid bin Sayeed and Nasim Jawed have argued in analyses of the separation of Bangladesh that the modernist Islam of the regime was much closer to the scripturalist and legalist Islam current in some circles in the West than to the Islam of Bengal. Bengal, with a population almost one-fourth Hindu, and with a tradition of openness to Bengali literature and folkways, was deemed religiously suspect.

The adoption of Urdu in Pakistan as a national language seemed only logical to the new rulers. It was the mother tongue of the *muhajir* who had migrated from north India and settled in cities of Pakistan and it was the second language of elite groups throughout the new country, among others of many of the *ashraf* of East Pakistan. Yet, the decisive factor in the choice of Urdu as national language was its position in Punjab where Urdu had long been, unlike in East Pakistan, the language of education for all communities. Yet, as described in Chapter 3, this 'cognitive map' lacked popular support in particular in East Pakistan. In fact, language proved to be a major source of tension between the two wings and before the first decade after partition was over, Bengali language riots had, at least on paper, assured equal status for Bengali as a national language. Yet, as was seen, this was the beginning of the downfall of the united Pakistani nation-state. Actually, by demanding that Bengali should be East-Pakistan's first language and not Urdu, the Bengali Muslims who had demanded it along with the Bengali Hindus in East Pakistan, had challenged the mental borders on the cognitive map of the Pakistani nation builders that were intended to unite the Muslims and separate them from the Hindus. Therefore, despite the 'grant' for accommodation of Bengali in East Pakistan a legacy of bitterness remained in both wings.

The elections of 1970 saw the decisive victory of Bhutto's Pakistan People's Party in West Pakistan and that of Shaikh Mujibur Rahman's Awami League in East Pakistan. Yet, now the Pakistani leaders were not prepared to make 'further concessions' and resorted to more aggressive policies to eradicate the alternative map in the minds of the East Pakistanis, which embodied borders that united Hindu and Muslim Bengalis and placed them against Pakistanis as an alternative 'other'. The Pakistani failure however to grant Mujib the premiership he had won and to accommodate the six demands for provincial autonomy he had requested, resulted in a civil war that altered the geographical borders of Pakistan as it had existed during these almost 25 years after the event of partition. In short, the process of partition in Pakistan cumulated in yet another partition through first the (successful) challenging of its mental borders and later on the removal of these borders by East Pakistani Bengalis, which caused the breakdown of Pakistan's geographical borders and saw the birth of a third nation-state: Bangladesh.

In Chapter 4, I have argued and illustrated that the new cognitive map in the new nation-state of Bangladesh was however not less hegemonic and its borders, supported by new history writing explicitly sought to unite the citizens of Bangladesh by making 'Bengali Hindus' the 'other' placed in antagonistic relation against 'Bengali Muslims'. I have illustrated how nation-builders transformed Bangladesh into a partitioned society by the enactment of partition rhetoric. According to Rafiuddin Ahmed:

> The role of the state in Bangladesh demonstrates the arbitrary nature of political control and manipulation of symbols by the post-colonial regimes. It also suggests that the historic process of systematisation and articulation of cultural symbols, which had earlier played a critical role in defining and redefining the cultural boundaries of Bengali Islam, has increasingly been replaced by a highly politicised and limited agenda sponsored by authoritarian regimes and fundamentalist groups.

As a result, among others, but not solely as Shelley Feldman (Ahmed 2001: 209-236) describes in the case of women in Bangladesh, 'Bengali Hindus' got marginalized. These Hindus who rather identified as 'Hindu Bengalis' were not only excluded from Bangladesh's historiography but also delinked from the nation-state and relinked with India. Thus this border making on the minds of Bangladeshi nation-makers involved both the spatial as well as the discursive field. The mental borders on the minds of Bangladesh's (self appointed) guardians of the nation-state not only marginalized these Hindus within the geographical borders of the state but also sought their exclusion from the state. The discursive field that remained for them was India.

Chapter 5 and 6, concern nation-building in partition in India. Like in Bangladesh, I illustrate that nation-builders reproduced a partitioned society by the adoption of a partition rhetoric that divides the Hindu majority against the Muslim minority, which as the scholar Vazira Zamindar (quoted in Van Schendel 2005: 395 note 94) concluded, caused Muslims in India to end up "in a discursive no man's land between two [actually three] nations". The discursive space left them neither with Pakistan (or Bangladesh), which they had to identify as 'the other,' nor with India (as they had to pay the price of partition).

The Threat from Within

By the end of Chapter 6 we have therefore arrived at the creation of two partitioned societies, Bangladesh and India through a "theory of the passive revolution" that has taken place ever after 1947 and which has made of partition a process that continues till date. Though partition for both countries also meant independence, this independence bore not many fruits rather partitioned countries faced many losses. Samaddar (2003: 34) so eloquently described what these partitioned nation-states affected that I start this section with his observations of what happens when nation-states adopt partition rhetoric as their main organizing principle:

> First, constitutionalism (whether or not it succeeds) in the new nations naturalizes the dark side, and, promising a return to normalcy, marginalizes the dissenters and heretics. Second, this normalcy, based on an act of violence and hatred, kills the spirit of reconciliation. The polity can then speak only of retributive justice and not of restorative justice. The promised restoration of dignity after the hour of retribution never arrives. Third, democracy becomes organic in other words, intolerant – and the people so defined by democracy refuse to accommodate other peoples, not so defined by democracy, and push the latter out. And finally, the issue of self-determination, which caused the political managers so many sleepless nights, resolves its own dilemmas by a bizarre technique. It kills all other selves to such an extent that there need not be any other self but only the geopolitical self of the aspirant.

Sadly, Samaddar's account above seems quite realistic going through the pages in these book where I describe how partition rhetoric is enacted again and again in both nation states intended to marginalize and even "push out" 'Hindus' in Bangladesh and 'Muslims' in Jharkhand. Yet, Samaddar forgets to mentions that till date not all have, though too many unfortunately have, been 'killed', nor has their selves been killed. This justifies hope that alternatives could be formulated, which can prevent that the grim prediction described above by Samaddar becomes a complete reality.

The example of happenings in East Pakistan and the birth of a new nation Bangladesh described in this book provide reasons for optimism but also should make 'political managers cause sleepless nights'. I have illustrated in the case of Pakistan that "political managers" did not manage to kill all "other selves". Rather, Hindu and Muslim Bengalis successfully resisted the "homogenizing Grand National Narratives" of these Pakistani nation builders and formulated their own narratives with alternative mental others. Furthermore, our example of Muslims in Jharkhand also demonstrates that though people's selves have been and are killed this 'killing' is only temporarily. Narratives described in Chapter 6 indeed describe this 'killing' or rather silencing of voices through the continuous enactment of partition rhetoric in the lives of Muslims in Jharkhand. Yet in Chapter 7, I illustrate that these Muslims did not remain silent however. Though they are still silenced and their narratives have no place in official the state-supported partition rhetoric, their narratives show the limited result of the homogenizing grand narrative that state managers try to impose upon them. Besides, Bihar has been divided and though, like the Hindus in Bangladesh, they have to find new 'others' and 'other selves' (thus new inner maps) in order to become accommodated within the new geographical boundaries of the states in which they now want to live, they are happy about these new geographical boundaries.

Yet, this should not allow nation-builders to sit back and stop worrying. The fact that Muslims in Jharkhand and Hindus in Bangladesh have not challenged their states' geographical borders and rather want to become accommodated within them does not mean that this always will remain so. The example of East Pakistan demonstrates that there is reason for worry. In another context, Jamal (2004: 433-471) showed that in Israel to ethnic citizenship model dominant in Israeli political culture does not incorporate the national or cultural identity of all Israeli citizens equally, rendering "Israeli patriotism" among Arab citizens more questionable. In this case and as a result, Arab patriotic attachment had gradually shifted from civic Israeli to Palestinian patriotism and demands for a separate homeland. In the case of Bangladesh, the continuous enactment of partition rhetoric in the lives of 'Pakistanis' made some people change their 'selves'. They identified as 'minorities' as Bengalis and separated themselves from the majority of Pakistanis. Yet, when this alternative cognitive map had not the desired results they fought for another division and 'got' Bangladesh and thus decisively altered geopolitical space with their alternative maps. As long as partition rhetoric remains reproducing partitioned societies the possibility of new geographical partitions remains real as some web messages demonstrate. On 5 February 2002 one Pratik Majumdar felt that, "Hindus in Bangladesh must demand a separate Homeland":

All Hindus in Bangladesh must unite and take up arms. They must all be together to defend themselves from Islamic terror. They all must start a movement against the Government like killing Bangladeshi Muslims, destroying mosques etc. They must demand a separate homeland for the minority Hindus where only Hindus will be allowed to stay. India must help the minorities and take this matter to U.N.O. Jai Hinduttva, Hindustan Zindabad.

Times New Network also mentioned on 4 February 2003 in a message written by one Aloke Banerjee in Kolkata (!) that a "provisional Hindu Republic" had been established in Bangladesh six months before with the declared objective of forming a "Hindu Republic of Bir Banga" having its "capital" at Shaktigarh in the Chittagong hills. Though the 'Republic' was still on paper, "a supreme revolutionary council" and a "17-member interim government in exile" had already been formed, "to launch an armed struggle" and "bring about a partition of Bangladesh and form the Hindu Republic comprising almost the entire southern half of the country". A "national flag" had also been designed "bearing pictures of symbolic weapons on a saffron background" and a national seal "with a picture of weapons of the Hindu Gods" (quoted in *Muslim India*, Vol. 21, nos. 1-7, January-July 2003: 313).

Though it is not surprising that the VHP, a conservative Hindu party in India extended its support, as this kind of 'partition' neatly fits in its mental map, from the interviews we conducted in Bangladesh I do not get an impression that this kind of 'solutions' are advanced by Hindu in Bangladesh themselves (yet it certainly is supported by some among those who left Bangladesh and ncw live in West Bengal as well as by some other West Bengali Hindus). They rather just leave Bangladesh, as illustrated by quite some scholars quoted in this book. Yet, I have also shown that this is not the only solution Hindu Bengalis propose. The narratives quoted in Chapter 4, illustrate this. Besides, these Hindus in Bangladesh have experienced, like the Muslims in Jharkhand, that another partition is not a solution for their problems. These minorities realize that if they use the changed borders of their mind in support of such demands for changes in the geographical borders of their native places, it only will attest the hegemony of official partition rhetoric that divides rather than unites populations with all bloody consequences and a repetition of gains and losses. And, what is more it remains always unsure who will gain and who loose after such a partition. My study therefore shows that partitions do neither provide long-term solutions to (ethnic-religious) conflicts nor do they prevent further conflict.[3] We therefore propose other solutions that can mitigate contemporary domestic and international conflicts between and within India and Bangladesh and which, certainly, will ease the contemporary suffering of Hindus in Bangladesh and Muslims in India caused by the assiduous enactment of partition in their lives. These 'solutions' might even be of use to populations in partitioned countries elsewhere Suchas in Pakistan CF. Kumar 2005.

Towards De-Partitioned Societies

The task is thus clear. Partition is causing more losses (and potential losses) than gains and the only way towards less suffering is to end partition, i.e. to stop the process of partition and make it an event. This is first of all needed in order to lessen the sufferings of Muslims in India and Hindus in Bangladesh who now live as minorities, silenced by the threat that their selves will be 'killed'. Yet, the example of Bangladesh (and in some respects Jharkhand as well) should make even political managers realize that this silencing does not work. Pakistani nation-builders eagerly protecting its geographical borders by the imposition of a mental map that imprisoned the voices of Bengalis lost a part of their nation and state. One therefore wonders what drives these nation-makers to sustain making partition "the universal act in the age of liberal democracy", and, "the institutionalised form" of their domestic and geopolitical histories" (Samaddar 2003: 34), as the (potential) losses seem much more than the gains. What is needed therefore are de-partitioned societies where nobody is the 'other' or at least not permanently so. To be sure, this surely is not an argument against (temporary) 'reservations'[4] for minorities per se but partition creates permanent others and antagonized others at that. In that sense partition is completely in contraction with the liberal democratic system propagated in both Bangladesh as well as India, as in these partitioned societies the otherness of people is imposed upon people. In a de-partitioned democratic society, people can choose and are allowed to be 'the other', which makes all the difference.

In present-day partitioned Indian and Bangladesh society however, which seek to guard their geographical borders, those who choose to identify as the other are not only 'suspect' but also silenced or pushed out. As I have illustrated in this book however silencing and deportation do not guarantee the stability of geographical borders. Instead what is needed is, rather than silencing, listening. Till date the two nation-states, who reproduce the partition rhetoric on daily basis or during particular and crucial moments, have considered no alternative than the imprisonment and silencing of alternative narratives that oppose the borders embodied in the partition narratives espoused by these nation-builders. Listening to the voices as exposed in Chapters 4 and 7 of this study reveals however that such suspicion is unfounded. Rather, as this study also shows, ignoring these alternative narratives or even oppressing them can produce much more threatening outcomes for nation-builders, as the case of East Pakistan clearly shows. These nation-builders have still time however, time to stop silencing and start listening to these alternative narratives. This not only concerns narratives of 'minorities' in both countries but also implies listening to alternative 'cognitive maps' proposed by members of so-called majority members.

O'Connell (2001: 201-202) for instance describes that in Bangladesh a tradition 'humanity (*manabata / lok-hitata*) exists "as a shared non-partisan trans-communal ideal" which O'Connell feels, "might reasonably hope to motivate a broad cross-section of citizens, each in his or her particular way, to contribute to such overriding national objectives as economic development and population control, social justice and responsible politics". Yet, O'Connell states that till date, none of the Bangladeshi 'nation-builders', have properly listened to these voices of members of the majority community let alone to those citizens delegated to the other side of the border. In fact, even these majority member narratives are "symbolically marginalized, its religio-cultural heritage apparently being ignored or neglected". This O'Connell severely regrets as,

> Moreover, to the extent that the ideal of humanity can be affirmed and accentuated in the life of any community, so much the more effectively can those

within that community who feel strong about human life, refute and challenge those who would project as a less humane, less tolerant interpretation of their own community and its ideals.

Yet, listening is just the beginning, the first step that nation-builders serious in their (self-appointed) task to protect the geographical borders of the nation have to take. The road towards the creation of de-partitioned societies is much longer and comprise much more than a patient listening. The narratives of our informants are clearly narratives of rooting and therefore exactly the opposite from what partition rhetoric wants or fears them to be, i.e. narratives of uprooting. The selves, formulated by our informants in both India as well as Bangladesh, are not 'the others' as partitioned rhetoric rules them to be. One could have expected that, as often is the case in other contexts, the experience of discrimination based on religion as caused by the enactment of the partition rhetoric among these religious minorities would have provoked the Muslims in Jharkhand and Hindus in Bangladesh to target *adivasis* and Bangladeshi Muslims respectively as a negative out-group. Instead, as illustrated in this book, Hindus in Bangladesh, or at least those interviewed by us, identify as Bangladeshis and label Hindus in West Bengal (India) as the (though not always antagonistic) 'others'. In similar fashion interviewed Muslims in Jharkhand strongly identify as Jharkhandis and label the 'Muslims in (if not of) Bihar as 'the other'.

In doing so, these Hindus in Bangladesh and Muslims in Jharkhand could therefore perfectly be accommodated in their place of residence as equal citizens along with citizens of other religious denominations with whom they share their 'selves'. Their problem is however that they are not. Partition rhetoric 'forbids' them to identify with the 'locals' or as 'locals', the majority: They have to pay the price of partition. If listened to properly, these nation builders who reproduce a rhetoric that even endangers their own geo-political projects, will realize however that these narratives actually constitute a redemption of partition and can be considered as the price they have paid for the losses caused by partition. Without having had to do so, these minorities have, however, now paid enough and it is time for them to exchange 'retributive justice' for 'restorative justice'. It is time not only for these minorities but also for nation-builders less they will face more partitions, as the selves of these minorities are neither monolithic nor unchangeable.[5] Once these nation-builders have properly listened to these minorities (as well as to members of the 'majority community' who project different cognitive maps), and have convinced themselves that it is in their own interest and thus the interest of the nation-state they want protect or rather built up, to pay them attention, they can then start extending 'restorative justice'.

This is however not a small task and does not necessarily encompasses the framing of new laws or even the constitutions in these countries. These are actually generally fine and can be accommodated in de-partitioned societies. Though, a few Acts might have to be changed or omitted as institutionalisation of partition rhetoric has taken place. O'Connell (2001: 202) for Bangladesh concluded:

> A national Bangladeshi commitment to humanity (or humanism) need not, though it might, involve alteration of the Bangladesh Constitution's declaration of principles. Clearly, however, it would entail a change in how Bangladeshi Muslims, especially the more modernized elite, think, talk, and feel about the meaning of being Muslim in relation to national identity and purpose.

Thus, and as argued in this book, it is rather the unwritten laws in both nation-states that have to be changed, i.e. the discursive space has to be opened up. In partitioned India, Muslims do not exist in any other shape than as 'the other' and border-making practices make them live in a discursive no man's land between three nations (Cf. Zamindar quoted in Van Schendel 2005: 395n94). In Bangladesh, Hindus do only exist as the 'other' and the only discursive space they have links them to India. The opening up of this discursive space by freeing alternative narratives both projected by members of the so-called majority as well as those by the 'minority communities', which are still imprisoned by partition rhetoric in both nation-states, is a tremendous task however as it encompasses the complete alteration of the 'internally stored cognitive maps' of the nation-builders (often members of the 'majority group') in both nation-states.

In other words, the minds of the majorities as well as minorities, in both countries have to be 'de-partitioned' or to use another word, 'de-colonized'. Though the minds of the people we interviewed in Bangladesh and India do appear to be already freed as they have formulated alternative narratives with different mental borders than those embodied in partition rhetoric, their accounts of suffering indicate that such a de-partitioning of the minds of other members who identify as religious minorities in both countries might also be needed as they, according to the narrative accounts we collected, also could act as 'perpetrators' who enacted partition rhetoric in the lives of these interviewed Muslims in Jharkhand and Hindus in Bangladesh. It will not suffice to address the problem only constitutionally as both nation-states have been exploiting "tho communal card in its politics", "not in constitutional terms but in actual behaviour" (Ahmed 2002: 27). Such a de-partitioning of minds is therefore a much more difficult task than the refashioning of laws as after all we are handling a "root-metaphor" (Cf. Gupta 2000: 51-60). Yet, of course, the judiciary has to be addressed as well but this task requires psychic, political and rhetorical work that reaches across religious and national divides. It needs to look, in other words, at what Ashis Nandy calls "isomorphic oppressions" and demands changing the "unconscious", "emotions" (Cf. Bhargava) and the "unwritten" as it is there where in particular partition rhetoric is reiterated (Cf. Cash and Schwab 2004: 137).

This, at first, might appear an impossible task but though I agree it is a tremendous task, it is only impossible if there is no (political) will among the nation-builders of the country to embark upon the task. If convinced however that this effort at de-partitioning might bear the fruits of independence so much desired but 'lost' due to partition, and avoid further partitioning, these nation-builders should start with the re-writing of (history) textbooks. In this respect it will not suffice, as advised by scholar Sumit Sarkar (The *Hindu*, July 5, 2005), to just modify "the dominant narratives" in order to, "recognise complications and cross currents" but more to develop books that introduce, what to Sarkar's mind (and to my mind) is the most important potential of the subject:

> This is a sense that, everything changes, nothing is eternal, sacred, or 'natural' since the social world is made by human beings and therefore open to transformation. The past in many ways was a different country (the best answer, really, for countering the charge that 'sentiments' are getting hurt, much heard in BJP times but not confined to them). Religious communities, nations, etc. do not have absolutely continuous histories, and so blaming the present generation for the misdeeds [or perceived misdeed] of some of their forefathers is no more than racism.

This also will require the replacement of history textbooks that approach history as a chronological study of 'nation-states' by an approach that studies various types of societies (not nation states per se) in a non-chronological and thematic way. The abolishment of the difference between 'history' and 'memory' is also recommendable or at least the revision of the (false) belief that 'history' (and in particular state-supported history, often written with a capital H) is somewhat outside systems of knowledge and power (Cf. Radstone and Hodgkin 2004: 11). Lastly, in order to avoid that stories of independence, do not end up as partition narratives, alternative narratives of independence such as those exposed in this book should be collected from among other heart- and borderlanders and included in state-supported narratives that then will stop being partition stories (only). Yet, in societies such as Bangladesh and India in which even among the 'majority' the literacy level is relatively extremely low, a transformation of history textbooks alone will not bear many fruits. In order to replace partition rhetoric with the 'counter voices' that will alter the existing mental maps in both countries that reproduce partitioned societies, we need to think of other means and media (Sebastian Periannan 2004: 52-61) (such as cinema, the press, television, radio, internet and literature), that will prevent that Hindus in Bangladesh are relegated to India and Muslims in India are ghettoised within their own country (Ravinder Kaur in: *Hindustan Times*, October 10, 2005). This might wash clean the "unclean partition" (Chaturvedi 2002: 149) and make an event out of partition. These alternative means and media possibly designed by national and international campaigns "for reconciliation and harmony" (Iyer 1996) and in which 'civil society' in both countries has to play a crucial role (Aiyar and Malik 2004) should emphasize that pluralism and diversity of selves do not necessarily mean a threat to the geographical boundaries that form nation states. This ideally should bring about nation-states without mental borders among its citizens, i.e. the end of partition and its "pathological politics" (Ahmed 2002: 27). This is the kind of nation-state Jinnah said he intended to establish in which, "You can belong to any religion or caste or creed- that has nothing to do with the business of the State. We are all citizens and equal citizens of one State" (Ainslie T. Embree quoted in *Outlook*, 23 August 2004: 18).

Referring to the discussion in India on the 'secular' credentials of Jinnah triggered of by Advani's speech during his momentous five days in Pakistan and presented in my introduction, this book has shown that these kind of discussions if not taken in the right spirit are if not harmful, quite futile. What matters is that Jinnah and for that matter Indian Nehru, Bangladeshi Sheikh Mujibur Rahman and a host of other nation builders, have not succeeded in formulating such policies that delivered the fruits of independence to all citizens of their countries. Yet, there might have been some political dividend in Advani's statement too, as Muralidharan (2005: 2381) rightly suggest:

> Advani's is the first high-profile political resignation (June 7) occasioned by conflicting readings of history. In this sense, it limits the potentiality of history being a quarry from which prejudices can be mined for political advantage. It is likely to provoke a re-examination of the 'Good Queen Bess and Bad King John's school of historiography that has long dominated pedagogy in the subject. And to the extent that the past is not dead– indeed not even past – it could trigger a reconstruction of a common history for the people of south Asia that allows room for reconciliation in the future.

References

1. With marvelous empirical material, Willem van Schendel (2005) demonstrates however how the Bengal borderlanders are not only negatively affected by these international borders, a border making that has not even been completed till date, but at times challenge and subvert them and turn them to their economic, political or social advantage.

2. Willem van Schendel (2005: 375-376) defines such "cognitive maps" as "organized representations of people's spatial environment and their own place in it". Yet, Van Schendel adds that sometimes these cognitive maps "can be stored externally in the form of physical maps, but usually they are

not. Studying the changing geographies of a borderland therefore requires us to access 'maps in minds', internally stored cognitive maps".

3. See for a similar conclusion: Radha Kumar, "Settling Partition Hostilities. Lessons Learnt, the Options Ahead", in: Deschaumes and Ivekovi (2003: 3-19).

4. See for a debate on Muslims and reservations in India, for instance: Sunita Gangwal, "Reservation V/s Social Justice", in: *Indian Journal of Secularism*, vol. 8, no. 2 (July-September 2004): 66-73. See related to this issue also an article on '*Dalit* Muslims': N. Jamal Ansari, "Oppression of *Dalit* Muslims through Constitution of India", in: *Indian Journal of Secularism*, vol. 8, no. 2 (July-September 2004): 73-77.

5 This means that at times and in some places 'Muslims' (and 'Hindus') will strongly identify as a religious community and at other instances and in other places as Pandey emphasized in the case of Muslims in India they will adhere "somewhat loosely to the label of Muslim". Pandey also emphasized that before partition, some people who later on became identified as 'Muslims' such as the "Meos of Mewat, the Momins of UP and Bihar and the Mapillas of Malabar", had, "for long adhered somewhat loosely to the label of Muslim", in Pandey (2001: 132). See also Joya Chatterjee, "The Bengali Muslim: A Contradiction in Terms? An Overview of the Debate on Bengali Muslim Identity," in *Islam Communities and the Nation: Muslim Identities in South Asia and Beyond* (New Delhi: Manohar, 1998: 265-283). In similar way, and corresponding to the narratives I collected in Jharkhand, Peter Gottschalk described the narratives of present-day Muslims in Bihar and avoiding the dichotomy between myth and history, he demonstrated how these narratives express group memories of the past in the context of social relationships in the present. These stories reveal that, this ever-changing context involves a complex interaction of multiple identities that often transcends the simple divide of Hindu and Muslim. See, Gottschalk, Beyond Hindu & Muslim. See also, Shail Mayaram, *Resisting Regimes: Myth, Memory and the Shaping of a Muslim Identity* (Delhi: Oxford University Press, 1997).

Bibliography

Note: The titles of those books/articles/archival/web material and newspaper reports fully enumerated in the main text or notes at the end of the main text and which are not referred to later on in the main text have not been included in this bibliography.

Adeney, Katherine. "Constitutional Centring: National Formation and Consociational Federalism in India and Pakistan", in: Commonwealth and Comparative Politics, Vol. 40, no. 3, (November), 2002: 8-33.

Adhikari, Abanti. "The Economic and Intellectual Origins of Movements of Protests in East Paksitan (1947-1971)", in: J.K. Ray (ed.) Asia Annual 2000 (New Delhi: Shipra 2000): 77-93.

Ahmad, Imtiaz and Helmut Reifeld (ed.) Lived Islam in South Asia. Adaptation, Accommodation & Conflict (New Delhi: Social Science Press, 2004).

Ahmad, Kamruddin. The Social History of East Pakistan (Dacca: Mrs. Amina Khatun, 1967).

Ahmad, Khan, Muin-ud-din. Muslim Struggle for Freedom in Bengal. From Blassey to Pakistan, A.D. 1757-1947 (Dhaka: Islamic Foundation of Bangladesh, 1982).

Ahmad, Riaz "Gujarat Violence: Meaning and Implications", in: Economic and Political Weekly, (18 May, 2002).

Ahmed, Imtiaz, Abhijit Dasgupta and Kathinka Sinha-Kerkhoff (eds.). State, Society and Displaced People in South Asia, Dhaka: The University Press Limited, 2004).

Ahmed, Ishtiaq. "The 1947 Partition of India: A Paradigm for Pathological Politics in India and Pakistan", in: Asian Ethncity, vol. 3, no. 1, (March) 2002: 9-28.

Ahmed, Ishtiaq. State, Nation and Ethnicity in Contemporary South Asia (London and New York, 1996).

Ahmed, Khaled. "Pakistan. Violation of the Rights of the Minorities in Pakistan", in: Sumanta Banerjee (ed.), Shrinking Space: Minority Rights in South Asia (Kathmandu: South Asia Forum for Human Rights, 1999): 119-137.

Ahmed, Rafiuddin. The Bengal Muslims, 1871-1906: A Quest for Identity (New York: Oxford University Press, 1981).

Ahmed, Rafiuddin. (ed.). Understanding the Bengal Muslims. Interpretative Essays (New Delhi: Oxford University Press, 2001).

Ahmed, Salahuddin. Bangladesh. Past and Present (New Delhi: A.P.H. Publishing Corporation, 2004).

Akbar, M.J. Riot after Riot: Reports on Caste and Communal Violence in India (New Delhi: Penguin, 1988).

Alam Javeed and Suresh Sharma. "Remembering Partition. A dialogue between", in: Seminar, 461 (January) 1998): 98.

Alavi, Hamza. "The State in Postcolonial Societies: Pakistan and Bangladesh", in: Kathleen Gough and Hari P. Sharma. Imperialism and Revolution in

South Asia (New York: Monthly Review Press, 1973): 145-173.

Alavi, Hamza. "Misreading Partition Road Signs", in: Economic and Political Weekly, vol. xxxvii, nos. 44-45 (November 2-8 / 9-15, 2002): 4515-4523.

Ali, A.F. Imam. Hindu-Muslim Community in Bangladesh (Delhi: Kanishka Publishing House, 1992)

Anisuzzaman. "Towards A Redifinition of Identity: The Case of the Bengali Language in East Bengal, 1947-71", in Sampark , (January-March, 1999): 23-42.

Ansari, Ashfaque Husain. Momin Conference Ki Dastavezi Tareekh (Documented History of the Momin Conference 1926-2001) (Delhi: All India Momin Conference, 2000): 237-255 (translated from Urdu by Md. Masoom Reza).

Ansari, Hasan Nishat. "Historical Geography of Bihar on the eve of the Early Turkish Invasions", in: Journal of the Bihar Research Society, vol. xlix, nos. 1-4 (January-December 1963): 253-260.

Ansari, Nishat Hasan. "Tirhut (North Bihar) and Bihar (South Bihar) under Mohammed Bin Tughluq: A.D 1325-1351," in: The Journal of the Bihar Research Society, L: Parts I-IV (January to December 1964): 59-72.

Arnold, T.W. The Preaching of Islam: A History of the Propagation of the Muslim Faith (New York: AMS Press, 1974).

Aziz, K.K. A History of the Idea of Pakistan, vol. 1 (Lahore, 1987).

Bagchi. Jasodhara and Subhoranjan Dasgupta (eds.). The Trauma and the Triumph: Gender and Partition in Eastern India (Calcutta: Stree, 2003).

Bajpai, Kanti. "Minorities and Majorities", in D.L. Sheth and Gurpreet Mahajan (eds.), Minority Identities and the Nation-State (New Delhi Oxford University Press, 1999): 220-242.

Bal, Ellen. "An Untold Story of the Partition: The Garos of Northern Mymensingh", in: Imtiaz Ahmed, Abhijit Dasgupta and Kathinka Sinha-Kerkhoff (eds.), State, Society and Displaced People in South Asia (Kolkata: The University Press Limited, 2004): 245-279.

Banerjee, Mangobinda. A Historical Outline of Pre-British Chhota Nagpur: From the Earliest Times to 1765 (Ranchi: Educational Publications, 1989) (reprint of 1942).

Banerjee, Sumanta. (ed.). Shrinking Space: Minority Rights in South Asia (Kathmandu: South Asia Forum for Human Rights, 1999).

Bannerji, Himani. "Partition and Its Meanings", in: Economic and Political Weekly, vol. xxxix, no. 34, 2004 (August 21-27): 3806-3810.

Barkat, Abul (ed.). An Inquiry into Causes and Consequences of Deprivation of Hindu Minorities in Bangladesh through the Vested Property Act (Dhaka: PRIP Trust, 2000).

Barkat, Abul. Shafique Uz Zaman, Azizur Rahman and Avjit Poddar, Political Economy of the Vested Property Act in Rural Bangladesh (Dhaka: Association for Land Reform and Development (ALRD), 1997)

Basu, Mrinal Kumar. "Self-assertion of local communities. Namasudra-Muslim Riots in early Twentieth Century East Bengal", in: Ranjit Kumar Roy, Retrieving Bengal's Past: Society and Culture in the Nineteenth and Twentieth Century (Calcutta: Rabindra Bharati University, 1995): 139-167.

Basu, Partha Pratim. "Religious Cleavage, Politics and Communalism in India", in: Rakhahari Chatterji, Politics India. The State-Society Interface (Delhi: Intl. Academic Publishers, 2001): 259-282.

Baxter, Craig and Syedur Rahman. Historical Dictionary of Bangladesh (New Delhi: Vision Books, 2004).

Bhargava, Rajeev. "History, Nation and Community. Reflections on Nationalist Historiography of India and Pakistan", in: Economic an Political Weekly, vol. xxxv, no. 4 (22-28 January), 2000: 193-200.

Bharucha, Rustom. "Muslims and Others. Anecdotes, Fragments and Uncertainties of Evidence", in: Economic and Political Weekly, (October 4-10), vol. xxxviii, no. 40 (2003): 4238-4250.

Bhowmick. N.C. and Bashudeb Dhar, Samprodaik Boisomya kar Swarthe? (In who's interest is communalism?) (Bengali) (Dhaka: Sasatta Prakashan, 1998).

Bruner, M. Lane. Strategies of Remembrance: The Rhetorical Dimensions of National Identity Construction (Colombia: University of South Carolina Press, 2002).

Cash, John and Gabriele Schwab. "'When they say that your people do not exist, how does that make you feel?'", in: Postcolonial Studies, vol. 7, no. 2 (2004): 133-137.

Chakrabarty, Bidyut (ed.). Communal Identity in India. Its Construction and Articulation in the Twentieth Century (New Delhi: Oxford University Press, 2003).

Chakrabarty, Bidyut. "Fluidity and Compartments. Hindus, Muslims and Partition", in: Bidyut Chakrabarty (ed.), Communal Identity in India. Its Construction and Articulation in the Twentieth Century (New Delhi: Oxford University Press, 2003): 75-109.

Chakrabarty, Dipesh. "Remembered Villages. Representation of Hindu-Bengali Memories in the Aftermath of the Partition", in: Economic and Political Weekly (August 10, 1996): 2143-2151.

Chakravartty, Gargi. Coming Out of Partition: Refugee Women in Bengal (New Delhi: Bluejay Books, 2005).

Chandhoke, Neera. "Rethinking Rights. A Response to the Needs of a Multi religious Society", in: Social Action, vol. 47, no. 3 (July-September 1997): 272-304.

Chatterji, Joya. "The Fashioning of a Frontier: The Radcliffe Line and Bengal's Border Landscape, 1947-52", in: Modern Asian Studies, vol. 33, no. 1 (1999): 185-242.

Chatterji, Joya. "The Aftermath of Partition: Muslims in West Bengal, 1947-67". On: http://www.aasianst.org/absts/2003abst/South/sessions.htm.

Chaturvedi, Sanjay. "Process of Othering in the case of India and Pakistan", in Tijdschrift voor Economische and Sociale Geografie, vol. 93, no. 2, (May) 2002: 149-159.

Chitkara, M.G. Bangladesh: Mujib to Hasina (New Delhi: APH Publishing Corporation, 1997).

Choudhury Niren C. and Bhowmik, Sharit K. "Migration of Chota Nagpur Tribals to West Bengal", in: M.S.A. Rao (ed.), Studies in Migration: Internal in India and International (Calcutta: ICSSR, 1986).

Choudhury, Serajul Islam. " Some Aspects of Nationalism of the Bengalis", in: The Journal of the Asiatic Society of Bangladesh (Humanities), vol. 42, no. 1 (June) 1997: 1-39.

Choudhury, Serajul Islam. Middle Class and the Social Revolution in Bengal. An Incomplete Agenda (Dhaka: Oxford University Press Limited, 2002).

Corbridge, Stuart; Jewitt, Sarah and Kumar, Sanjay. Jharkhand. Environment, Develoment, Ethnicity (New Delhi: Oxford University Press, 2004).

Cunningham, Hilary and Josiah McC. Heyman, "Introduction: Mobilities and Enclosures at Borders", in: Identities. Global Studies in Culture and Power, vol. 11 (2004): 289-302.

Das, Suranjan. Communal Riots in Bengal 1905-1947 (Delhi: Oxfod University Press, 1991).

Dasgupta, Subhoranjan. "Imagined Authenticity and State Formation: Afghanistan and Bangladesh", in: Mainstream (January 26) 2002: 19-23.

Datta, Nonica "Partition and Many Nationalisms", in: Economic and Political Weekly, xl, no. 28 (July 9), 2005: 3000-3002.

Datta, Sreeradha. Bangladesh. A Fragile Democracy (New Delhi: Shipra, 2004).

Datta, V.N. "Islam and Pakistan's Identity", in: Economic and Political Weekly,vol. xxxix, no. 39, 25 (September-October 1) 2004: 4329-4333.

Desai, Radhika. "Tryst with Fate. India and Pakistan in the War on Terrorism", in: Economic and Political Weekly, vol. xxxvii, no. 33 (August 17-23) 2002: 3456-3464.

Deschaumes, Chislaine Glasson and Rada Ivekoviæ (eds.) Divided Countries, Separated Cities. The Modern Legacy of Partition (New Delhi: Oxford University Press, 2003) (First published as Transeuropéennes, no. 19/20, winter, 2000-2001).

Dixit, J.N. Liberation and Beyond (Dhaka: University Press Limited, 1999).

Eaton, Richard. The Rise of Islam and the Bengal Frontier, 1204-1760 (Delhi: Oxford University Press, 1997).

Fazal, Tanveer. "Religion and Language in the Formation of Nationhood in Pakistan and Bangladesh" in: Robinson, Rowena (ed.)., Sociology of Religion in India (New Delhi: Sage, 2004): 275-302.

Fein, Lisa C. "Symbolic Boundaries and National Borders: The Construction of an Estonian Russian Identity", in: Nationalities Papers, vol. 33, no. 3 (September 2005): 333-344.

Feldman, Shelley. "Gender and Islam in Bangladesh: Metaphor and Myth", in: Ahmed, Rafiuddin. (ed.)., Understanding the Bengal Muslims. Interpretative Essays (New Delhi: Oxford University Press, 2001): 209-236.

Foucault, Michel. "Is it Useless to Revolt?" in: Philosophy and Social Criticism, vol. 8 (1981): 5-9.

Franda, Marcus. Bangladesh: The First Decade (New Delhi: South Asian Publishers, 1982).

Frøystad, Kathinka. Blended Boundaries. Caste, Class, and Shifting Faces of 'Hinduness' in a North Indian City (New Delhi: Oxford University Press, 2005).

Gankovsky, Y.V. and Polanskaya, L.R. History of Pakistan (Moscow: Nauka, 1964).

Ghosh, Gautam (ed.)., "God is a Refugee: Nationalism, Morality and History in the 1947 Partition of India", Partition, Unification, Nation: Imagined Moral Communities in Modernity. Special Issue of Social Analysis (South Australia: University of Adelaide, vol. 42, no.1, 1998): 33-62.

Ghosh, Papiya. "Muttahidah qaumiyat in aqalliat Bihar: The Imarat i Shariah, 1921-1947", in: The Indian Economic and Social History Review, vol. 34, no. 1 (1997): 1-20.

Ghosh, Papiya. "Partition's Biharis," in: Mushirul Hasan (ed.), Islam, Communities and the Nation: Muslim Identities in South Asia and Beyond (New Delhi: Manohar, 1998): 229-264.

Gordon, Leonard A. Bengal: The Nationalist Movement 1876-1940 (New Delhi: Manohar, 1979).

Gottschalk, Peter. Beyond Hindu and Muslim: Multiple Identity in Narratives from Village. India (Oxford / New York: Oxford University Press, 2000).

Grare, Frédéric (ed.), The Muslims of the Indian Sub-continent after the 11th September Attacks (New Delhi: India Research Press, 2002).

Greenberg, Jonathan D. "Divided lands, phantom limbs: partition in the Indian subcontinent, Palestine, China, and Korea", in: Journal of International Affairs, vol. 57, no. 2 (Spring): 2004: 7-31 (Special issue on Land: Borders, Identity, Rights).

Guha, B.S. Studies in Social Tensions among the Refugees from Eastern Pakistan, Memoir no. 1 (Delhi: Manager of Publications, Department of Anthropology, Government of India, 1959).

Guhathakurta, Meghna, "Communal Politics in South Asia and the Hindus of Bangladesh", in: Hussain, Monirul and Ghosh Lipi (eds.), Communal Politics in South Asia and the Hindus of Bangladesh (India: Manak Publications, 2002): 70-87.

Guhathakurta, Meghna. "Minority Rights, Identity Politics and Gender in Bangladesh: Current Problems and Issues", on: www.meghbarta.org/2004/january/gender.html (2004).

Guhathakurta, Mehgna and Suraiya Begum. "Bangladesh: Displaced and Dispossessed", in: Paula Banerjee, Sabyasachi Basu Ray Chaudhury and Samir Kumar Das, Internal Displacement in South Asia. The Relevance of UN's Guiding Principle (New Delhi: Sage, 2005): 175-213.

Gupta, Dipankar. "Secularisation and Minoritisation. Limits of Heroic Thought", in: Economic and Political Weekly, vol. xxx, no. 35 (September 2) 1995: 2203-2207.

Gupta, Dipankar. Culture, Space and the Nation-state. From Sentiment to Structure (New Delhi: Sage, 2000).

Gupta, Dipankar. "Limits of Tolerance. Prospects of Secularism in India after Gujarat", in: Economic and Political Weekly, vol. xxxvii, no. 46 (16-22 November), 2002: 4615-4620.

Haque, C. Emdad. "The Dilemma of 'Nationhood' and Religion: A Survey and Critique of Studies on Population Displacement Resulting from the Partition of the Indian Subcontinent", in: Journal of Refugee Studies, vol. 8, no. 2, (1995): 185-209.

Hartmann, Betsy and James Boyce. A Quiet Violence: View from a Bangladesh Village, (London: Zed Press, 1983).

Hasan, Mushirul. "Memories of a Fragmented Nation: Rewriting the Histories of India's Partition", in: Economic and Political Weekly, vol. xxxiii, no. 41 (10 October) 1998: 2667.

Hasan, Mushirul. Islam in the Subcontinent. Muslims in a Plural Society (New Delhi: Manohar, 2002).

Huq, Abul F. "The Problem of National Identity in Bangladesh", in: Journal of Social Studies, vol. 24, no.1, 1984: 47-73.

Hussain, Monirul and Lipi Ghosh. Religious Minorities in South Asia, vol. I (India: Manak Publications, 2002): 70-87.

India's Minorities (Delhi: Publications Division, Ministry of Information and Broadcasting, Old Secretariat, 1948).

Iyer, Ramaswamy, R. "Hindus and Muslims: Towards a New Modus Vivendi", in: Economic and Political Weekly, vol. xxxi, no. 30 (July 27), 1996: 2034-2040.

Jalal, Ayesha. The Sole Spokesman: Jinnah, the Muslim League, and the Demand for Pakistan (Cambridge: Cambridge University Press 1985).

Jamal, Amal. "The Ambiguities of Minority Patriotism: Love for Homeland versus State among Palestinian Citizens of Israel", in: Nationalism and Ethnic Politics, vol. 10, no. 3 (Autumn), 2004: 433-471.

Jha, Jata Shankar. Aspects of the History of Modern Bihar (Patna: Kashi Prasad Jayaswal Research Institute, 1988).

Jha, Shefali. "Secularism in the Constituent Assembly Debates, 1946-1950", in: Economic and Political Weekly, vol. xxxvii, no. 30 (July 27-August.2, 2002): 3175-3180.

Kabir, Muhammad Ghulam Minority Politics in Bangladesh (New Delhi: Vikas Publishing House, 1980).

Kabir, Muhammad Ghulam. Minority Politics in Bangladesh (Dacca: Nawroze Kitabistan, 1980).

Kamal, Justice Mustafa. Bangladesh Constitution: Trends and Issues (Dhaka: University of Dhaka, 1994).

Kamaluddin, A.F.M. 'Refugee Problems in Bangladesh', in: Kosinski, L.A. and Elahi, K.M. (eds.), Population and Development in South Asia (Holland: D. Reidel Publishing Company, 1985): 221-236.

Kaul, S. Partitions of Memory. The Afterlife of the Division of India (New Delhi: Permanent Black, 2001).

Kaviraj, Sudipta. "The Imaginary Institution of India", in Partha Chatterjee and Gyanendra Pandey (eds), Subaltern Studies VII: Writings on South Indian History and Society (Delhi: Oxford University Press, 1992).

Khan, Mohammed Roya. What Price Freedom (Chennai, 1969) (quoted in A.G. Noorani (ed.), The Muslims of India (New Delhi: Oxford University Press, 2003).

Khan, Rasheeduddin. "Muslim Identity in Contemporary India", in: Indian Horizons, vol. 48, no. 2 (2001): 54-78.

Khan, Zafarul-Islam, "Muslims in post-Independence India, with special reference to anti-minority policies of the Sangh Parivar", in: Muslim India, vol. 22, no. 2 (February 2004): 131-140.

Khilnani, Sunil. "Nehru's Faith", in: Economic and Political Weekly, vol. xxxvii, no. 48 (November 30 to December 6, 2002): 4793-4799.

Kumar, Anuradha. "Partition, Congress Secularism and Hindu Communalism", in: Economic and Political Weekly, vol. xxxv, no. 31 (July 29-August 4), 2000: 2732-2734.

Kumar, Krishna. Prejudice and Pride. School Histories of the Freedom struggle in India and Pakistan (New Delhi: Penguin Books India, 2001).

Kumar, N. Gazetteer of India: Bihar: Ranchi (Patna: Government of Bihar, 1969). Kumar, Radha. Making Peace with Partition

Kuwajima, Sho. Muslims, Nationalism and the Partition: 1946 Provincial Elections in India (New Delhi: Manohar, 1998).

Lobo, Lancy. "Adivasis, Hindutva and Post-Godhra Riots in Gujarat", in Economic and Political Weekly, vol. xxxvii, no. 48: 4844-4849.

Mahajan, Vidya Dhar. Fifty Years of Modern India [1919-1969] (Delhi: S. Chand & Co. 1970).

Mahato, Pashupati Prasad. "The Status of the Kudmi-Mahatos in the Hor-Mitan and Hor-Diku dichotomy: A Study of Ethno-history and Inter-ethnic relations in Jharkhand", in: Religion and Society, vol. xli, no. 1 (March 1994): 51-74.

Mamdani, Mahmood. Good Muslim, Bad Muslim. Islam, the USA, and the Global War Against Terror (New Delhi: Permanent Black: 2004).

Mascarenhas, Anthony. Bangladesh: A Legacy of Blood (London: Hodder and Stoughton, 1986).

Mehdi, Syed Sikander, "Migration, Multiculturalism and 'Peace City': The Experience of Karachi", in: Imtiaz Ahmed; Abhijit Dasgupta and Kathinka Sinha-Kerkhoff (eds.), State, Society and Displaced People in South Asia, Dhaka: The University Press Limited, 2004): 312-325.

Metcalf, Barbara D. Islamic Contestations. Essays on Muslims in India and Pakistan (New Delhi: Oxford University Press, 2004).

Mishra, Omprakash and Anindyo J. Majumdar (eds.). The Elsewhere People: Cross-border Migration, Refugee Protection and State Response (New Delhi: Lancer Books, 2003).

Mishra Ratneshwar (ed.). Region in History. Perspectivising Bihar (Patna: Janaki, 2002).

Mishra, Shushila. History of the Freedom Movement in Chhota Nagpur (1885-1947) (Patna: Kashi Prasad Jayaswal Research Institute, 1990).

Mondal, Seik Rahim. "Social Structure, OBCs and Muslims", in: Economic and Political Weekly, vol. xxxviii, no. 46 (November 15-21). 2003: 4892-4897.

Muralidharan, Sukumar. "L.K. Advani's Pakistan Yatra. Historical Revisionism". in: Economic and Political Weekly, vol. xl, no. 24 (June 11) 2005: 2381-2383.

Murshid, Tazeen M. The Sacred and the Secular. Bengal Muslims Discourses 1871-1977 (Dhaka: University Press, 1996).

Nag, Sajal. "Nationhood and Displacement in Indian Subcontinent", in: Economic and Political Weekly, vol. xxxvi, no. 51 (22-28 December 2001): 4753-4760.

Nahar, Sultana. A Comparative Study of Communalism in Bangladesh and India, (Dhaka: Dhaka Prokashon, 1994) (in Bengali and English).

Narayan, J. "Regional Studies on Communal Problems: A Case Study of Bihar", in: Ratneshwar Mishra (ed.), Region in History. Perspectivising Bihar (Patna: Janaki, 2002): 65-70.

Narayan, Jitendra. Communal Riots in India. A Case Study of an Indian State (New Delhi: Ashish Publishing House, 1992).

Narayan, S. Jharkhand Movement. Origin and Evolution (New Delhi: Inter India Publications, 1992).

Nauriya, Anil. "Some Portrayals of Jinnah: A Critique", in: D.L. Sheth and Gurpreet

Mahajan (eds.). Minority Identities and the Nation-State (New Delhi: Oxford University Press, 1999): 73-113.

Nicholas, Ralph W. "Islam and Vaishnavism in the Environment of Rural Bengal", in: Rafiuddin Ahmed, Understanding the Bengal Muslims Interpretative Essays (New Delhi: Oxford University Press, 2001): 52-71.

Noorani, A.G. (ed.). The Muslims of India. A Documentary Record (New Delhi: Oxford University Press 2003).

O' Malley, L.S.S. Bengal. District Gazetteers: Santhal Parganas (Calcutta: The Bengal Secretariat Book Depot, 1910).

O'Malley, L.S.S. Bihar and Orissa District Gazetteers: Palamau. Revised edition by P.C. Tallents (Patna: Government Printing Press, 1926).

O'Connell, Joseph. "The Bengali Muslims and the State: Secularism or Humanity for Bangladesh?", in: Rafiuddin Ahmed (ed.) Understanding the Bengal Muslims. Interpretative Essays (New Delhi: Oxford University Press, 2001): 179-209.

Pandey, Gyanendra. "Can A Muslim be an Indian", in: Comparative Studies in Society and History, vol. 41, no. 4 (1999).

Pandey, Gyanendra. "India and Pakistan, 1947-2002", in: Economic and Political Weekly, vol. xxxvii, no. 11 (16-22 March) 2002: 1032 (also available on: http://www.sacw.net/partition/gpandey2002.html).

Pandey, Gyanendra. "Partition and Independence in Delhi: 1947-1948", in: Economic and Political Weekly, vol. xxxii, no. 36, (6 September) 1997: 2261-2272.

Pandey, Gyanendra. Remembering Partition: Violence, Nationalism and History in India (Cambridge: Cambridge University Press, 2001).

Prakash, Amit. Jharkhand: Politics of Development and Identity (New Delhi: Orient Longman, 2001).

Puniyani, Ram. Communal Politics. Facts versus Myths (New Delhi: Sage, 2003).

Puri, Balraj. Indian Muslims Since Partition (New Delhi: Institute of Objective Studies, 1994).

Radstone, Susannah and Katharine Hodgkin (eds.) Regimes of Memory (London and New York: Routledge, 2003).

Rahman, Lutfor Khan Md. "Minorities of Bangladesh and Their Alienation: Causes and Implication", in: Journal of the Asiatic Society of Bangladesh, vol. 41, no. 2, December (1996): 299-315.

Rahim, Enayetur. "Bengali Muslims and Islamic Fundamentalism: The Jama't-I-Islami in Bangladesh", in: Rafiuddin Ahmed (ed.) Understanding the Bengal Muslims. Interpretative Essays (New Delhi: Oxford University Press, 2001): 209-236.

Rahman, Mahbubar and Van Schendel, Willem. "I am not a Refugee': Rethinking Partition Migration", in: Imtiaz Ahmed; Abhijit Dasgupta and Kathinka Sinha-Kerkhoff (eds.), State, Society and Displaced People in South Asia, Dhaka: The University Press Limited, 2004): 207-243.

Rahman, Md. Shah Noorur. Hindu-Muslim Relations in Mughal Bengal (Calcutta: Progressive Publishers, 2001).

Ramachandran, Sujata. "Of Boundaries and Border Crossings: Undocumented Bangladeshi 'Infiltrators' and the Hegomony of Hindu Nationalism in India", in: Interventions, vol. 1, no. 2 (1999): 235-255 (Special Issue on The Partition of the Indian Sub-continent edited by Ritu Menon).

Report of the Indian Commission of Inquiry on Communal Disturbances in Ranchi-Hatia: August 22-29, 1967 (New Delhi: Ministry of Home Affairs, 1968).

Rizvi, Syed Sifarish Husain. Partition. End Product of the Trend (Patna: Khuda Bakhsh Oriental Public Library, 1998).

Robinson, Francis "History of Muslim Societies", in: Economic and Political Weekly, vol. xxxix, no. 44 (October 30-November 5) 2004: 4782-4784.

Rosser, Yvette Claire. Indoctrinating Minds. A Case Study of Bangladesh (New Delhi: Rupa & Co. 2004).

Roy Choudhury, P.C. Hazaribagh District Gazetteers (Patna: State Press, 1957).

Roy, Beth. Some Trouble with Cows. Making Sense of Social Conflict (New Delhi: Vistaar Publications, 1994).

Roy, Sanjay K. (ed.). Refugees and Human Rights. Social and Political Dynamics of Refugee Problem in Eastern and North-Eastern India (Jaipur and New Delhi: Rawat Publications, 2001).

Roy, Tathagata. My People, Uprooted: A Saga of the Hindus of Eastern Bengal (Kolkata: Ratna Prakashan, 2002).

Roy Choudhury. Hazaribagh District Gazetteers (Patna: State Press, 1957).

Sajjad, Mohd. "Interrogating the Metanarratives of Congress Nationalism: Muslim Resistance to Communal Separatism in Colonial Bihar", in: Islam and Modern Age, vol. 33, no. 3 (August 2002): 53-85.

Salahuddin, Ahmed. Bangladesh. Past and Present (New Delhi: A.P.H. Publishing Corporation, 2004).

Salat, F. "Telling Tales of Muslims in India", in: Shernaz Cama and Sudhir Chandra Mathur, (eds.). The Muse and the Minorities. Social Concerns and Creative Cohesion. International Seminar: Papers and Proceedings (New Delhi: The Steering Committee, 1998): 186-189.

Samad, Saleem. "Bangladesh. State of Minorities in Bangladesh", in: Sumanta Banerjee (ed.). Shrinking Space: Minority Rights in South Asia (Kathmandu: South Asia Forum for Human Rights, 1999): 75-96.

Samad, Saleem. "State of Minorities in Bangladesh: From Secular to Islamic Hegemony", country paper presented at the Regional Consultation on Minority Rights in South Asia (20-22 August) organized by South Asian Forum for Human Rights (SAFHR), Kathmandu. Also available on internet: mukto-mona.com / Articles / saleem / secular_to_Islamic.htm (1998).

Samad, Yunas. A Nation in Turmoil. Nationalism and Ethnicity in Pakistan, 1937-1958 (Karachi: Oxford Univrsity Press, 1995).

Samaddar, Ranabir. "The Last Hurrah that Continues", in: Ghislaine Glasson Deschaumes and Rada Ivekoviæ (eds.), Divided Countries, Separated Cities. The Modern Legacy of Partition (New Delhi: Oxford University Press, 2003): 21-35.

Satyani, Pirbhu Lal. Hamey Bhi Jeeney Do: Pakistan mai acchoot logon ki suratehal (in Urdu) (Let us also live: the situation of the untouchables in Pakistan) (Lahore: ASR Resource Centre, 2005).

Sebastain Periannan, S. "Methodological Issues in Analyzing the Perception of Religious Minorities in the Media", in: Indian Journal of Secularism, vol. 8, no. 3 (October-December, 2004): 52-61.

Sen, Satadru. "Border of Insanity. Deporting Bangladeshi Migrants", in: Economic and Political Weekly, vol. xxxviii, no. 7 (February 15-21), 2002: 611-612.

Sengupta, Roshini. "Communal Violencce in India. Perspectives on Causative Factors", in: Economic and Political Weekly, vol. xl, no. 20 (May 14-20): 2046-2050.

Shankar Jha, Jata. Aspects of the History of Modern Bihar (Patna: Kashi Prasad Jayaswal Research Institute, 1988).

Sherwani, Latif Ahmed. Pakistan Resolution to Pakistan 1940-1947 (Dacca: National Publishing House Limited, 1969).

Sheth, D.L. and Gupreet Muhajan (eds.). Minority Identities and the Nation-State (New Delhi: Oxford University Press, 1999).

Siddiqui, M.K.A. Marginal Muslim Communities in India (New Delhi: Institute of Objective Studies, 2004).

Singer, Wendy. Creating Histories. Oral Narratives and the Politics of History-Making (Delhi: Oxford University Press, 1997).

Singh, Amrik (ed.). The Partition in Retrospect (New Delhi: Anamika Publishers/National Institute of Panjab Studies, 2000).

Sinha, S.P. "Tribal Leadership in Bihar. Genesis and Development", in: S.P. Sinha (ed.), Tribal Leadership in Bihar (Ranchi: The Bihar Tribal Welfare Research Institute for the Government of Bihar Welfare Department, 1991): 146.

Sinha-Kerkhoff, Kathinka. "Futurising the Past: Partition Memory, Refugee Identity and Social Struggle in

Champaran, Bihar", in: South Asian Refugee Watch (SARWATCH), vol. 2, no. 2, (December), 2000: 74-93.

Sinha-Kerkhoff, Kathinka. "Left Behind or Staying Put? Muslims in India and Hindus in Bangladesh after the Partition of India in 1947", in: Indian Journal of Secularism. A Journal of the Centre for the Study of Society and Secularism, vol. 7, no. 3, (October-December), 2003: 27-44.

Sinha-Kerkhoff, Kathinka. "Permanent Refugees: Female Camp Inhabitants in Bihar", in: Philomena Essed, Georg Frerks and Joke Schrijvers (eds.). Refugees and the Transformation of Societies. Agency, Policies, Ethics and Politics (New York and Oxford: Berghahn, 2004a): 81-94.

Sinha-Kerkhoff, Kathinka, "Partition memory and multiple identities in the Champaran district of Bihar, India", in: Peter Gray and Kendrick Oliver (eds.). The Memory of Catastrophe (Manchester and New York: Manchester University Press, 2004b): 147-158.

Sinha-Kerkhoff, Kathinka. "From 'Displaced Person' to being 'a Local': Cross-Border Refugees and Invisible Refugees in Ranchi", in: Imtiaz Ahmed; Abhijit Dasgupta and Kathinka Sinha-Kerkhoff (eds.). State, Society and Displaced People in South Asia, Dhaka: The University Press Limited, 2004c): 149-168.

Sinha-Kerkhoff, Kathinka. "Voices of Difference: Partition Memory and Memories of Muslims in Jharkhand, India", in: Critical Asian Studies, vol. 36, no. 1 (March) 2004d: 113-143.

Spear, Percival (ed.). The Cultural Heritage of Pakistan (Karachi: 1955).

Sundar, Nandini. "Teaching to Hate. RSS Pedagogical Programme", in: Economic and Political Weekly, vol. xxxix, no. 16 (April 17-23, 2004): 1605-1612.

Tajuddin, Mohammad. "Minorities in Bangladesh: A Conspectus", in: Sumanta Banerjee (ed.), Shrinking Space: Minority Rights in South Asia (Kathmandu: South Asia Forum for Human Rights, 1999): 97-119.

Talukdar, Mohammad H.R . Memoirs of Huseyn Shaheed Suhrawardy (Dhaka, University Press Ltd. 1987).

Umar, Badruddin. Language Movement in East Bengal (Dhaka: Jatiya Grontha Prakashan 2000).

Upadhyay, Archana. "The 'Infitrator' Issue", in: Economic and Political Weekly, vol. xl, no. 28 (July 9-15), 2005: 3002.

Vajpeyi, Dhirendra. "Muslim Fundamentalism in India: A Crisis of Identity in a Secular State", in: Dhirendra Vajpeyi and Yogendra K. Malik (eds.), Religious and Ethnic Minority Politics in South Asia (New Delhi: Manohar, 1989): 51-71.

Van Bijlert, Victor A. "Hindus and Muslims in Bengal: Is Religious Experience a Unifying Factor?", in: Religion, Conflict and Reconciliation. Multifaith Ideals and Realities. (ed), Jerald D. Gort, Henry Jansen and Hendrick M.Vroom (Amsterdam / New York: Rodopi, 2002): 37-51

Van Houtum, Henk and Van Naerssen Ton. "Bordering, Ordering and Othering", in: Tijdschrift voor Economische en Sociale Geografie, vol. 93, no. 2, 2002: 125-136.

Van Schendel, Willem and Erik Zürcher (eds.), Identity Politics in Central Asia and the Muslim World. Nationalism, Ethnicity and Labour in the Twentieth Century (London and New York: I.B. Tauris, 2001).

Van Schendel, Willem. "Stateless in South Asia: The Making of the India-Bangladesh Enclaves", in: The Journal of Asian Studies, vol. 61, no.1 (February) 2002: 115-147.

Van Schendel, Willem. The Bengal Borderland. Beyond State and Nation in South Asia (London: Anthem Press, 2005).

Varshney, Ashutosh. Ethnic Conflict and Civic Life. Hindus and Muslims in India (New Delhi: Oxford University Press, 2002).

Verkaaik, Oskar. "The Captive State. Corruption, Intelligence Agencies, and Ethnicity in Pakistan", in: Thomas Blom Hansen and Finn Stepputat, States of Imagination. Ethnographic Exploration of the Post-colonial State (Durham and London: Duke University Press, 2001): 345-364.

Verma, Arbind Prasad. Development of Land Revenue Administration (Delhi: Jindaram Publications, 1980).

Weiner, Mysron. Sons of the Soil: Migration and Ethnic Conflict in India (Delhi: Oxford University Press, 1978).

Zavos, John , Thomas Blom Hansen and Christophe Jaffrelot (eds.), Hindus Nationalism and Indian Politics (New Delhi: Oxford University Press, 2004).

Zinkin, Maurice."Minorities, Immigrants and Refugees: The problems of integration", in: International Relations, vol. x, no. 3 (1991): 267-276.

Ziring, Lawrence, Bangladesh: From Mujib to Ershad (Karachi: O.U.P., 1992).

Fig. 1. Weaves.

Fig. 2. Pottes.

Source: Author's personal collection.
Muslim weaver and Hindu pottes in Bangladesh.
"Weavers can work throughout the year. Potters like us, have to stop working during raining season. That is the only difference between us'

(Informat in Bangladesh)

Fig. 3. Man with Cow.

Fig. 4. School Children.

Source: Author's personal collection.
Rooted in own place: Be it India or Bangladesh.

Index

I

J

N

O

P

Q

R